A History of Ancient Persia

Blackwell History of the Ancient World

This series provides a new narrative history of the ancient world, from the beginnings of civilization in the ancient Near East and Egypt to the fall of Constantinople. Written by experts in their fields, the books in the series offer authoritative accessible surveys for students and general readers alike.

Published

A History of Ancient Persia

The Achaemenid Empire

Maria Brosius

WILEY Blackwell

This edition first published 2021
© 2021 John Wiley & Sons, Inc.

The right of Maria Brosius to be identified as the author of this work has been asserted in accordance with law.

Registered Office
John Wiley & Sons, Inc., 111 River Street, Hoboken, NJ 07030, USA

Editorial Office
111 River Street, Hoboken, NJ 07030, USA

For details of our global editorial offices, customer services, and more information about Wiley products visit us at www.wiley.com.

Wiley also publishes its books in a variety of electronic formats and by print-on-demand. Some content that appears in standard print versions of this book may not be available in other formats.

Library of Congress Cataloging-in-Publication Data

Names: Brosius, Maria, author.
Title: A history of ancient Persia : the Achaemenid empire / Maria Brosius.
Other titles: Achaemenid empire
Description: Hoboken, New Jersey : Wiley-Blackwell, 2021. | Series:
   Blackwell History of the Ancient World | Includes bibliographical
   references and index.
Identifiers: LCCN 2020023647 (print) | LCCN 2020023648 (ebook) | ISBN
   9781444350920 (paperback) | ISBN 9781119702542 (adobe pdf) | ISBN
   9781119702535 (epub)
Subjects: LCSH: Achaemenid dynasty, 559 B.C.-330 B.C. | Iran–History–To
   640. | Iran–Civilization–To 640.
Classification: LCC DS281 .B76 2021 (print) | LCC DS281 (ebook) | DDC
   935/.05–dc23
LC record available at https://lccn.loc.gov/2020023647
LC ebook record available at https://lccn.loc.gov/2020023648

Cover Design: Wiley
Cover Image: © Maria Brosius

Set in 10.5/12.5pt Plantin by SPi Global, Pondicherry, India

10 9 8 7 6 5 4 3 2 1

Contents

List of Illustrations

List of Maps

List of Special Topics

List of Sources in Translation

List of Boxed Texts

List of Abbreviations

A¹Pa	Inscription of Artaxerxes I, Persepolis (a)
A²Sa	Inscription of Artaxerxes II, Susa (a)
A²Sd	Inscription of Artaxerxes II, Susa (d)
A²Sf	Inscription of Artaxerxes II, Susa (f)
ABC	Grayson, A.K., 1985, *Assyrian and Babylonian Chronicles*, Locust Valley, NY: J.J. Augustin (Texts from Cuneiform Sources 55)
AchHist 2	Sancisi-Weerdenburg, H., and A. Kuhrt, eds., 1987, *Achaemenid History 2: The Greek Sources*, Leiden: Nederlands Instituut voor het Nabije Oosten
AchHist 3	Kuhrt, A., and H. Sancisi-Weerdenburg, eds., 1988, *Achaemenid History 3: Method and Theory*, Leiden: Nederlands Instituut voor het Nabije Oosten
AchHist 8	Sancisi-Weerdenburg, H., A. Kuhrt, and M.C. Root, eds., 1994, *Achaemenid History 8: Continuity and Change*, Leiden: Nederlands Instituut voor het Nabije Oosten
AchHist 11	Brosius, M., and A. Kuhrt, eds., 1998, *Studies in Persian History. Essays in Memory of Professor David M. Lewis*, Leiden: Nederlands Instituut voor het Nabije Oosten
AchHist 13	Henkelman, W., and A. Kuhrt, eds., 2003, *Achaemenid History 13. A Persian Perspective. Essays in Memory of Heleen Sancisi-Weerdenburg*, Leiden: Nederlands Instituut voor het Nabije Oosten
Ael. *var. hist.*	Aelianus, *varia historia*
Akk.	Akkadian
Andoc.	Andocides
ANET	Pritchard, J.B., ed., 1969, *Ancient Near Eastern Texts relating to the Old Testament* (3rd. rev. edn.), Princeton, NJ: Princeton University Press

AOAT	Alter Orient und Altes Testament
ap.	apud
App.*Syr.*	Appian, *Syriaca*
Arr.*an.*	Arrian, *anabasis*
ARTA	Achaemenid Research on Texts and Archaeology
Athen.	Athenaios
Bab.	Babylonian
BCE	Before Christian Era
BE X	Clay, A.T., 1904, *Business Documents of Murashu Sons of Nippur dated to the Reign of Darius II (424–404 BC)*, Philadelphia, PA: University of Pennsylvania
BM	siglum of the British Museum, London
BN	siglum of the Bibliothèque Nationale, Paris
CAH IV²	*Cambridge Ancient History IV: Persia, Greece and the Western Mediterranean*, 1988, ed. by J. Boardman, N.G.L. Hammond, D.M. Lewis, and M. Ostwald, Cambridge: Cambridge University Press
CAH VI²	*Cambridge Ancient History VI: The fourth century BC*, 1994, ed. by D.M. Lewis, J. Boardman, S. Hornblower, and M. Ostwald, Cambridge: Cambridge University Press
CE	Christian Era
col.	Column
Curt.Ruf.	Curtius Rufus
D²Sa	Inscription of Darius II, Susa (a)
D²Sb	Inscription of Darius II, Susa (b)
DB	Inscription of Darius I, Bisitun
DNa	Inscription of Darius I, Naqsh-e Rustam (a)
DPd	Inscription of Darius I, Persepolis (d)
DPe	Inscription of Darius I, Persepolis (e)
DSaa	Inscription of Darius I, Susa (aa)
DSc	Inscription of Darius I, Susa (c)
DSe	Inscription of Darius I, Susa (e)
DZf	Inscription of Darius I, Suez Canal (f)
Dem.	Demosthenes
Diod.Sic.	Diodorus Siculus, *Geographia*

ed./eds.	edited, editor/editors
Elam.	Elamite
FGrH	Jacoby, F., 1923–1958, *Die Fragmente der Griechischen Historiker*, Leiden: Brill
Gr.	Greek
Hdt.	Herodotus, *Histories*
Isocr.	Isocrates
Isocr.*Evag.*	Isocrates, *Evagoras*
Just.	Justinus, Epitome of the *Philippic Histories* of Pompeius Trogus
l./ll.	line/lines
LE	Left Edge
mod.	modern
m	meter
MDP IX	Scheil, V., 1907, *Textes élamites-anzanites*, Paris: Ernest Leroux (3ème série, Mémoires de la Délégation Française en Perse IX)
Mt.	Mount
NCh	Nabonidus Chronicle
Nep.*Dat.*	Cornelius Nepos, *Lives of the Great Generals XIV: Datames*
no.	number
nr.	near
obv.	obverse
OGIS	Dittenberger, W., 1903, *Orientis Graeci Inscriptiones*, Leipzig: Hirzel
OP	Old Persian
Paus.	Pausanias
PF	siglum for Persepolis Fortification Tablets
PFa	Hallock, R.T., 1978, Selected Fortification Tablets, *Cahiers de la Délégation Française en Iran* 8: 109–136
PF NN	siglum for Persepolis Fortification Tablets transliterated, but unpublished
PFS	Persepolis Fortification Seal
pl.	plural
Plut.*Alex.*	Plutarch, *Life of Alexander*
Plut.*Art.*	Plutarch, *Life of Artaxerxes*

Plut.*Demetr.*	Plutarch, *Life of Demetrius*
Plut.*Per.*	Plutarch, *Life of Perikles*
PMG	Papyrus Michigan
PN	Personal Name
Poly.	Polyaenus, *Strategemata*
Ps.-Arist.	Pseudo-Aristotle
PT	siglum for Persepolis Treasury Tablets
rev.	reverse
RIMA	*Royal Inscriptions of Mesopotamia: Assyrian Rulers* I–, Toronto 1987–
SAA	State Archives of Assyria
Schol.Dem.	Scholia to Demosthenes
Simonides	Page, D.L., 1981, *Further Greek epigrams: epigrams before 50AD from the Greek Anthology and other sources, not included in Hellenistic epigrams or the garland of Philip,* Cambridge: Cambridge University Press
sg.	Singular
SXf	Seal of Xerxes, (f)
Tac.Ann.	Tacitus, *Annals*
TAM	Tituli Asia Minoris TBER, Durand, J.-M., 1982, *Textes babyloniens d'époque récente,* Paris: A.D.P.F. (Recherche sur les grandes civilisations 6; études assyriologiques)
Thuc.	Thucydides, *History of the Peloponnesian War*
TMHC	Texte und Materialien der Hilprecht Collection
transl.	translated
Xen.*an.*	Xenophon, *anabasis*
Xen.*Cyr.*	Xenophon, *Cyropaedia*
Xen.*hell.*	Xenophon, *hellenika*
XPf	Inscription of Xerxes, Persepolis (f)
XPg	Inscription of Xerxes, Persepolis (g)
XPh	Inscription of Xerxes, Persepolis (h)

The Achaemenid Dynasty

The Achaemenid Dynasty

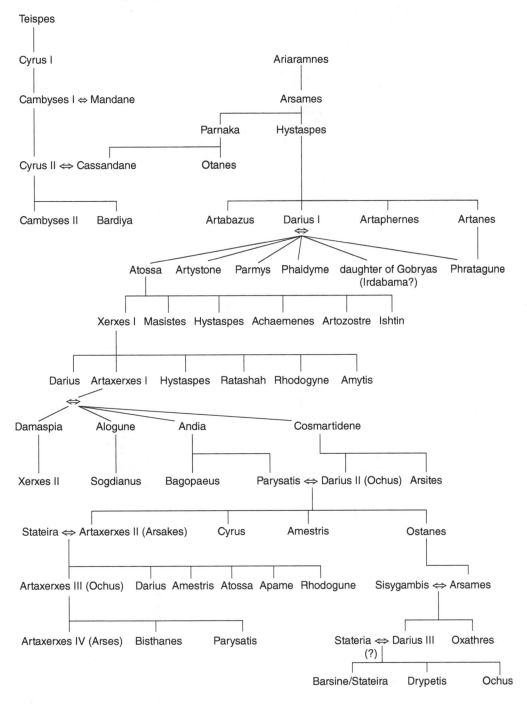

Teispes

Cyrus I

Ariaramnes

Cambyses I ⇔ Mandane

Arsames

Parnaka   Hystaspes

Cyrus II ⇔ Cassandane   Otanes

Cambyses II   Bardiya   Artabazus   Darius I   Artaphernes   Artanes
⇔

Atossa   Artystone   Parmys   Phaidyme   daughter of Gobryas   Phratagune
(Irdabama?)

Xerxes I   Masistes   Hystaspes   Achaemenes   Artozostre   Ishtin

Darius   Artaxerxes I   Hystaspes   Ratashah   Rhodogyne   Amytis
⇔

Damaspia   Alogune   Andia   Cosmartidene

Xerxes II   Sogdianus   Bagopaeus   Parysatis ⇔ Darius II (Ochus)   Arsites

Stateira ⇔ Artaxerxes II (Arsakes)   Cyrus   Amestris   Ostanes

Artaxerxes III (Ochus)   Darius Amestris Atossa Apame Rhodogune   Sisygambis ⇔ Arsames

Artaxerxes IV (Arses)   Bisthanes   Parysatis   Stateira ⇔ Darius III   Oxathres
(?)

Barsine/Stateira   Drypetis   Ochus

Preface

In the past few decades, Achaemenid history has established itself as an exciting and multifaceted area of study and research. Thanks to many academic publications looking at aspects of the empire or indeed covering the history in its entirety, the subject has become accessible to students and graduates, while concise histories offer non-specialists and general readers a way into the subject. Several recent exhibitions on ancient Persia, some of them travelling across the globe, have brought the splendour of the Persian court, the immensely rich art found across its territories and in the far corners of the empire, to life. Most recently, a magisterial sourcebook on the Persian empire written by Amélie Kuhrt has given the academic community an invaluable tool to learn about the wealth of written sources on Achaemenid Persia.

This has not always been the case. A few years ago, an exhibition on the Persian empire in the British Museum in London was aptly entitled 'Forgotten Empire. The World of Ancient Persia.' For the longest time the study of Persian history had fallen, figuratively speaking, 'between the cracks'. It was a history outside the core of Near Eastern studies whose focus was ancient Mesopotamia, and a time period which fell out of its remit. For Classical Studies and Ancient History, it lay outside their European core. It popped up only when its history brushed against the Greek world, and the emphasis then was on the wars, not the diplomatic relations. It is due to the pioneering work of a few individuals over the past centuries, who doggedly beat the odds, went astray, either from their classical path or their Near Eastern studies, and pursued their interest in the language, history and archaeology of Achaemenid Persia, that the empire, indeed, was not forgotten.

The present book is intended as a textbook for students and interested readers who wish to learn about the first Persian empire, whether they are ancient historians, archaeologists or students of Biblical studies or Iranian civilization. It has been written with the aim to show the Persian empire and its diversity and cultural richness, using key sources and archaeological data to gain insights into the way the empire operated, how its kings ruled and, as far as possible, how its people lived. I have tried to show how carefully we need to read and assess the Greek sources which provide the main narrative of Persia's political history, by pointing out how their narrative is often subject to a literary construct and traditional stereotype rather than depicting historical reality – merely for the sake of creating a specific image of the Persians. Frequently, we have contrary reports or at least indications of matters looking different when viewed from an eastern perspective, using Near Eastern sources including Assyrian, Babylonian, Persian, Egyptian and Aramaic. Sometimes these are not easy to understand; their text might be fragmented or partly destroyed. In many cases, we are not yet able to offer translations for terms used in the texts. These shortcomings constitute a problem in itself, but the reader might nevertheless gain an appreciation of the type of these documents and how far they can help us to complement our view of ancient Persia. It was most important to me to include the Persian royal inscriptions, our primary written sources for the Persians, to let them tell their story wherever possible. But others also were fundamental in this presentation. Administrative records from archives recovered from across the empire, both imperial and private ones, allow us to gain an insight into the daily life of officials, administrators and even ordinary people – from imperial orders to land leases, lower officials and marriage settlements of people in the cities of the empire, or the ration payments of the men, women and children who built the royal palaces.

This brings me to another aspect of this book. As an introduction, it serves to guide the reader in a comprehensive manner through a diversity of material. In doing so, my goal was to incorporate current research, pointing out areas of contemporary debate. What may be less clear in this book is that our sources are not evenly balanced, that royal inscriptions are plentiful for Darius I and Xerxes I, but peter out by the fourth century. Equally, the richness of the Persepolis texts is not matched with an equal wealth of Persian documents in the later empire. Many of our sources are strewn across the empire, from different cultures and different periods within the 230-year rule of the Persians. We can only show the diversity of the empire with the building blocks we have, and these sometimes amount only to a small aspect of the whole.

But taken together, these sources, I hope, reveal a wondrous empire, unmatched in its size and longevity compared to any other empire of the ancient Near East, and splendid in its concept, ruled by kings who adhered to the principle that, in order to govern such a vast multi-ethnic, multicultural and multi-confessional empire, respect and tolerance for others was key. In our current climate of growing nationalism worldwide, and the growing fear of foreigners and of the religions of others, it appears that the Achaemenid empire can still show us that 'national identity' and the acceptance of others do not have to be mutually exclusive values.

FURTHER LITERATURE ON THE ACHAEMENID EMPIRE

Briant, P. (2006). *From Cyrus to Alexander*. Winona Lake, IN: Eisenbrauns.

Curtis, J. and Simson, St. J. (eds.) (2010). *The world of Achaemenid Persia. History, Art and Society in Iran*. London: Tauris.

Curtis, J. and Tallis, N. (eds.) (2005). *Forgotten Empire: The World of Ancient Persia*. London: British Museum Press.

Gramiccia, A. and d'Inzillo Carranza, G. (eds.) (2001). *Antica Persia*. Rome: I tesori del Museo Nazionale di Tehran e la ricerca italiana in Iran.

Jacobs, B. and Rollinger, R. (eds.) (in press). *A Companion to the Achaemenid Persian Empire*. Oxford: Wiley Blackwell.

Kuhrt, A. (2010). *The Persian Empire: A Corpus of Sources of the Achaemenid Period*. London: Routledge.

Potts, D.T. (ed.) (2013). *The Oxford Handbook of Ancient Iran*. Oxford: Oxford University Press.

Rehm, E. and Externbrink, H. (eds.) (2006). *Das Persische Weltreich: Pracht und Prunk der Grosskönige*. Stuttgart: Thesis.

Rollinger, R., Truschnegg, B., and Bichler, R. (eds.) (2011). *Herodot und das persische Weltreich. Herodotus and the Persian Empire*. Wiesbaden: Harrassowitz.

Waters, M. (2014). *Ancient Persia. A Concise History of the Achaemenid Empire 550–330 BCE*. New York: Cambridge University Press.

Wiesehöfer, J. (2001). *Ancient Persia: From 550 BC to 650 AD* (trans. Azizeh Azodi), 231–242. London: Tauris.

Acknowledgements

My deep thanks go to the series editor, Haze Humbert, for her patience and support throughout the conception of the book, as well as to the copy-editor, Giles Flitney. I am also grateful to the anonymous reviewers for their helpful comments and suggestions. The resources of the Robarts Library, University of Toronto, proved invaluable, and I thank the staff and librarians for their continuous help and assistance. A brief period at the Getty Villa and Getty Research Center in Los Angeles provided me with the opportunity to discuss some ideas for this book with friends and colleagues, including Rahim Shayegan at UCLA, Rolf Strootman, and Jake Nabel; I am especially indebted to the Director of the Scholars' Program, Alexa Sekyra – thank you! I warmly thank friends and colleagues for their readiness to provide their photographs, including Michael Alram, Gian Petro Basello, Marion Cox, Elsbeth R.M. Dusinberre, Pontus Hellström, Mark Garrison, Deniz Kaptan, Florian Knauss, Javier Álvarez-Mon, Joaquin Velasquez Muñoz, Dan Potts and Rolf A. Stucky, as well as the Antikenmuseum Basel and Sammlung Ludwig, The Getty Museum, The National Museum Tehran, The Musée du Louvre RMN-Grand Palais, and The State Heritage Museum, St Petersburg. Above all, I wish to thank two people without whose unfailing support through a difficult time in the past I would not have been able to write this book, Gill Paczynski and Seamus Ross. It is dedicated to both.

Author's Note

The basis for many of the translated texts has been Amélie Kuhrt's sourcebook *The Persian Empire: A Corpus of Sources from the Achaemenid Period* (2010). It is a fundamental tool for the study of Achaemenid history and sets a standard to which one ought to adhere. As her translated passages are accompanied by valuable comments and references, the reader will benefit from using the present volume in conjunction with her sourcebook. Old Persian inscriptions and Elamite texts have been translated by the author. Digital libraries for cuneiform texts can be found in the Cuneiform Digital Library Initiative (http://cdli.ox.ac.uk) and the Open Richly Annotated Cuneiform Corpus (http://oracc.museum.upenn.edu/). Greek and Latin translations have been taken from Loeb editions. Most of these can be accessed through www.perseus.tufts.edu.

In the translations of Near Eastern and Greek texts, words inserted to facilitate reading are indicated by round brackets (word); omissions are indicated by round brackets and ellipses (…); explanations are given in round brackets with the equal sign (= …); spaces where the text is broken or illegible are marked with square brackets and ellipses […]; restorations of letters and words are indicated with square brackets [word]; a description of an issue is written in italics in round brackets. An asterix (*) attached to a number of a Persepolis seal indicates that the seal is inscribed. All dates are BCE unless otherwise stated.

1

Introduction

The first Persian empire, which is known as the Achaemenid empire after the eponymous ancestor Achaemenes, was founded in 550 by Cyrus II. He is one of the few rulers in world history who received the epithet 'the Great'. It is more than apt. Cyrus II established an empire which, at its largest extent, stretched from Egypt and the eastern Mediterranean to the Indus River. It included the whole of modern Turkey and Europe to the Danube River; it controlled the lands of Central Asia now bordering on Russia. If the conquests themselves were an impressive achievement, it was at least equally formidable that this empire remained in the control of one dynasty for over 200 years, until its conquest by Alexander III of Macedon and the death of its last king, Darius III, in 330. It was Cyrus II who set the course for the success of a political concept which ensured the longevity of his empire, which, at its core, was characterised by tolerance: the subject peoples of the empire were allowed to continue their own way of life, adhere to their own languages, follow their own religious cults and practices and maintain their own cultural habitat. This is not to claim that Cyrus II and his successors, far ahead of their time, were enlightened or humane rulers. Rather, their decision to tolerate other peoples' and nations' beliefs and cultural habits was anchored in the concept of political expediency. The less state force was used on the inhabitants of any land, the less likely was the chance of opposition to the governing power. Permitting people their own language, culture and religion greatly reduced the grounds for resistance to Persian rule.

There were two areas where this political tolerance met its limits: in the payment of taxes and tribute, and in rebellion. While there is no record that any of the lands of the empire ever refused the former, rebellions did happen, and they were severely punished. Persian kings did not tolerate disloyalty or disobedience, and any land which tried to secede from the empire faced a relentless Persian might, no matter how long it took to recover a province. The most extreme case undoubtedly was Egypt, never a willing subject of the Persian king, but which began a revolt in 404 which was only quashed in 343/2 by Artaxerxes III. While such rebellions were staged in a bid for independence, others were directed at the king, challenging his authority. Several revolts occurred in

A History of Ancient Persia: The Achaemenid Empire, First Edition. Maria Brosius.
© 2021 John Wiley & Sons, Inc. Published 2021 by John Wiley & Sons, Inc.

the period between the death of one king and the accession of his successor. If that succession was not clear-cut, that is, if there was no son alive born to the king and his Persian queen, the succession was fought over by half-brothers, leading to rebellion or, in the case of Artaxerxes II and his brother Cyrus the Younger, to war. Yet despite these upheavals, royal power remained within the same dynasty and often led to long reigns, such as that of Artaxerxes I, who ruled for 40 years, or that of Artaxerxes II, whose reign lasted 45 years.

Royal inscriptions and the palatial building programme reflect an inherent sense of continuity among the Achaemenid kings and an awareness of the place they took within their own imperial history. The 'king of kings' was eager to manifest his heritage and his position within the line of kings his family had created. Building projects begun by his predecessor were proudly completed, and existing palaces restored, remembering the ancestor who had built it. At their investiture, the kings observed a ritual in Pasargadae, the first royal city of the Persians, in commemoration of the founder of the empire, Cyrus II.

For many scholars, students and general readers, especially in the western world, the Persian empire conjures up two images in particular: firstly, the Persian Wars against Greece in 490 and 480/79, and secondly, the conquest of Persia in 330 by the Macedonian king Alexander the Great. The focus on the Persian defeats in the Greek sources which reported them led to the overwhelming impression of a weak empire in a perpetual state of decline. This view finds its origin in our earliest surviving Greek sources on Persian history, the *Histories* of Herodotus (lived c.484–425), and the tragedy *The Persians* written by Aeschylus (lived 525/4–456), first performed in 472. Both works created, in the aftermath of the Persian War of 480/79, the antithesis between Greeks and barbarians, the latter becoming a stereotyped reference to the Persians in the fifth and fourth centuries in Greek written and visual arts. Together, these sources shaped the idea of the antithesis between (Greek) freedom and (Persian) despotism, as well as between Europe and Asia. This theme found itself perpetuated in classical scholarship for about 200 years, educating generations of students of Classics and Ancient History to accept the 'traditional' view as given. In the nineteenth century, it led the German philosopher Georg W. Friedrich Hegel (1770–1831 CE) to declare in one of his lectures on the philosophy of history:

> If we ask which [powers] were confronting each other in this war (= the Persian War), it is on the one hand the oriental despotism, the entire oriental world united under one master, thus, on the outside, with great advantage. (...) On the other hand against these sometimes very warlike peoples a few peoples of free individuals stand to fight. Never in world history has the superiority of spiritual power over a mass, and a not inconsiderable one at that, presented itself in such glory. (...) These are world-historical victories: they saved education and spiritual power, pulling them away from the Asiatic principle. (G.W.F. Hegel, 1961: 363; my translation)

Yet opportunities to challenge the stereotyped view of Persia arose in the early nineteenth century when Georg Friedrich Grotefend (1775–1853 CE), a student at the University of Göttingen in Germany, deciphered the cuneiform script, the wedge-shaped form of writing used in the Near East to write – mostly – on clay. This achievement was followed by another advance made in the mid-nineteenth century by the British officer

Henry Creswicke Rawlinson (1810–1895 CE), who copied the text of the Bisitun Inscription, a monumental trilingual inscription and relief carved high on Mt. Bisitun in northwest Iran by the Persian king Darius I in which he recorded the events that led to his accession to the Persian throne in 522. For the first time, scholars were able to learn about the ancient Persians from their own voice. Even more far-reaching, the decipherment of the cuneiform scripts opened an entire new gateway to our understanding of the ancient Near East and ancient Persia, as it enabled scholars to read the royal inscriptions and the thousands of cuneiform tablets from the archives of the ancient Near East written in Akkadian. The decipherment of the Bisitun Inscription led to the birth of a new discipline, Assyriology, while it also paved the way for ancient Persian studies. Subsequent archaeological excavations of Iranian sites such as Susa, Pasargadae, Naqsh-e Rustam and Persepolis from the late nineteenth century until 1979, brought to light more inscriptions, and enabled a new generation of scholars to study Persian history using primary sources.

Had it been, up to this point, down to many individual scholars across the world who ventured into the fields of Iranian archaeology, languages and history, it was a series of workshops on Achaemenid History organised by Heleen Sancisi-Weerdenburg of the University of Groningen, The Netherlands, and Amélie Kuhrt of University College London, England, which propelled Achaemenid Studies into an established research area. This was not least due to their endeavour to bring together scholars from different disciplines, Classics, Ancient History, Archaeology, Egyptology, Semitic Studies and Old Testament Studies, to name but a few, to find common ground and enable a diverse discussion on the Persian empire. At the same time in the early 1980s, the monumental endeavour of the *Encyclopaedia Iranica* project based at Columbia University, USA, was initiated by Ehsan Yarshater, and has now become an invaluable research tool for Iranian studies, including the study of Achaemenid Persia.

In order to understand what Achaemenid history entails and to study it in a meaningful way, the interdisciplinary approach which began with the Achaemenid History Workshops is key, for we are dealing not only with a vast range of different languages and scripts, from Elamite, different dialects of Akkadian and Old Persian cuneiform scripts to Phoenician, Aramaic, Hebrew, Hieroglyphic, Demotic, Lycian and Greek, but also with a wide array of scholarly disciplines, including History, Archaeology, Old Testament Studies, Art History, Numismatics and Papyrology. For a single scholar, the mastery of all these languages and disciplines is hardly feasible, and thus the co-operation and collaboration with colleagues from other fields is essential. The Achaemenid History Workshops, which met annually between 1981 and 1990, began this innovative approach, which has since then been successfully adopted by other conferences and workshops on Achaemenid history and the history of pre-islamic Iran. They were the inspiration for a website for Achaemenid research, www.achemenet.com, and the research journal ARTA, as well as new series publications on Persian history such as Oriens et Occidens and Classica et Orientalia.

It is easy to appreciate that the demands and challenges faced by scholars and students of Achaemenid history thus are far more complex than for most of these individual disciplines, whose research is contained to a restricted geographical space or a specific language. Since scholars have become open to incorporating material and approaches from other disciplines, many discoveries have been brought to light which have had a considerable impact on the way we view the Persian empire today. Some critics continue to argue that, due to a lack of historiographical writing from Persia itself, we are still, ultimately, dependent on the Greek sources to write a history of the Achaemenid empire. Yet the inclusion of the richness of the Near Eastern and Egyptian sources which have come to light in the past decades, the archaeological excavations which have taken place in the periphery of the empire, and even the study of Achaemenid artefacts in their own right, have made significant contributions to illuminate the way this empire functioned and the king, his governors and the court expressed themselves within their realm. Not only have they enabled us to gain deeper insights into the structure and organisation of the empire and its provinces, into practical aspects of legal positions between the Persian authority and local communities, the way the economy functioned at imperial and local level, the recruitment and payment of troops and the relationship between the centre and local cults. In quite a few instances they also have shown that many of the views expressed in the classical sources are subject to literary constructs, while others are simply inaccurate, if not plain false. In other cases, such as in the publication of the Aramaic texts from the Jewish colony of Elephantine, of the Babylonian bankhouse of the Murashu family of Nippur, the Persepolis archives, the correspondence of Arsames, the Persian governor of Egypt, or, most recently, the correspondence of Akhmavazda, probably the Persian satrap of Bactria, we have been provided with unique insights into the daily life of local governors, high-ranking and ordinary people, estate owners and tax payers, administrators, officials, workers and servants in the royal cities of the Persian empire which are unparalleled anywhere else in the sixth to fourth centuries BCE.

FURTHER READING

For an overview of the Greek sources on Persia see Brosius, M. (2013). Greek sources on Achaemenid Iran. In: *Oxford Handbook of Ancient Iran* (ed. D. Potts), 658–668. Oxford: Oxford University Press. The story of the decipherment of the cuneiform script is described in Wiesehöfer, J. (2001). *Ancient Persia: From 550 BC to 650 AD* (trans. A. Azodi), 231–242. London: Tauris. The conference volumes of the *Achaemenid History Workshops* were edited by Heleen Sancisi-Weerdenburg and different co-editors in eight volumes and were published between 1983 and 1994. Since then the Achaemenid History series continues to publish monographs and edited volumes on the subject. The *Encyclopaedia Iranica* is now an online tool and can be accessed at www.iranicaonline.org.

For the impact of the Persian Wars on world history see the seminal article by Wiesehöfer, J. (1993). "Denn es sind welthistorische Siege" – nineteenth and twentieth-century views of the Persian Wars. In: *The Construction of the Ancient Near East* (ed. A.C. Gunter), 61–83. Copenhagen: Academic Press (Culture and History 11).

2

The Arrival of the Persians on the Iranian Plateau

2.1 The Persians

Around the first millennium BCE Persian tribes migrated to the Iranian plateau, the landmass defined by the mountain range of the Zagros in the west, the Caucasus Mountains in the northwest, the Caspian Sea in the north, the Indus River in the east and the Indian Ocean and the Persian Gulf in the south and southwest. The Iranian plateau features a rich geographical diversity ranging from the mountainous regions of the Zagros range and the Alburz range, which reaches its highest peak with Mt. Damavand (5610 m), to the lush and fertile regions south of the Caspian Sea, the Central Asian steppe with its grasslands and savannah, interrupted only by the two large rivers, the Oxus (mod. Amu Darya) and the Jaxartes (mod. Syr Darya), the desert regions of the Dash-e Kavut and Dasht-e Lut and the mountain and desert regions of the southeast. In the southwest, the plateau borders on the Mesopotamian lowlands, and in the northeast on the mountain ranges of the Hindukush and the Himalayas (Map 2.1). Agriculture allowed for the planting of wheat, emmer and barley, while pastures secured the breeding of small livestock, such as sheep, goats and fowl, as well as horses and camels.

The Persians were an Indo-Iranian people who spoke an Iranian language which we now refer to as Old Persian. Theirs was an oral society which, prior to their settlement on the Iranian plateau, had had no need for written records. What triggered the undoubtedly hazardous and arduous migration of Persian tribes from the east is not known; we can only hypothesise that the reasons were economic, namely the need to find new land to feed families and livestock. It may have been due to political pressure in their original homeland or wars and military conflicts which had threatened or destroyed their way of life. The overland routes these tribes took before finally settling on the Iranian plateau remain an unresolved issue. What we do know, based on our extant sources, is that this migration movement and the processes of settlement happened peacefully, neither using military aggression towards the indigenous populations they encountered, nor forcing their displacement in turn for Persian settlement.

A History of Ancient Persia: The Achaemenid Empire, First Edition. Maria Brosius.
© 2021 John Wiley & Sons, Inc. Published 2021 by John Wiley & Sons, Inc.

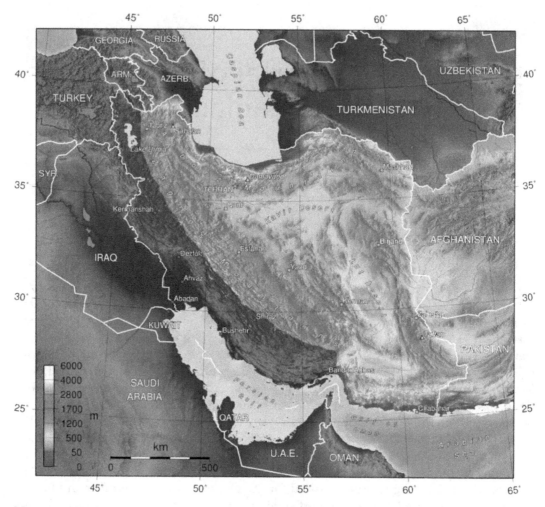

Map 2.1   Physical map of the Iranian plateau. *Source*: Google Earth.

To achieve such a successful process of acculturation, the Persians must have met with the acceptance of the local population, while they, in turn, must have shown a significant willingness to adapt to their new cultural surroundings, to accept their hosts' way of life while offering their own expertise to them.

2.1.1   Parsua and Parsumash

From the ninth to the sixth centuries, Assyrian and Babylonian records identify two distinct tribal Persian groups, the Parsua located in the western Zagros, either east of modern Senandaj or in the Mahidasht region, and those who settled in the region of Parsumash, which included Anshan in the southwest, and later came to be known as Parsa (mod. Fars). There is no evidence to suggest that the migrations of the Persian tribes occurred as a single movement in which they entered the Iranian plateau from the north and then separated to settle in these different regions. It is more plausible to assume that the various Persian tribes moved over an extensive period of time via different routes from the east to find the new areas of settlement. The earliest mention of the Persians and the land of Parsua occurs in 836/5 in the so-called Black Obelisk inscription of the Assyrian king Shalmaneser III (ruled 858–824).

> In my 24th regnal year I (= Shalmaneser III) crossed the Lower Zab (River), crossed Mt. Hashimur, and went down to the land Namri. Ianzu king of the land Namri, took fright in face of my mighty weapons and ran away to save his life. I captured Sihishalah, Bit-Tamul, Bit-Shakki, (and) Bit-Shedi, his fortified cities. I massacred them, plundered them, razed, destroyed, (and) burned (those) cities. The survivors fled up a mountain. I laid siege to the mountain peak, captured (it), slaughtered them, plundered them, (and) brought their property down. Moving from the land Namri I received the tribute of 27 kings of the land of Parsua. I went down to the lands Messu, Media (= Amadãiia), Araz-iash, (and) Harhar, (and) captured the cities Kuakinda, Hazzanabi, Ezamul (and) Kinab-bila, together with the cities in their environs. (BM 118885, Black Obelisk Inscription, transl. after Grayson 1995: 67–68, ll.110–123)

One of Shalmaneser's successors, Adad-Nirari III (ruled 810–783) lists the land of Parsua, located in the central Zagros, among his tribute-paying subjects:

> Property of Adad-nerari, Great King, legitimate king, king of the world, king of Assyria (...); Conqueror from Mt. Siluna in the east, (from) the country of Namri, the country of Ellipi, the country of Harhar, the country of Araziash, the country of Messu, the country of the Medes, the country of Gizilbunda in its totality, the country of Munna (= Mannea), the country of Parsua, the country of Allabria, the country of (Bīt-)Apdadani, the country of Na'iri to its full extent, the country of Andia, which is far away, (from) the mountain of BADhu in its totality until the shore of the Great Sea in the east. I made them submit all to my feet, imposing upon them tribute. (RIMA 3, A.0.104.85–12; transl. Radner 2003: 43)

According to the annals of the Assyrian king Sargon II (ruled 722–705), Parsua was a principality bordering on Media in the east, Mannea in the north, northwest at Zamua and southwest at Ellipi. Sargon's son and successor Sennacherib (ruled 705–681) mentioned Parsua as one of the allies of the Elamite king Humban-umena against the Assyrians in the battle of Khalule (probably 691) in the region of Samarra. The contingents came from Parsua, Anshan, Pashiru and Ellipi, as well as from Chaldaean and Aramaean tribes, that is, the principalities and tribal groups of Babylonia and the Zagros region south of the Khorassan route. Parsua and Anshan were clearly regarded as separate entities. By 643, the principality of Parsumash was mentioned in the annals of Ashurbanipal (ruled 668–627) in which he recorded two Iranian rulers, 'Kurash, king of Parsumash' and 'Pizlume, king of Hudimiri', who sent tribute to the Assyrian king after the latter's victory over Elam. Kurash even gave his son Arukku as a hostage to the Assyrian court: 'After the victorious weapons of Assur had overcome and destroyed all of Elam (...) [fear came upon the nations round about]. The fear of my majesty overwhelmed them, and they sent their messengers to win friendship and peace with costly presents. They enquired after the well-being of my majesty; they kissed my feet and besought my lordship. (When) Kurash, king of Parsumash heard of the mighty victory which I had inflicted on Elam, with the help of Ashur, Bel, Nabu, and the great gods, my lords, (and that) I had overwhelmed the whole of Elam like a flood, he sent Arukku, his eldest son, together with his tribute, as hostage to Nineveh, my lordly city, and implored my lordship' (Nassouhi Prism, transl. after Kuhrt 2010: 53–54, no. 2).

2.1.2   Kurash of Parsumash

Since Ernst Weidner's publication of this text in 1931–1932, Kurash of Parsumash, mentioned in the Nassouhi Prism, has been equated with Cyrus I of Anshan, the son of Teispes and grandfather of Cyrus II (ruled 559–530), the founder of the Persian empire. This assumption has been subject to considerable scholarly controversy, especially considering the timeline this identification establishes, dating the rule of Cyrus I to the mid-seventh century, and that of his grandson Cyrus II to almost one hundred years later. Alternatively, scholars have proposed a chronology of the ancestors of Cyrus II based on an average reign of 25 years, which would date Cyrus I's reign between c.610 and 585, in which case he cannot be identical with the Kurash of Parsumash mentioned in Ashurbanipal's prism. But chronological uncertainties apart, it is plausible to suggest that Ashurbanipal's destruction of Susa in 646 forced the Persians and Elamites of Parsumash to react and avoid further Assyrian military aggression east of the Zagros.

2.2   The Indigenous Population of the Iranian Plateau: The Elamites

Settlements of Persian tribes in the southwestern region of the plateau meant that these came to live alongside the indigenous population, the Elamites. They were an ancient people, attested as early as the third millennium BCE in the region west of the Zagros, with its royal capital Susa, as well as in the region east of the Zagros, Anshan, with its second royal capital bearing the region's name. The site of this city has been identified with modern Tall-e Malyan. The language of the Elamites is autochthonous which means that it is related neither to Indo-Iranian nor to Semitic languages.

The ethnic name we now use for the country of Elam is in fact the Hebrew name for this kingdom; it was known as 'NIM' in Assyrian, and 'uja' in Old Persian; the Elamites themselves referred to their land as 'Hatamti', 'Lord Country'. For the kings of Mesopotamia, Elam described the entire Iranian plateau, but for the people of the plateau, Elam meant the land of Anshan.

In the Neo-Elamite period (c.1000–539), Elamite troops were repeatedly found as supporters of the Babylonian army against Assyria. Thus, in 720, as an ally of the Babylonian king Merodach-Baladan II (ruled 721–710 and 703 [for nine months only]), the Elamite king Huban-nukash fought against Sargon II (ruled 721–705) at Der. Sargon II launched attacks against the Elamite king Shutruk-Nahhunte II (Akk. Ishtar-hundu, ruled c.717–699); his successor Sennacherib (ruled 705–681) fought a first campaign against Babylon, which received the support of Elamite troops including bowmen and horses:

> Merodach-Baladan, king of Kardu[niash...] (= Babylonia) a rebel plotting treachery, a criminal abhorring justice, turned to Shutruk-Nahhunte, king of E[lam, for help] and bestowed upon him gold, silver, (and) precious stones and asked him for support. As help for him (= Merodach-Baladan) he (= Shutruk-Nahhunte) sent to Sumer and Akkad Imbappa, the general, [...] Tannanu, the *tashlishu* official, ten *rab kisri* commanders, together with Nergal-nasir, the Sutian chieftain, fearless in battle, eighty thousand bowmen [...] [and] horses with them. (transl. after Brinkman 1965: 164–165)

The enmity between Assyria and Elam reached its zenith in the mid-seventh century, when Ashurbanipal (ruled 668–c.631) killed the Elamite king Tepti-Huban-Inshushinak (Akk. Te Umman, ruled 664–653), as well as his son Tammaritu, in a battle at the Ulai River. Unable to maintain control over Elam, Ashurbanipal marched against this country and destroyed 29 cities, including Susa, which was sacked in 646. Yet despite this level of destruction, several smaller principalities emerged in Elam after Susa's destruction. Within a few decades, the city itself was resettled. An archive recovered on the Acropole revealed 298 administrative texts written on clay and dealing in the main with weapons and tools, textiles and leather, as well as metal vessels. These texts, dated between either c.646 or c.605 and 539, name rulers such as Huban-kitin, who may be identical with the son of Shutur-Nahhunte, and Ummanunu, father of Shilhak-Inshushinak II and grandfather of Tepti-Huban-Inshushinak. Together with inscriptional evidence, the documents from Susa allow the reconstruction of a sequence of rulers, including Shutur-Nahhunte, the son of Humban-umena III, Hallutash-Inshushinak, son of Humban-Tahra II, and Atta-hamti-Inshushinak, son of Hutran-tepti, in the second half of the seventh century. These kings still used the royal title 'king of Anshan and Susa', even though the settlement of Anshan was abandoned by the mid-seventh century. The archive texts from Susa also refer to the lands of Un-sak, Zari, Huhnur, Ayapir and Parsirra or Persia, and these may identify the different principalities which arose in Elam after 646. At Shekaft-e Salman, two reliefs which originate in the Middle Elamite period and depict an Elamite royal family were (re-)claimed by a Neo-Elamite ruler of Ayapir (mod. Izeh in Khuzestan), named Hanni, who had his name, as well as those of his wife Huhun and his two daughters, Ammaten and, only partially legible, Hah-[x], carved on the reliefs (Figure 2.1). The spectacular find of a cache of precious silver objects in the Kalmakareh cave near Khorramabad in 1989 bore Elamite inscriptions of a series of kings bearing the title 'king of Samati', which may have formed a further Elamite principality in the northeast of the region.

Apart from the remains of the city of Anshan, further Elamite evidence in Fars is visible at Naqsh-e Rustam where a relief depicts an Elamite king and his queen. The central relief has been destroyed by a superimposed Sasanian relief, but the figure of the king and the head of the queen are still visible, both figures framing what most likely had been a scene depicting a religious ceremony. The king wears a long robe and is adorned with a cap-like headcover; the queen is wearing a turreted crown. Very distinctive is the position of the king's hands, clasped around one another in a gesture classed as hand-over-wrist, a feature that was adopted into Achaemenid art. Naqsh-e Rustam maintained its importance under the Persians, when Darius I and his successors chose this rock formation as the royal burial site of several Achaemenid kings. Features of Elamite kingship and court life were adopted as well as elements of Elamite administration: The Persians continued their bureaucratic system, conducting the day-to-day administration and record-keeping using Elamite language and script, even continuing to use Neo-Elamite seals, possibly heirlooms, in their administration. On example is a seal bearing the Elamite inscription '(I am) Sherash, daughter of Hubannahpi' (PFS 77*). The name Hubannahpi is known from a bronze plaque and from several documents from Susa in which he is referred to as 'son of the king' (MDP IX 167). They also mention his son Addaten. More importantly, both documents refer to Ammaten, which identified the daughter of Hanni in the inscription of Shekaft-e Salman II. If these two names refer to the same female, Hanni's daughter

Figure 2.1 Elamite relief with inscriptions of Hanni at Shekaft-e Salman II. The relief dates to the twelfth century BCE and shows a ruler of the Middle Elamite period with his queen and their heir. In the Neo-Elamite period, the ruler Hanni re-used this relief and carved his name and that of his wife and daughters alongside the older images. *Source*: Photograph with kind permission of Javier Álvarez-Mon.

may have entered the royal household of Hubannahpi through a marriage alliance. The conclusion of such a dynastic alliance between the rulers of Susa and Ayapir was by no means unusual and would have served to strengthen their respective positions. Most famous, no doubt, is the seal carved in Neo-Elamite style which shows a warrior on horseback pursuing his enemies, with two slain bodies already on the ground. The accompanying Elamite inscription identifies the warrior as 'Cyrus son of Teispes, of Anshan' (PFS 93★) and is no other than Cyrus I. The inscription and the artistic style reminiscent of that of the Neo-Elamite period allude to the close political and cultural affinity the Persians must have developed towards their Elamite neighbours over the more than one hundred years of acculturation (Figure 2.2).

2.3 The Neighbours in the North: The Medes

Like the Persians, the Medes were an Iranian people, who had settled in the northwest of the Iranian plateau, roughly covering the area between Harhar (mod. Kermanshah) and Ecbatana (mod. Hamadan). Due to the scarcity of the archaeological data and the lack of written sources, scholars encounter considerable problems in securely identifying the Medes through their language and art. As a result, it is challenging to grasp even an idea of Median culture. Faced with such difficulties, scholars have traditionally depended on Herodotus's account of Media. However, his presentation of this region as an empire united under a single ruler recently has proved untenable in

Figure 2.2 Seal of Cyrus of Anshan (PFS 93*). The seal image depicts a warrior on horseback pursuing a fleeing enemy already injured by a long spear. Two slain men are lying on the ground. The Elamite inscription reads '(I am) Cyrus son of Teispes'. Composite line drawing of impressions from the seal of Cyrus of Anshan. *Source*: Courtesy of M.B. Garrison, M.C. Root and the Persepolis Seal Project.

light of written Assyrian sources as well as of the extant archaeological record from this region itself.

2.3.1 Media in Herodotus

In his Median *logos*, the story of the Medes (Hdt.I.95–130), Herodotus presents the image of a unified Median kingdom which began with a man called Deiokes son of Phraortes and his royal city Ecbatana. In line with Herodotus's accounts of the rise and fall of other kingdoms, Median rule ended with its fifth king, Astyages, and his defeat by Cyrus II in 550. According to Herodotus, the Medes were comprised of different tribes, among them the Busae, Paretaceni, Struchates, Arizanti, Budii, and the Magi. After a 53-year reign, Deiokes (ruled c.700/699–647/6) was succeeded by his son Phraortes (ruled c.647/6–624/3). His campaign against the Persians result-ed in the latter becoming subjects of the Medes (Hdt.I.102.1). Phraortes engaged in battle with the Assyrians, continuing his father's policy, and besieged the city of Niniveh. His successor, Cyaxares (ruled c.624/3–585), was then attacked by hordes of Scythians invading from the north, resulting in the defeat of the Medes in battle. After an interregnum of 28 years, the Scythians were driven out of Media by Cyaxares. He also took the Assyrian city of Niniveh in 612, and Assyria, except for Babylon, came under Median control. Cyaxares died after 40 years of reign, and was succeeded by his son Astyages (ruled 585–550), the last king of Media.

2.3.2 Near Eastern Sources on the Medes

Of Herodotus's account only the latter period dating from the reign of Cyaxares can be credited with some historical accuracy, while his description of the 'early empire' is strongly contradicted by Near Eastern sources. Attempts to identify Deiokes with the ruler Daiukku mentioned in Assyrian texts have proved untenable, as the annals do not identify Daiukku as king of the Medes but as governor of the province Mannea. Likewise, the alleged Median king Phraortes, who has been identified with Kashtaritu, was in fact the leader of a people located in the Zagros Mountains, as mentioned in omen queries of the Assyrian king Esarhaddon (ruled 680–669):

> [Shamash, grea]t [lord, give me a f]irm, positive answer to what I am ask[ing you! Should Esarhad]don, ki[ng of Assyria, send] the messenger of his choice [to Kash]tar[itu, city ruler] of Karkashi? [and if Esarhaddo]n, king of Assyria, [sends his messenger to K] ashtaritu [will he, on the advice of his advi]sors, [seize] that messenger, [question him], kill him? (SAA 4 no. 56 obv.ll.1–9; transl. Kuhrt 2010: 28, no. 9)

Recent research shows that Media was a region governed by local chiefs or city-lords, called *bēl āli* in Akkadian. The main settlements of these Median chiefs were fortified places, such as Nush-e Jan and Godin Tepe, with storerooms, a ceremonial space with columned halls and cultic buildings (Figure 2.3).

Collectively, the Medes were referred to as Madāyu. From the time of Shalmaneser III to Ashurbanipal, Assyrian texts refer to them as Umman-manda, and they are variously described as 'the distant Medes', 'the mighty (greater) Medes of the east', the Medes 'whose country lies far off', the 'distant Medes on the borders of Mt. Bikni' (mod. Mt. Alvand) and the Medes 'who live near the salt desert'. Media was known

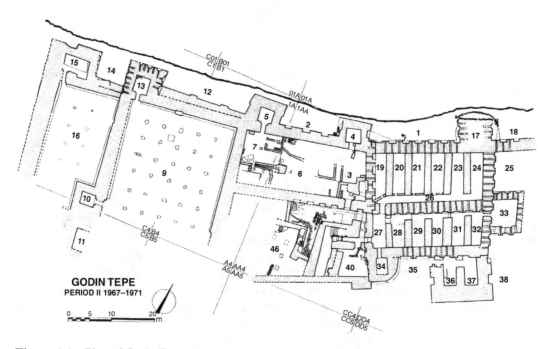

Figure 2.3 Plan of Godin Tepe. The Median site is dated to the seventh/sixth century and shows a central columned hall with a square ground plan. It is considered an architectural predecessor to the columned halls of Persepolis and Susa. A similar structure is found at the Median site of Nush-e Jan. To this we may now add the construction featuring a columned hall in the United Arab Emirates at Muweilah, Sharjah, dated to the eighth century. *Source*: After Young and Levine 1974, fig. 87.

for its horses and horse breeding, and Assyrian raids to capture the famed animals provide our earliest evidence for the Medes. In addition, they benefited from an ideal geographical position which linked the Mesopotamian lowlands to Central Asia. As enemies of the Assyrians they were repeatedly subject to raids and campaigns into their territory, first attested in 843 under Shalmaneser III. For the year 715/4 the annals of Sargon II from Dur-Sharrukin (mod. Khorsabad) attest to 22 city-lords of Media who had to pay tribute to the Assyrian king: 'For the subjugation of the land of the Medes, I strengthened Dur-Sharrukin, [...] of 22 city rulers of the mighty Medes [I received] tribute [...] the city of Kimirra of the land Bit-Hamban 2530? people, together with their possessions, I carried off [...].' In the following year, their number increased to 45: 'The tribute of Ullusunu, the Mannean, of Dalta of Ellipi, of Bel-apal-iddina of Allabria, of 45 city-rulers of the mighty Medes, 4609 horses, mules, cattle, sheep in countless numbers, I received' (Annals of Sargon II from Khorsabad, 713; transl. Kuhrt 2010: 25, no. 2 (ii), (iv)). Probably in 676, during the reign of Esarhaddon, the city-lords Uppis of Partakka, Zanasana of Partukka and Ramateia of Urakazabarna, referred to as 'Medes from a distant place who during the reign of the kings, my fathers, have not crossed the border of Assyria nor trodden its ground', paid tribute in the form of horses and lapis lazuli and asked for the king's support against other cities (Borger 1956: 54–55, episode 15; transl. Radner 2003: 58).

While these sources leave no doubt that the Median country was governed by a great number of city-lords, the political landscape changed after 614 with the emergence of a single ruler known as Umakishtar in Assyrian documents and identified with Cyaxares in Herodotus. Due to a lack of sources in the period immediately preceding Umakishtar's reign, it is not possible to explain this political development. But it is interesting to note that in this period we find political marriage alliances between a daughter of Umakishtar/Cyaxares and the Babylonian king Nabu-kudurru-usur/Nebuchadnezzar II (ruled 604–562), as well as an alliance between Cyaxares's son Ishtumegu/Astyages and the Lydian princess Aryenis daughter of Alyattes. We may surmise a link between Media's newly found political energy and the military decline of Assyria following the death of Ashurbanipal in 626 and culminating in the sack of Nineveh in 612:

> The king of Akkad mustered his army and [marched to Assyria.] The king of the Umman-manda hordes (marched) towards the king of Akkad [...] ... they met one another. [The k]ing of Akkad [... U]makishtar (= Cyaxares) and brought across, and they marched along the bank of the Tigris, and [... they encam]ped against Niniveh. Fom (the month) Simanu (= May/June) until (the month) Abu (= July/August), for three [months ...] they subjected the city to heavy fighting. Abu, [day ... a] huge [defeat] on a grea[t people(?)]. On that day, Sinsharishkun (= a son of Ashurbanipal), king of Assy[ria ...] ... [...] ... they carried off vast booty of the city and the temple and [turned] the city into a ruin he[ap...] of Assyria grasped the feet of the king of Akkad to plead for his life. (Month) Ululu, day 20 (= 8 September), Umakishtar and his army went home. After he had gone, the king of Akka[d...] they marched to Nasibina (= Nisibis). Booty and exile [...] and they brought (the people of) Rusapu to the king of Akkad at Niniveh. In [X, day X ...] in Niniveh [...f]rom day 20 of [month X], the king of [...] set out and in [...]. (Fall of Nineveh Chronicle, transl. Kuhrt 2010: 31, no. 10)

Oddly, from then on until the defeat of king Ishtumegu/Astyages by the Persian Cyrus II in 550, Near Eastern sources are silent on Media's political development. Archaeological data reveal that the fortified settlements were abandoned peacefully after 614. Whether this indicates an end of the rule of city-lords and the rise of a single king centred on Ecbatana can only be surmised. For all their military success against Assyria, the Medes did not extend their territorial control, as there is no suggestion of Median presence in Assyria. This also holds true for Median control over the territory bordering on the Lydian empire in the northwest, marked by the Halys River, as alleged in Herodotus. Rather, there is reason to consider the continued existence of a loose coalition of different peoples, as implied in a Babylonian inscription of king Nabonidus (ruled 556/5–539), which refers to the Umman-manda and 'the kings going at his sides' (Schaudig 2001: 417). References to multiple kings of Media can also be found in the Old Testament, where they are in coalition with Urartians, Manneans and Scythians (Jeremiah 51.27–28).

The 'Median Spring' of political thriving marked by its independence from Assyria ended in 550 when the Median army led by Astyages was defeated by the Persian king Cyrus II. Recorded in the Nabonidus Chronicle, the entry for the year 550 notes: '(Ishtumegu) mustered (his army) and marched against Kurash, king of Anshan, for conquest [...]. The army rebelled against Ishtumegu and he was taken prisoner. Th[ey handed him over?] to Kurash [...]. Kurash marched to Ecbatana, the royal city. Silver, gold, goods, property, [...], which he carried off as booty (from) Ecbatana, he took to Anshan. The goods (and) treasures of the army of [...]' (NCh col.II:1–4). It was an event allegedly foretold to Nabonidus by Marduk, the city-god of Babylon, in a vision which occurred to the Babylonian king at the onset of his reign: 'Marduk said to me: "The Mede of whom you spoke – he, his land and the kings who went at his side, are no more." When the third year (= of Nabonidus's reign, 553) arrived he aroused against him Kurash king of Anshan, his (= Marduk's) young servant. With his few troops he scattered the multitude of the Medes. Ishtumegu king of the Medes he seized and took him captive to his land' (Dream-text of Nabonidus, transl. after Kuhrt 2010: 56, no. 6).

Taking the available sources into account, Media was far from the unified kingdom Herodotus describes. Rather, we have to envisage Media as a territory of chiefdoms which, between 614 and 550, may have combined their military strength under one city-lord, and that this city-lord based his power at Ecbatana as the most splendid of the Median fortified settlements. Considering Media's political set-up, as well as her lack of interest in extending her territorial power, as can be observed in her retreat from Assyria, it is unlikely that Parsumash ruled by king Cyrus II could have been a vassal state of Media.

FURTHER READING

A most current and excellent discussion on the Persian migration is provided by Potts, D.T. (2014). *Nomadism in Iran. From Antiquity to the Modern Era*, especially 1–87. Oxford: Oxford University Press. On the problem of Parsua and Parsumash see Rollinger, R. (1999). Zur Lokalisation von Parsu(m)a(š) in der Fars und zu einigen Fragen der frühen persischen Geschichte. *Zeitschrift für Assyriologie* 89: 115–139. Weidner, E.F. (1931–1932). Die älteste Nachricht über das persische Königshaus. *Archiv für Orientforschung* 7: 1–7. For the Black Obelisk inscription see Grayson, A.K. (1996). *Assyrian Rulers of the Early First Millennium BC II (858–745BC)*, 62–71. Toronto: Toronto University Press (RIMA 3). see also Brinkman, J.A.

(1965). Elamite military aid to Merodach-Baladan. *Journal of Near Eastern Studies* 24: 161–166. The seal of Cyrus is extensively discussed by Garrison, M.B. (2011). The seal of "Kuraš the Anzanite, son of Šispiš" (Teispes), PFS 93*: Susa – Anšan – Persepolis. In: *Elam and Persia* (eds. J. Álvarez-Mon and M.B. Garrison), 375–405. Winona Lake, IN: Eisenbrauns. For Elam see Álvarez-Mon, J. and Basello, G.P. (eds.) (2018). *The Elamite World*. London: Routledge; Potts, D.T. (2016). *The Archaeology of Elam. Formation and Transformation of an Ancient Iranian State*, 2e. Cambridge: Cambridge University Press. The Neo-Elamite texts from Susa were published by Scheil, V. (1907). *Textes élamite-anzanites, troisième series*. Paris: Leroux (MDP IX).see also Pedersén, O. (1998). *Archives and Libraries in the Ancient Near East 1500–300 B.C*, 214–216. Bethesda, MA: CDL Press. The debate about Media and the thorny question of empire was triggered by Sancisi-Weerdenburg, H. (1988). Was there ever a Median empire? *AchHist* 3: 197–212;, and is given further in-depth consideration in a volume edited by Lanfranchi, G.B., Roaf, M., and Rollinger, R. (2003). *Continuity of Empire (?): Assyria, Media, Persia*. Padova: S.a.r.g.o.n Editrice e Libreria. From this volume, the following articles are of particular interest: Mario Liverani, The Rise and Fall of Media: 1–12, and Karen Radner, An Assyrian view of the Medes: 37–64.

3

The Establishment of Empire: Cyrus the Great

3.1 Cyrus II and Media

The history of the first Persian empire begins with the reign of Cyrus II (Elam. Kurush) on whom western historians bestowed the epithet 'the Great'. We know little more than the names of his ancestors. His father was Cambyses I (Elam. Kambujiya), his grandfather Cyrus I, and his great-grandfather Teispes (Elam. Shishpish), all of whom are accredited with the title 'king of Anshan'. The heirloom seal of Cyrus I with the Elamite inscription '(I am) Cyrus the Anshanite, son of Teispes' (see Figure 2.2) is the earliest record for the Persian royal family in Persia proper. It is preserved only as an imprint on clay tablets from Persepolis. Yet the seal's inscription and the image contain valuable information: The image was carved in the artistic style of the Neo-Elamite period, and Cyrus I used the Elamite script to embellish the seal. It may be argued that, as an oral society, the Persians' adoption of an already existing script is not surprising, but, more importantly, the use of Elamite expresses the Persians' affinity with the Elamites, and indeed Cyrus's own identification as an Anshanite. As noted in the previous chapter, the city of Anshan had been abandoned in the mid-seventh century, yet the following decades saw Elamite rulers of smaller principalities use the traditional royal title, referring to both Elamite cities. Perhaps Cyrus I referred to the region, rather that the city of Anshan, but he also may be alluding to the Elamite royal title 'king of Anshan and Susa'.

Cyrus's family belonged to the tribe of the Pasargadae, considered by Herodotus to have been one of the three highest ranking settled tribes alongside the Maraphians and the Maspians (Hdt.I.125.1). Cyrus II entered the political stage with his victory over the Median king in c.550/549. The Babylonian and Greek sources provide different reasons for the battle. According to the Nabonidus Chronicle, Astyages invaded Persis and attacked Cyrus's army, but was defeated when all or part of his troops deserted and defected to Cyrus. Astyages was taken prisoner and Cyrus claimed the Median city of Ecbatana and took possession of its treasury. Against the minimal matter-of-fact report of the Nabonidus Chronicle stands Herodotus's elaborate narrative, which

A History of Ancient Persia: The Achaemenid Empire, First Edition. Maria Brosius.
© 2021 John Wiley & Sons, Inc. Published 2021 by John Wiley & Sons, Inc.

claims that the conflict between the Medes and the Persians arose due to the Persians' political dependency on the Median king. Striving for political freedom, Cyrus called upon the Persians to fight for independence.

3.1.1 A Folktale or a Tool for Legitimacy?

Herodotus tops his story with the claim that Cyrus was Astyages's grandson, the offspring of the union between his daughter Mandane and Cambyses I. As a Persian, Cambyses I was considered politically and socially inferior by the Median king, who had his reasons for marrying his daughter beneath her status. In a dream, Astyages was foretold that a stream flowing out of his daughter's womb would cover the whole of Media. Interpreting this to mean that Mandane's offspring would deprive him of his throne, Astyages set about to deceive fate, firstly, by marrying Mandane to a man of low social rank, and secondly, by ordering the murder of the couple's son Cyrus at the hands of his courtier Harpagus. But instead of killing the infant, Harpagus entrusted the child to the cowherd Mithradates and his wife Cyno. At the age of 10, however, Cyrus's true identity was revealed and Astyages returned the child to his parents. In time, Cyrus rose against the Median king and deposed him.

Several versions of this story circulated in antiquity, the most intriguing being one recounted in the *Histories* of Nicolaus of Damascus (born c.64), according to which Cyrus was the son of the brigand Atradates and his wife Argoste, a goat-herder. They belonged to the Mardians, one of the lowest clans of the Persians. Regardless of his low rank, the young Cyrus found employment on the royal estate under the care of a royal servant, first beautifying the garden inside the palace compound, and then being promoted to the king's cupbearer. This story echoes the legend of the Assyrian king Sargon I of Akkad (ruled 2334–2279), preserved in an eighth-century BCE copy:

> Sargon, the mighty king, king of Akkad, am I. My mother was an *entum* (= a cultic functionary holding very high status), my father I knew not. My father's brother(s) dwell(?) in the mountains. My city is Azupiranu, situated on the banks of the Euphrates. My mother, the *entum*, conceived me, in secret she bore me. She placed me in a basket of rushes, with bitumen she sealed 'my door' (= the lid). She cast me into the river which did not rise over me. The river bore me up and carried me to Aqqi, the water-drawer. Aqqi, the water-drawer lifted me out as he dipped his ewer. Aqqi, the water-drawer, adopted me, brought me up. Aqqi, the water-drawer, set me up as his gardener. As a gardener, Ishtar loved me. For [56] years I exercised kingship. (ANET: no. 119; transl. Kuhrt 1995: 48)

What we observe here is the fact that the literary tradition of the Ancient Near East cast its influence as far as the Persian heartland. It suggests that the story of Cyrus's childhood was a fictional creation which, through oral and written traditions, eventually reached the Greek world where it was preserved with its variant versions. Such a story could only have derived from the royal or aristocratic levels of Persian society and had required the aid of Mesopotamian scholars to transfer the story of Sargon of Akkad to Cyrus's court.

However fictional the account of Cyrus's childhood may be, there is a strong possibility that there was no male heir to the Median throne, and that accordingly

Astyages's power would pass via his daughter Mandane to his grandson. Cambyses I, whom Cyrus II refers to as 'king of Anshan' in a brick inscription from Uruk, was certainly not the low-standing Persian Herodotus claimed. Perhaps this union expressed a diplomatic alliance between Media and neighbouring Persia. As we have seen in Chapter 2, a Persian political dependence on Media must be considered unlikely. Certainly, Herodotus's idea of a Persian fight for freedom imposes Greek fifth-century thought onto a non-Greek society and has to be discarded. There is no indication that the Persians (and the indigenous Elamite population) had any cause, political or military, to have submitted to a Median sovereignty. With the end of Assyrian political and military dominance in 612 and the revival of Elam with the principalities in the decades following the sack of Susa in 646, Cyrus II was recognised as a Persian king whose ancestors had long established their role as leaders of the people of Anshan.

If we trust the Greek historian Ctesias, who denies any pre-existing familial link between Astyages and Cyrus II, the Persian king married Astyages's daughter Amytis after his Median conquest (Ctesias FGrH 688 F9 (21)). Such an alliance would have been in accordance with a long-established Near Eastern practice of affirming political treaties or peace agreements with a royal marriage.

3.2   The Conquest of the Lydian Kingdom

With Media now in his possession, Cyrus II had at his disposal over a substantial army and the resources necessary to secure its logistics – bowmen, armour, horses for chariots and cavalry, as well as the fodder they consumed, pack animals, food and supplies for the army. Probably as a result of his victory over Media, Cyrus II also gained control over the principality to the north, Urartu. This ancient kingdom centred on the city Tushpa (mod. Van), but had been exposed to attacks from the Assyrian king Sargon II, who campaigned there in 714. About one hundred years later, it became subject to Scythian attacks. The sources are silent for the early sixth century, but perhaps Urartu was then loosely allied with Media, and, following its demise in 550, submitted to Persian sovereignty without offering resistance.

Cyrus's next military target was Lydia, ruled by king Croesus, son of Alyattes. The traditional date of this conquest, 547, has recently been contested on account of the partial illegibility of our primary source, the Nabonidus Chronicle, and, alternatively, a later date of c.542 has been suggested. Lydia, the wealthiest kingdom in western Asia Minor, was sovereign over the Ionian Greeks of the coastal cities, who paid tribute to its king. Aware of the imminent Persian attack, Croesus marched towards the city of Pteria in Cappadocia, its exact location still unknown but thought to be located near the Black Sea, to meet Cyrus's army in battle. When that fight ended in a draw, Croesus returned to Sardis to call upon military support from his allies Sparta, Babylonia and Egypt, but Cyrus's army destroyed any hope of enlarging the Lydian army with foreign support. The Persian king had marched with great speed towards Sardis, leaving Croesus with no choice but to meet him in battle outside the city walls. His army was routed by the Persians, and Croesus was forced to withdraw to the city. After a 14-day siege, Sardis was taken and Croesus, like Astyages before him, became a prisoner of the Persian king. Following the subjection of Lydia, the Ionian cities also came under Persian rule.

3.3   Cyrus and the Ionian Greeks

Herodotus informs us about the first encounter between Cyrus and the Ionians in the form of a parable which appears to echo a fable recounted in Aesop (lived c. 620–564). Prior to his attack on Sardis, Cyrus had sent messengers to the Ionians offering them favourable conditions if they were to switch sides and surrender to him peacefully. They declined, but faced with Croesus's defeat, the Ionians and Aeolians sent messengers to Sardis offering their submission to the new sovereign on the same terms as those under which they had been under the Lydian king. Cyrus responded with an allegoric tale: There once was a flute player who saw some fish in the sea and played his flute to them in the hope that they would come ashore. When they refused to do so, he took a net, netted a large catch, and hauled them in. Seeing the fish jumping about, he said to them: 'You had best cease from your dancing now; you would not come out and dance then, when I played to you' (Hdt.I.141). The moral of the tale was to demonstrate to the Ionians and Aeolians that they were ready to obey him only after Cyrus's victory, but had refused beforehand when Cyrus had asked them to revolt against Croesus. Accordingly, the Ionian cities began to prepare their defence against a Persian attack. Only Miletus had accepted the Persian sovereignty from the outset and thus was spared. In this allegory, Herodotus depicted a Persian king with shrewd political skills: his diplomacy was peaceful as long as it met with no opposition. Whoever failed to comply with the king's demand, or, in the case of the Ionians and Aeolians, accepted it too late, had to reckon with military action.

Before leaving for his next campaigns, which probably led the king towards Bactria and other eastern territories, Cyrus made arrangements to secure Persian power in Lydia, installing the Persian Tabalus as governor of Sardis, assisted by a Lydian, Pactyes, who was in charge of the treasury. Pactyes made an unsuccessful attempt to rebel against the new Persian power, but as a result of his disloyalty the Mede Harpagus took over as treasurer.

3.4   The First Royal City of the Persians: Pasargadae

No records illuminate Cyrus's eastern conquests; accordingly we cannot account for the time between the Lydian conquest in the 540s and the date of the conquest of Babylonia, 539. Herodotus has him move east only after taking Babylon, first subjecting Bactria, then Scythia and Egypt, although the latter conquest was only achieved by his son and successor Cambyses II. Other indications of Cyrus's eastern campaign are a reference in later sources to the city of Cyropolis at the northeastern frontier zone of the empire and the presence of an Indian delegation in the palace reliefs from Persepolis dated after c.518. It is possible that Cyrus returned to Persis after the Lydian conquest, and oversaw the building of the first Persian capital, Pasargadae, located in the plain of Dasht-e Murghab in Parsa. Pasargadae, known as Batrakatash in the archival texts from Persepolis, was named after Cyrus's own tribe. There is no evidence for Strabo's claim that it was built in the plain where the decisive battle against Astyages was fought (Strabo XV.3.9). Among the labourers who built the palace were Ionian Greeks who Cyrus will have brought with him after the Lydian conquest. What is visible of the city today are the royal quarters, including Cyrus's private palace, an audience hall, pavilions and an entrance gate. Slightly set aside is the tower-like structure of the Zendan-e Soleiman, and, built atop a hill, a large unfinished palace complex, the Tall-e Takht. Cyrus's palace features a *para-daida-*, an Old Persian word which was translated into Greek as *paradeisos*, 'paradise', meaning 'walled space, garden'. This garden was shaped in a large rectangular space, itself divided into rectangular units by water channels. Recent geomagnetic surveys revealed that a much wider area of the palace complex had been landscaped, and thus we may envisage that the entire compound was set in a constructed garden. The entrance gate which allowed access to the complex features a unique relief on its inner side, a male bearded figure with a double pair of wings, dressed in a long, fringed Elamite dress and wearing a triple crown. Initial suggestions that it represents Cyrus himself have been contradicted by the argument that this figure is an adaptation of the winged genius known from Neo-Assyrian palaces. In the case of the Pasargadae genius, we see an amalgamation of artistic features from Elam, Assyria and Phoenicia (Figure 3.1). Together with the Ionian stonemasons, Cyrus obviously intended to have the conquered lands of his empire reflected in his palatial art.

At a distance to the two palatial buildings, Cyrus II built his tomb atop a six-stepped platform (Figures 3.2 and 3.3). In its simple structure and design the tomb of Cyrus presents a truly elegant piece of architecture; it is perfectly proportioned with pyramidal steps and a single chamber structure with a gabled roof, each section measuring about 5.5 m.

Figure 3.1   Winged genius from Pasargadae. The single relief figure is placed at the Entrance Gate at the Pasargadae complex (Gate R). The figure wears a long Elamite dress and a headdress known from Phoenicia, though it originates in Egypt. The figure is double-winged, reminiscent of the double-winged genii of Neo-Assyrian palaces. *Source*: Author photograph.

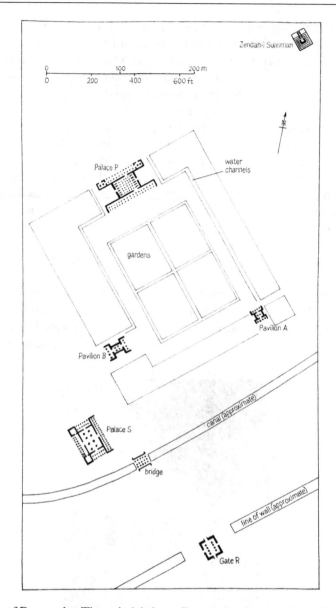

Figure 3.2   Plan of Pasargadae. The palatial site at Pasargadae features the palace of Cyrus (Palace P), looking out onto a rectangular spaced garden watered by means of water channels, still visible today. Two pavilions (Pavilion A and B) complete the immediate palace site. To the south, a second palace was built (Palace S). The site was accessed via the Entrance Gate (Gate R), and then by crossing a bridge. North of Cyrus's palace is a tower-like structure, the Zendan-e Suleiman, whose function is not yet fully understood. *Source*: Drawing by Marion Cox.

The bottom three pyramidal steps measure 1 m in height, the upper three only half a metre. The origin of its architectural design remains a question of debate: on the one hand it has been proposed that this is an adaptation of the so-called Pyramid tomb near Sardis, the tomb of Alyattes, or the tomb of Taş Kule near Phocaea, while

Figure 3.3   The tomb of Cyrus II is a single chamber space with a gabled roof placed on a six-stepped platform. The whole structure is perfectly proportioned, with the steps measuring 5.5 m, and the gabled tomb chamber measuring slightly less, achieving an overall height of almost 11 m. *Source*: Author photograph.

on the other we find a similar structure built on a smaller scale and executed in a more humble style at Gur-e Duhktar (mod. Buzpar) in Persis. The suggested solution to this problem may be the Ionian stonemasons who are attested as the builders of Pasargadae; Lydo-Ionian architecture may well have served as a model for Cyrus's tomb, copied and adapted by the Ionian workers at Pasargadae.

Pasargadae remained the royal memorial of the Persian kings, the place where Cyrus's tomb was maintained and sacrifices made. An administrative text from Persepolis records the dispensing of grain given to the priest (Elam. *shatin*) at Pasargadae for the *akris* of the god(s) (PF 774), a term which we have not yet been able to translate. Cyrus's successors celebrated their investiture at Pasargadae and commemorated the founder of the empire. Two centuries after Cyrus's death, Alexander III of Macedon (ruled 336–323), who considered himself a *philocyros*, a 'lover of Cyrus', paid homage to Cyrus and was enraged when his orders of protecting the tomb had been disobeyed.

> He (= Alexander) was distressed by the outrage on the tomb of Cyrus son of Cambyses since (as Aristobulus relates) he found it broken and rifled. The tomb of the famous Cyrus was in Pasargadae in the royal park; a grove had been planted around it with all sorts of trees and irrigated, and deep grass had grown in the meadow; the tomb itself in the lower parts was built of stones and a door leading into it so narrow that it was hard and caused much distress for a single man of low stature to get through. In the chamber lay a golden sarcophagus in which Cyrus's body had been buried; a couch stood by its side with feet of wrought gold; a Babylonian tapestry served as a coverlet and purple rugs as a carpet. There was placed on it a sleeved mantle and other garments of Babylonian workmanship. According to Aristobulus, Median trousers and

robes dyed blue lay there, some dark, some of other varying shades, with necklaces, scimitars and earrings of stones set in gold, and a table stood there. It was between the table and the couch that the sarcophagus containing Cyrus's body was placed. Within the enclosure and by ascent to the tomb itself there was a small building put up for the *magi* who used to guard Cyrus's tomb, from as long ago as Cambyses, son of Cyrus, an office transmitted from father to son. The king used to give them a sheep a day, a fixed amount of meal and wine, and a horse each month to sacrifice to Cyrus. (Arr.*an*.VI.29.4–7)

3.5   The Conquest of Babylon

At the time of Cyrus's conquest of Babylon in October 539, the city was ruled by king Nabonidus (ruled 556–539). He had usurped the Babylonian throne after a conspiracy removed the ruler, Labashi-Marduk, son of king Nergal-sharru-usur/Neriglissar (ruled 559–556). Nabonidus may well have been acquainted with Babylonian court life because of his mother, Adad-guppi, who seems to have held an eminent position at the court of previous Babylonian kings. Despite military successes in north Arabia, Nabonidus met with resentment among the Babylonian elite due to his favouring the moon god Sin over the city god of Babylon, Marduk. The Babylonian king devoted much attention to the temple of Sin at Harran in northern Babylon, and declared his daughter En-nigaldi-Nanna the high priestess of the sanctuary of Sin in Ur. In addition, a campaign against northern Arabia which began in 553 meant that Nabonidus was absent from Babylon for 10 years. His continued emphasis on the cult of the god Sin to the point of neglect of that of Marduk seems to have fostered the resentment of the Babylonian population, an emotion which we find strongly expressed in Cyrus's account of his Babylonian conquest. This report makes for the best-documented conquest of all of Cyrus's campaigns. 'Best' in the sense that we possess a unique primary source documenting the event in the form of an inscription, seemingly by Cyrus himself, in which he recounted his entry into Babylon under the divine protection of Marduk.

The original text was written in Babylonian on a clay cylinder, a shape which is reminiscent of Assyrian building inscriptions, and was found in 1879 in Babylon by Hormuzd Rassam (1826–1910 CE), an archaeologist from Ottoman Mesopotamia. The Cyrus Cylinder is now housed in the British Museum, London. There, the recent find of fragments of a Babylonian clay tablet, which turned out to be part of a copy of the same Cyrus Cylinder text, not only allowed the restoration of the first five lines of the inscription and an improved reading of the last four lines following line 44, but also revealed that this text, far from being a unique document, was copied – most likely more than once – and thus made available to a wider audience. It may be surmised that Cyrus had a vested interest in distributing his version of events widely amongst the Babylonian population for the simple reason of convincing them of his peaceful and god-approved rule over Babylonia. In order to 'create' this version, Cyrus enlisted the advice of Babylonian scholars who composed a text which, in the tradition of Babylonian literature, maligned the ruling king Nabonidus, emphasising the religious sacrileges committed by him, and Cyrus's own support of the Babylonian god Marduk.

Sources in Translation 3.1

The Cyrus Cylinder

The text of the Cyrus Cylinder consists of two parts. Lines 1–19 are written in the third-person singular, creating a detached, 'objective' description of the situation in Babylon, outlining Nabonidus's neglect of the city and the god Marduk's selection of Cyrus as the city's saviour. The second part, lines 20–45, switches to the first-person singular, seemingly having Cyrus speaking directly to the reader/the audience, recounting his restoration of the cult of Marduk and the sanctuaries and the restoration of the city wall Imgur-Enlil. Cyrus's 'peaceful' entrance into Babylon allows him to claim the Babylonian royal title, which is being combined with his Persian title as 'king of Anshan': '(ll.20–21): I am Cyrus, king of the universe, the Great King, the powerful king, king of Babylon, king of Sumer and Akkad, king of the four quarters of the world, son of Cambyses, the Great King, king of the city of Anshan, grandson of Cyrus, the Great King, ki[ng of the ci]ty of Anshan, descendant of Teispes, the Great King, king of the city of Anshan.'

[When ... Mar]duk, king of the whole of heaven and earth, the ... who, in his ... lays waste his ... [...] broad? in intelligence, ... who inspects (?) the wor]ld quarters (regions) [...] his [first]born (= Belshazzar), a low person, was put in charge of his country, but [...] he set [a ... counter]feit over them. He ma[de] a counterfeit of Esagil, [and ...] ... for Ur and the rest of the cult-cities. Rites inappropriate to them, [impure] fo[od-offerings ...] disrespectful [...] were daily gabbled, and, as an insult, he brought the daily offerings to a halt; he inter[fered with the rites and] instituted [...] within the sanctuaries. In his mind, reverential fear of Marduk, king of the gods, came to an end. He did yet more evil to his city every day; ... his [people ...], he brought ruin on them all by a yoke without relief. Enlil-of-the-gods became extremely angry at their complaints, and [...] their territory. The gods who lived within them left their shrines, angry that he had made (them) enter into Babylon. Ex[alted Marduk, Enlil-of-the-Go]ds, relented. He changed his mind about all the settlements whose sanctuaries were in ruins, and the population of the land of Sumer and Akkad who had become like corpses, and took pity on them. He inspected and checked all the countries, seeking for the upright king of his choice. He took the hand of Cyrus, king of the city of Anshan, and called him by his name, proclaiming him aloud for the kingship over all of everything. He made the land of Guti and all the Median troops prostrate themselves at his feet, while he shepherded in justice and righteousness the black-headed people whom he had put under his care. Marduk, the great lord, who nurtures his people, saw with pleasure his fine deeds and true heart, and ordered that he should go to Babylon. He had him take the road to Babylon, and, like a friend and companion, he walked at his side. His vast troops whose number, like the water in a river, could not be counted, were marching fully-armed at his side. He had him enter without fighting or battle right into Babylon; he saved his city Babylon from hardship. He handed over to him Nabonidus, the king who did not fear him. All the people of Babylon, of all Sumer and Akkad, nobles and governors, bowed down before him and kissed his feet, rejoicing over his kingship and their faces shone. The lord through whose help all were rescued from death and who saved them all from distress and hardship, they blessed him sweetly and praised his name.

I am Cyrus, king of the universe, the Great King, the powerful king, king of Babylon, king of Sumer and Akkad, king of the four quarters of the world, son of Cambyses, the Great King, king of the city of Anshan, grandson of Cyrus, the Great King, ki[ng of the ci]ty of Anshan, descendant of Teispes, the Great King, king of the city of Anshan, the perpetual seed of kingship, whose reign Bel (Marduk) and Nabu love, and with whose kingship, to their joy, they concern themselves. When I went as harbinger of peace i[nt]o Babylon I founded my sovereign residence within the palace amid celebration and rejoicing. Marduk, the great lord, bestowed on me as my destiny the great magnanimity of one who loves Babylon, and I every day sought him out in awe. My vast troops were marching peaceably in Babylon, and the whole of [Sumer] and Akkad had nothing to fear. I sought the safety of the city of Babylon and all its sanctuaries. As for the population of Babylon [..., w]ho as if without div[ine intention] had endured a yoke not decreed for them, I soothed their weariness; I freed them from their bonds(?). Marduk, the great lord, rejoiced at [my good] deeds, and he pronounced a sweet blessing over me, Cyrus, the king who fears him, and over Cambyses, the son [my] issue, [and over] my all my troops, that we might live happily in his presence, in well-being. At his exalted command, all kings who sit on thrones, from every quarter, from the Upper Sea to the Lower Sea, those who inhabit [remote distric]ts (and) the kings of the land of Amurru who live in tents, all of them, brought their weighty tribute into Babylon, and kissed my feet. From [Babylon] I sent back to their places to the city of Ashur and Susa, Akkad, the land of Eshnunna, the city of Zamban, the city of Meturnu, Der, as far as the border of the land of Guti – the sanctuaries across the river Tigris – whose shrines had earlier become dilapidated, the gods who lived therein, and made permanent sanctuaries for them. I collected together all of their people and returned them to their settlements, and the gods of the land of Sumer and Akkad which Nabonidus – to the fury of the lord of the gods – had brought into Babylon, at the command of Marduk, the great lord, I returned them unharmed to their cells, in the sanctuaries that make them happy. May all the gods that I returned to their sanctuaries, every day before Bel and Nabu, ask for a long life for me, and mention my good deeds, and say to Marduk, my lord, this: 'Cyrus, the king who fears you, and Cambyses his son, may they be the provisioners of our shrines until distant(?) days, and the population of Babylon call blessings on my kingship. I have enabled all the lands to live in peace.' Every day I increased by [... ge]ese, two ducks and 10 pigeons the [former offerings] of geese, ducks and pigeons. I strove to strengthen the defences of the wall Imgur-Enlil, the great wall of Babylon, and [I completed] the quay of baked brick on the bank of the moat which an earlier king had bu[ilt but not com]pleted its work. [I... which did not surround the city] outside, which no earlier king had built, his workforce, the levee [from his land, in/int]o Babylon. [...with bitum]en and baked brick I built anew, and [completed] its [work]. [...] great [doors of cedar wood] with bronze cladding, [and I installed] all their doors, threshold slabs and door fittings with copper parts. [...]. I saw within it an inscription of Ashurbanipal, a king who preceded me; [...] in its place. May Marduk, the great lord, present to me as a gift a long life and the fullness of age, [a secure throne and an enduring rei]gn, [and may I ... in] your heart forever.

Written and check]ed. [from a...]; (this) tablet (is) of Qishti-Marduk, son of [...]. (BM 90920, BM 47134 & BM 47176; transl. after Finkel 2013)

With this text Cyrus revealed a well-thought-out political strategy with which to appeal to a subjected country and to secure his acceptance as king. He also demonstrated his own awareness of the importance of history. Until recently, only the shape of the cylinder itself, as well as the reference to Ashurbanipal as his predecessor in line 43, hinted at a deliberate link to a historical past and therefore to a claim of continuity and legitimacy of kingship. With the find of the fragments of a second copy of the Cyrus Cylinder text, however, this connection has become markedly stronger. The text also points to Cyrus's desire to create a link to the Babylonian past. Hanspeter Schaudig has demonstrated that the text is a testament to Babylonian intellectual heritage, which is being used to allow Cyrus II to present himself as a legitimate successor to the Babylonian kingship (Schaudig 2018). It borrows phrases and sentiments from the second-millennium BCE Babylonian Epic of Creation called *enuma elish*, 'When on high', after the first lines of the text, as well as from the Esagil Chronicle, a religious text also dating to the second millennium BCE. It was written by a king of Ishin to the Babylonian king Apil-Sin (ruled 1830–1813) and contains references to the sins of earlier kings. Sentiments and phrases expressed in these two texts are being echoed in the Cyrus Cylinder with the intention to present Nabonidus in a negative light. Simultaneously, of course, they are to show that Cyrus regarded himself as following in the footsteps of his Assyrian and Babylonian predecessors. Without a doubt, Cyrus II relied on Babylonian scholars to advise him on how best to present himself as the new king of Babylon, placing himself within a Babylonian literary tradition as well as appearing as the saviour of the cult of Marduk and, with it, of Babylon itself.

In order to settle affairs without causing a major interruption, Cyrus's main concern dealt with the religious policy of Babylon, returning the statues of the gods of Akkad, which Nabonidus had taken away, to their appropriate place (NCh col.III.21–22). The Cyrus Cylinder explicitly shows Cyrus's respect for the Babylonian city god Marduk and for Nabu, the god of writing. It becomes clear from the reading of the text that Marduk sanctioned Cyrus's war against Nabonidus. For both Cyrus, as the new king of Babylonia, and his son Cambyses, Marduk requested the people's support. In return, Cyrus restored the cult centres in Babylon that apparently had been abandoned, and all the gods returned to their homes at the command of Marduk.

3.5.1   A Peaceful Conquest?

With the conquest of Babylonia, and simultaneously, with the conquest of Mesopotamia and the lands up to the eastern Mediterranean including the cities of Phoenicia, Cyrus II had successfully brought the Near Eastern realms under Persian control. Whether the conquest of Babylon was indeed as 'peaceful' as he claimed in his account may be doubted. The Nabonidus Chronicle gives a different view from Cyrus's version and shows Cyrus less as the 'humane' king than a military conqueror. According to this text, Cyrus, on his approach towards Babylon, took the city of Opis at the bank of the River Tigris by force, plundering the city and killing its inhabitants. At the news of such brutal fighting, the neighbouring city of Sippar surrendered without any resistance: '(...) In the month Tashritu (= September/October) when Cyrus did battle at Opis on (the bank of?) the Tigris against the army of Akkad, the people of Akkad retreated. He carried off the plunder (and) slaughtered the people. On the fourteenth day Sippar was captured without a battle. Nabonidus fled' (NCh col.III: ll.12–15). In Herodotus's version, the Babylonians met Cyrus in battle outside the city, only to retreat behind the city walls. Cyrus's troops then entered the city via a channel of the Euphrates River. In order to do so, his troops drew off the river by a canal which lowered the water level of the Euphrates channel, thus allowing the Persian troops to enter the city (Hdt.I.190).

3.5.2   Political Astuteness

In either case, Cyrus staged an official entry into Babylon as a symbol of his peaceful and god-approved conquest 17 days after Babylon's actual surrender. 'On the sixteenth day (= 12 October 539) Ugbaru, governor of the Guti, and the army of Cyrus entered Babylon without a battle. (...) On the third day of the month Arahshammu (= 29 October 539) Cyrus entered Babylon. [...] were filled with [...] before him. There was peace in the city while Cyrus spoke (his) greeting to all of Babylon' (NCh col. III ll.15–20). Cyrus immediately concerned himself with the seamless take-over of the city: he appointed Ugbaru governor of Babylon, who, in turn, was charged with appointing the district officers. It was also in Babylon that Cyrus installed his son and heir Cambyses II as king of Babylon. This seems to be indicated in a further passage of the Nabonidus Chronicle: 'When on the fourth day (of Nisan) (= 28 March 538) Cambyses, the son of Cyrus, went to E-ningiedar-kalamma-summu, the official of the sceptre-house of Nabu [gave him?] the sceptre of the land. When [Cyrus?] came, in Elamite attire, he [took] the hands of Nabu [...] lances and quivers he picked [up, and?] with the crown-prince [he came down?] into the courtyard' (NCh col.III: 24–27; transl. after Kuhrt 2010: 51, no. 1).

Special Topic 3.1

Cyrus and the Jewish Exiles

Soon after establishing his power in Babylon, Cyrus released the Jewish prisoners of war who had been captured during the campaign of the Babylonian king Nabu-kudurru-usur II/Nebuchadnezzar II against Judaea in 587 and allowed their return to their homeland, promising to take care of the rebuilding of the Temple, which had been destroyed during the war. 'In the first year Cyrus, king of Persia, in order to fulfil the word of the Lord spoken by Jeremiah, the Lord moved the heart of Cyrus, king of Persia to make a proclamation throughout his realm and to put in writing: This is what Cyrus king of Persia says: "The Lord, the God of Heaven, has given me all the kingdoms of the earth and he has appointed me to build a temple for him at Jerusalem in Judaea. Anyone of his people among you – may the Lord his God be with him and let him go up"'

(2 Chronicles 36: 22–23). Similarly the Book of Ezra records: 'In the first year of king Cyrus, the king issued a decree concerning the God in Jerusalem: Let the temple be replaced as a place to present sacrifices, and let its foundations be laid. It is to be ninety feet high and ninety feet wide, with three courses of large stones and one of timbers. The costs are to be paid by the royal treasury. Also the gold and silver articles of the house of God which Nebuchadnezzar took from the Temple in Jerusalem and brought to Babylon are to be returned to their places in the Temple in Jerusalem; they are to be deposited in the House of God' (Ezra 6.3–5).

There is a striking resemblance between Yahweh's selection of Cyrus as the ruler of the world and Marduk's identification of Cyrus as the saviour of Babylon in the Cyrus Cylinder text: 'Thus says Yahweh, your Redeemer, who fashioned you from birth (...), who says to Cyrus: "You shall be my shepherd to carry out all my purpose, so that Jerusalem may be rebuilt and the foundations of the temple may be laid." Thus says the Lord to Cyrus, his anointed, Cyrus, whom he has taken by the hand to subdue the nations before him and undo the might of kings' (Isaiah 44: 24–45:1; transl. after Kuhrt 2010: 83, no. 26 (iv)). We may see here the repetition of a literary motif adapted from Mesopotamian tradition.

About 20 years later, in the winter of 520 or 519, Cyrus's successor Darius I (ruled 522–486) ordered a search for Cyrus's decree in the royal archives at the behest of Tattenai, the governor of Transeuphratene. This satrapy described the lands west of the Euphrates River to the eastern Mediterranean. The construction of the temple had come to a halt, and the people of Jerusalem wanted confirmation of the pledge Cyrus had made to them. The document was finally recovered in the archive of Ecbatana. The restoration work could be continued and the temple was finally completed on the third day of the month Adar (= February/March) in the sixth year of Darius, which was 12 March 515 (Ezra 6:13–15).

There can be no doubt that as a result of his policy Cyrus gained considerable political support from the Jewish community. However, before we conclude that Cyrus was exceptional in his religious tolerance, it needs to be pointed out that this carefully planned strategy had a predecessor. Cyrus's association with the Assyrian king Ashurbanipal as 'the king who preceded me' clearly was intended to show his association with the Assyrian king. In addition, it was a standard procedure for Babylonian rulers to ascertain that their rule was legitimised by the respective god. Cyrus's engagement in the restoration of city-cults and cult centres is attested elsewhere in Babylonia, as can be gauged from several building inscriptions from Uruk and Ur. The picture thus emerging shows that Cyrus pursued a deliberate policy in order to consolidate his power over the people of Mesopotamia and Judaea by exercising a level of religious tolerance which saw him as the new king who was the protégé of all the gods as well as the protector of their cults and sanctuaries on earth. We may assume that this attitude was also expressed in the conquered kingdoms of Media, Lydia, Bactria and the other eastern regions, though evidence is lacking.

3.6   The Scythian Campaign

For information about Cyrus's final conquest, we are exclusively dependent on Greek sources. Herodotus recounts a campaign against the Massagetae, a Scythian tribe who inhabited the lands northeast of the Caspian Sea. At the time of Cyrus's attack, the Massagetae were ruled by queen Tomyris; when her son Spargapises became a captive of the Persians, rather than being imprisoned by them, he committed suicide. In a call for revenge, Tomyris's army defeated the Persians in a hard-won battle during which Cyrus himself was killed. Herodotus even has Tomyris ordering the mutilation of Cyrus's body, having his head cut off and immersed in a pail of blood. Later Greek writers such as Ctesias (lived end of the fifth/early fourth century) and Xenophon (lived c.430–354), however, have him die peacefully in his palace, though not before he could resolve the issue of his succession and divide control of the empire between his sons, appointing Cambyses as royal heir and Bardiya, who is known in these sources as Tanyozarkes or Tanoxares, as satrap of the eastern lands of the empire.

3.7   Cyrus II, Conqueror and Empire-Builder

Within the space of 20 years, Cyrus II king of Anshan had conquered the known Near Eastern world and its kingdoms, from Media in the north, Lydia in the northwest, Babylonia and the adjacent lands to the eastern Mediterranean in the west, as well as the eastern and northeastern territories of the Iranian plateau up to the steppes of Central Asia in the north and the Indus River in the east. Through his conquests, he had amassed an unfathomable amount of wealth from the royal treasuries of the conquered palaces, controlled a substantial naval force comprised of Ionian, Cypriote and Phoenician ships, increased the manpower to serve in his army and gained access to a wealth of natural resources of the conquered lands. The success of his conquest, moreover, lay in the balance he struck between conquest and consolidation. Immediately following a conquest, he concerned himself with the governance of the land as well as demonstrably showing his respect for the local gods. He passed himself off as the guarantor of the different religions of his subjects, safeguarding their cults and sanctuaries. In seeking the co-operation of local elites, as is evidenced in the Babylonian take-over, he was able to recruit an influential class of the ruling society for his purposes, empowering them through the award of high office. He built the first Persian royal capital, Pasargadae, with his private palace and reception palace, and thus gave Persian power a visual and representational expression. His inscriptions reveal that he saw himself following in the footsteps of Assyrian and Babylonian kings, establishing a link to their idea of kingship both in written and visual form. It imbedded the Persian king in a Near Eastern tradition, and through it Cyrus created his own place in the history of the Ancient Near East. His success as an empire-builder becomes apparent not least in the smooth transition of power to his heir, Cambyses II. No source recounts any attempt at rebellion – a political base had been established which was sufficiently strong to allow Cambyses II to take over the kingship unchallenged and to carry on his father's conquests. His military target was the only kingdom remaining in the Near East: Egypt.

FURTHER READING

For the legend of Sargon I and its literary tradition see Drews, R. (1974). Sargon, Cyrus and Mesopotamian folk history. *Journal of Near Eastern Studies* 33: 387–394. Kuhrt, A. (2003). Making history. Sargon of Agade and Cyrus the Great of Persia. *AchHist* 13: 347–361. On the disputed date of the Lydian conquest see Rollinger, R. (2009). The Median 'empire', the end of Urartu, and Cyrus' campaign in 547 (Nabonidus Chronicle II 16). *Ancient West & East* 7: 49–63. For the Cyrus Cylinder and the conquest of Babylon see: Finkel, I. (2013). *The Cyrus Cylinder*. London: Tauris. Lambert, W.G. (2013). *Babylonian Creation Myths*. Winona Lake, IN: Eisenbrauns. Kuhrt, A. (2007). Cyrus the Great: images and realities. In: *Representations of Political Power: Case Histories from Times of Change and Dissolving Order in the Ancient Near East* (eds. M. Heinz and M.H. Feldman), 169–192. Winona Lake, IN: Eisenbrauns. Rollinger, R. (1993). *Herodotus' Babylonischer Logos, eine kritische Untersuchung der Glaubwürdigkeitsdiskussion. Innsbrucker Beiträge zur Kulturwissenschaft* Special Issue 84. Schaudig, H. (2001). *Die Inschriften Nabonids von Babylon und Kyros' des Grossen samt den in ihrem Umfeld entstandenen Tendenzschriften. Textausgabe und Grammatik*. Münster: Ugarit (AOAT 256). Schaudig, H. (2018). The magnanimous heart of Cyrus. The Cyrus Cylinder and its literary models, In: *Cyrus the Great. Life and Lore* (ed. M. Rahim Shahyegan), 16–25. Boston: Ilex Foundation. Beaulieu, P.-A. (2018). *A History of Babylon 2200 BC – AD 75*. Oxford: Wiley Blackwell.

For Cyrus and the Old Testament see Kuhrt, A. (2007). Problems in writing the history of Israel: the case of Cyrus the Great of Persia. In: *Understanding the History of Israel* (ed. H. Williamson), 107–127. Oxford, London: Oxford University Press for the British Academy. The palace site of Pasargadae is discussed by Benech, C., Boucharlat, R., and Gondet, S. (2012). Organisation et aménagement de l'espace à Pasargades: Reconnaissances archéologiques de surface 2003–2008. *Arta* 3: 1–37. Boucharlat, R. (2001). The palace and the Royal Achaemenid City: two case studies – Pasargadae and Susa. In: *The Royal Palace Institution in the First Millennium BC*, 113–123. Aarhus: Aarhus University Press (Monographs of the Danish Institute at Athens 4); Boucharlat, R. (1997). Susa under Achaemenid rule. In: *Mesopotamia and Iran in the Persian Period. Conquest and Imperialism 539–331 BC. Proceedings of a Seminar in Memory of Vladimir G. Lukonin* (ed. J. Curtis), 54–67. London: British Museum Press. Stronach, D. (1969). *Pasargadae*. Oxford: Oxford University Press.

4

A Worthy Successor: Cambyses II

4.1 The Succession of Cambyses II

Following the death of his father in 530, Cambyses II, king of Babylon since 538, succeeded to the Persian throne. The earliest document attesting the commencement of his reign originates from Babylon and is dated to '12 Ulul (= 31 August 530), accession year of Cambyses, king of Babylon, king of lands' (Strassmaier 1890: no. 1). A member of the Pasargadae tribe on his father's side, Cambyses also belonged to the Achaemenid clan through his mother Cassandane, the daughter of the Achaemenid Pharnaspes (Elam. Parnaka). As the first-born son, Cambyses became the designated heir to the throne ahead of his brother Bardiya; in addition, there were two known sisters, Atossa and Artystone (Elam. Irtashduna), and a niece, Bardiya's daughter Parmys (Elam. Uparmiya). Cambyses II was married to Phaidyme, daughter of the Persian noble Otanes and the granddaughter of Pharnaspes, and thus Cassandane's niece. Ctesias mentions a wife called Roxane but there is no information about her background. More critically, Herodotus also claims that Cambyses married two full sisters, one of whom was Atossa. The other, who remains unnamed, died during Cambyses's campaign in Egypt. Whatever the truth of these marriages, no son and heir was born to Cambyses, a fact which had implications for the events following Cambyses's early and unexpected death, which assigned a crucial role to his sisters and his niece. His reign ended after only after eight years, due either to illness or to a fatal accident, some time after 1 July 522. Yet within this brief period, he succeeded in subjecting Egypt to Persian rule, and even (parts of) Nubia (mod. Sudan). Following Egypt's submission to the king, Libya, with the city of Cyrene, also recognised the sovereignty of Persia (Map 4.1).

Cambyses not only continued his father's expansion of the empire and his religious policy, he also adhered to Cyrus's imperial policy in Parsa. Early excavators ascribed to him a palace site in Dasht-e Gohar which resembles the architectural style of Pasargadae, and the remains of an unfinished tomb with a stepped platform comparable to the one we observe at Cyrus's tomb (Figure 4.1). While it remains a possibility that Cambyses wanted to emulate his father's idea of palatial and funerary architecture,

A History of Ancient Persia: The Achaemenid Empire, First Edition. Maria Brosius.
© 2021 John Wiley & Sons, Inc. Published 2021 by John Wiley & Sons, Inc.

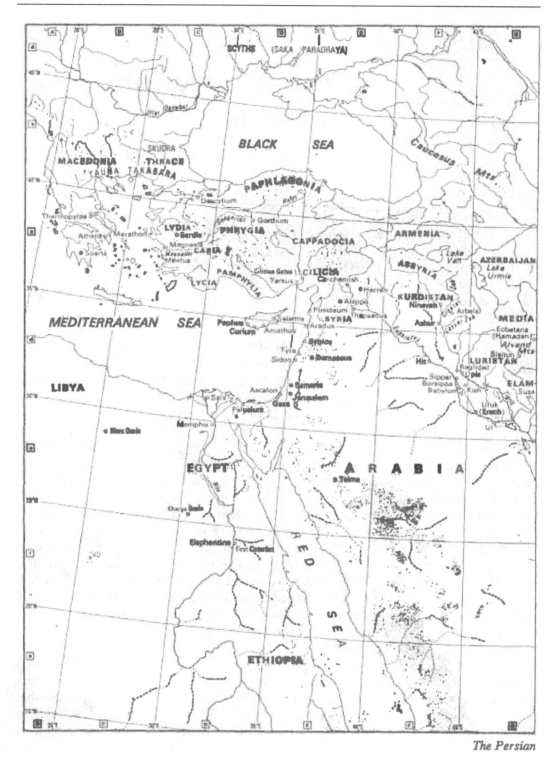

The Persian

Map 4.1   Map of the Persian empire in 526/5. *Source*: With kind permission of the Cambridge University Press.

Empire

Map 4.1   (Continued)

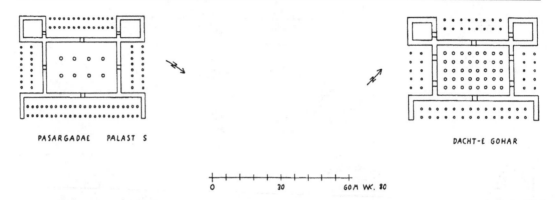

PASARGADAE   PALAST S

DACHT-E GOHAR

0   30   60 M WK. 80

Figure 4.1 Plan of the palace at Dasht-e Gohar. The ground plan shows a striking similarity to Palace S at Pasargadae and therefore has been dated to the reign of Cambyses II. *Source*: After Kleiss 1980, Abb. 3.

recent scholarly debate has cast doubt on this interpretation, attributing the two structures to Darius's father, Hystaspes. Cambyses's burial place thus remains unknown, though recently it has been suggested that this might be at Narezzash (mod. Niriz, southeastern Fars). Yet, although some Persepolis texts refer to the *shumar* of Cambyses being honoured there, no archaeological evidence has come to light which could corroborate the suggestion that Narezzash was Cambyses's burial place. It is possible that we need to ascribe to Cyrus, and possibly Cambyses, more intensive building activity in Parsa, if we consider the palace sites at Dasht-e Gohar, and those near Borazjan (Bardak-e Siah, Charkhab, Sang-e Siah), as early Persian, despite the Achaemenid style reliefs. The recent archaeological discoveries at Tol-e Ajori are among the most striking in recent years. The Italian-Iranian excavators of the site, which is located 3.5 km southwest of the Persepolis terrace, identified a monumental gate with walls more than 10 m thick. It implies the planning there of a palatial complex comparable to that of Pasargadae. The mythical creatures on the relief tiles of the gate, the striding bull and the *mahkhusshu*, the dragon-snake, allow a direct parallel to the Ishtar Gate of Babylon. The bricks, differing in their consistency from those at Susa, confirm that this gate must belong to the early Persian period, that is, after Cyrus's conquest of Babylon in 539, but before the start of Darius's building complex at Persepolis in c.518. This has several implications: on the one hand it confirms that the site had been identified as a base for a new city-foundation before Darius. On the other, the replica of the Babylonian city gate supports the idea that Cambyses, like his father before him, regarded himself as a successor to the Babylonian kings. The construction of the Babylonian city gate in Parsa meant more than an architectural copy – it was to be understood as a symbol of the continuity of power and of the Babylonian heritage of Persian kingship.

4.2 The Power of Propaganda

Primary sources from Egypt written in Hieroglyphs as well as Demotic indicate that Cambyses expressed his respect for Egyptian religion, taking the Pharaonic name Mesuti-Re, 'son of Re', restoring neglected temples and celebrating divine cults. With the exception of three temples, he did, however, curb the wealth of the Egyptian

Sources in Translation 4.1

The Inscription of Udjahorresnet

One of the key Egyptian sources for assessing Cambyses's attitude towards Egypt and its religious cults is the autobiography of the Egyptian official Udjahorresnet. A high official already under the king Khnemibre (Gr. Amasis, ruled 570–526/5) and his son Ankhare III (Gr. Psammetichus III, ruled 526/5), he held the position of chief physician as well as of chief scribe, administrator of the palace, king's friend and admiral of the fleet, to name just a few, and now found himself as advisor of Cambyses II, whom he advised on his Egyptian royal title Mesuti-Re, 'son of Re', and guided him to become the protector of the temple of the goddess Neith at Saïs. This temple had fallen into disrepair, but due to Cambyses's concern it was purified and restored, the festivals in honour of Neith revived. Udjahorresnet even described Cambyses's own devotion to the goddess, as he visited the temple and prostrated himself before the deity. The action shows the Persian king expressing all due respect to a foreign divinity, and his endeavours to restore the cult and the buildings hold up to a comparison with Cyrus's activities in Babylon, Ur and Uruk. On a smaller scale, the Hieroglyphic inscription on a seal of Cambyses allows the conclusion that his respect for Egyptian gods was not limited to Neith. The text, a dedication to the goddess Wadjet, the deity of the city of Imet (mod. Tell Nabasha, nr. Husseiniya in the eastern Nile Delta), declares: 'The King of Upper and Lower Egypt, Cambyses, beloved of (the goddess) Wadjet, ruler of (the city of) Imet, the great one, Eye of the Sun, ruler of the sky, mistress of the gods, given life like (that of) Re (the sun god)'. (transl. Brosius 2000: 14, no. 19).

'[...] The one honoured by Neith the Great One, the mother of the god, and by the gods of Saïs, the prince, count, royal seal-bearer, sole companion, true king's acquaintance, his beloved, the scribe, inspector in the assembly, overseer of scribes, great leader, administrator of the palace, commander of the king's navy under the King of Upper and Lower Egypt Ankhkare (= Psammetichus III), Udjahorresnet; engendered by the administrator of the castles (of the red crown), chief-of-Pe priest, *rnp*-priest, he who embraces the Eye of Horus, priest of Neith who presides over the Nome of Saïs, Peftuaneith. He says: "The Great King of all foreign Lands, Cambyses, came to Egypt, and the foreigners of all foreign lands were with him. He ruled the entire land. They made their dwellings therein, and he was the Great King of Egypt, the Great King of all foreign Lands. His Majesty assigned to me the office of chief physician. He caused me to be beside him as a companion administrator of the palace. I made his royal titulary, his name being the King of Upper Egypt and Lower Egypt Mesuti-Re (= Cambyses).

I caused His Majesty to perceive the greatness of Saïs, that it is the seat of Neith the Great, the mother who bore Re, who began birth when no birth had yet been; and the nature of the greatness of the temple of Neith: that it is heaven in every aspect; and the nature of the greatness of the temples of Neith and also of all the gods and goddesses who are in them; and the nature of the greatness of the Temple of the King, that it is the seat of the Sovereign, the Lord of Heaven (= Osiris); and the nature of the greatness of the Resenet and Mehenet sanctuaries; and of the House of Re and the House of Atum; that is, the mystery of all gods (...).

I petitioned the Majesty of the King of Upper and Lower Egypt, Cambyses, about all the foreigners who were dwelling in the temple of Neith, so that they should be expelled from it in order to let the temple of Neith be in all its splendour, as it had been in existence since the beginning. His Majesty commanded to expel all the foreigners who dwelt in the temple of Neith; all their houses were demolished and their pollution that was in this temple. They carried [all their] personal belongings outside the wall of the temple. His Majesty commanded to purify the temple of Neith and to return all its personnel, the [...] and the hour-priests of the temple. His Majesty commanded that offerings should be given to Neith the Great, the mother of the god, and to the great gods who are in Saïs, as it was before. His Majesty commanded (to perform) all their festivals and all their processions, as had been done since antiquity. His Majesty did this because I had caused His Majesty to perceive the greatness of Saïs, that it is the city of all the gods, who remain on their thrones in it forever."

The one honoured by the gods of Saïs, the chief physician, Udjahorresnet, says: "The King of Upper and Lower Egypt, Cambyses, came to Saïs. His Majesty proceeded himself to the temple of Neith. He touched the ground with his forehead before Her Majesty very greatly as every king has done. He made a great offering of all good things to Neith the Great, the mother of the god, and the great gods who are in Saïs, as every excellent king has done. His Majesty did this because I had caused His Majesty to perceive the greatness of Her Majesty, for she is the mother of Re himself."

The one honoured by Osiris of Hemag, the chief physician, Udjahorresnet, he says: "His Majesty completed all that is useful in the temple of Neith. He established the libation for the Lord of Eternity in the temple of Neith as every king did earlier. That did his Majesty do, because I had caused him to recognise how everything useful had been fulfilled in this temple by every king, because of the importance of this temple; for it is the place of all the gods, who live eternally.'" (transl. after Kuhrt 2010: 117–119, no. 11).

priesthood, a measure which may have led to their resentment of the new foreign ruler. Herodotus's account of Cambyses's rule in Egypt is beset with stories of sacrilege and immoral acts, resulting in the depiction of a king devoid of self-control and respect for other religions. Together with employing a historiographical story pattern, in which a successful, or good, king alternated with an unsuccessful, or bad, king, Herodotus declared Cambyses to be a 'mad' king, an attribute which until recently had been readily accepted in scholarship. It is tempting to suggest that Herodotus's view of Cambyses was informed by the disenfranchised Egyptian priesthood which saw itself deprived of their regular income. A fresh and unbiased look at the classical sources reveals the shortcomings of Herodotus's view, and, together with the Near Eastern and Egyptian sources, arrives at a more balanced view of Cambyses II. He must be regarded as a king who, despite his brief rule, proved himself to possess leadership qualities of a calibre comparable to that of his father's: a successful conqueror and a king who recognised the importance of consolidating his empire.

While Cambyses respected Egyptian gods and their cults to the point that he even observed the Egyptian custom to regard their pharaoh as divine, taking the royal name Mesuti-Re, he objected to the wealth of the temples themselves and took measures to restrict it. Thus, the temple economy of the Egyptian priesthood was dramatically curbed by a decree issued by Cambyses. His measures undoubtedly caused resentment among the priests. However, we must recognise that they are distinct from Cambyses's attitude towards Egyptian gods and cults. The original text is lost, but it survives in a Demotic copy written, probably, in the late third century.

4.2.1   The Demotic Papyrus

The matters which are ordered with respect to the law of the sanctuaries which is in the house of justice.

Building-wood, firewood, flax and shrubs, which used to be given to the sanctuaries of the gods, in the time of Pharaoh – life, prosperity, health – Amasis – life, prosperity, health –, – with the exception of the temples of Memphis, temple of *Wn-khm* (Letopolis?) and the temple of Perapis (Nilopolis?) [...](?) those sanctuaries – Cambyses ordered the following: 'Do not permit that one gives them as much as (?) [...] They should be given a place in the copse of the Southern Land (= Upper Egypt) and it shall be permitted that building-wood and firewood come from there and that they bring it to the gods!' The copse of the three sanctuaries above, Cambyses ordered this, i.e.: 'They shall receive this as before.'

The cattle which used to be given to the sanctuaries of the gods, in the time of Pharaoh – life, prosperity, health – Amasis – life, prosperity, health –, – with the exception of the three temples above – Cambyses ordered the following: 'Their share is what they are given.' What was given to them, (i.e.) the three sanctuaries above, this was ordered: 'It shall continue to be given to them.'

The birds, which used to be given to the sanctuaries of the gods, in the time of Pharaoh – life, prosperity, health – Amasis – life, prosperity, health –, – with the exception of the three sanctuaries above – Cambyses ordered the following: 'They shall not be given to them! The priests will obtain them (for the sanctuaries) and they will give them to the gods.'

The silver, cattle, birds, cereal (and) all the other things which used to be given to the sanctuaries of the gods, in the time of Pharaoh – life, prosperity, health – Amasis – life, prosperity, health –, – with the exception of the three sanctuaries above – Cambyses ordered the following: 'Do not give them to the gods; the value of the goods registered at 160 532 pieces(?), [...], cereal 70 210, [...] 6000; or 376 400 [...] (?).'

Aromatics, firewood, shrubs(?), papyrus, building wood; copy of [...] another papyrus. Building wood; copy [...] (transl. after Kuhrt 2010: 125, no. 14).

4.3   Cambyses's Depiction in Herodotus

The identification of Egypt as the source of the negative views about Cambyses can easily be made from Herodotus's account of Cambyses's conquest of Egypt. All atrocities the Persian king is said to have committed are linked to Egypt, including the humiliation of the conquered Pharaoh Psammetichus III by parading his daughter in public and sending his son to his death, the unearthing and mutilation of Amasis's body, the attack on the oasis of Ammon in Siwa, the killing of the sacred Apis bull, the order to kill his brother and the murder of his sister-wife who was with him in Egypt at the time. Herodotus leaves no doubt that Cambyses's conquest of Egypt was beset with acts of sacrilege and immoral deeds.

According to Herodotus, even Cambyses's reason for the conquest itself contains an irrational element, thus setting the tone for the description of Cambyses as a despot. In his view, the conquest was undertaken as an act of revenge because Cambyses had been deceived by the ruling Pharaoh when he demanded to marry the daughter of the Egyptian Pharaoh Ahmose II, (Gr. Amasis, ruled 570–526). He, being afraid that his daughter would never be given the status of a royal wife, instead sent a daughter of the previous Pharaoh Wahibre (Gr. Apries, ruled 589–570), called Nitetis. Discovering the deceit, Cambyses set out to conquer Egypt. In yet another version, Herodotus claims that Cambyses II was already the product of a marriage between Wahibre's daughter Nitetis and Cambyses's father, Cyrus II, though the historian dismisses this story, preferring the Persian account according to which Cambyses was the son of Cassandane. Herodotus's choice is correct: Egypt has a long history in concluding international marriage alliances as part of political diplomacy, yet it stands out from all other kingdoms in that it accepted foreign princesses to the Egyptian court but, unlike her allies, never allowed an Egyptian princess to be married to a foreigner. Thus, while the idea of Cambyses as the son of an Egyptian princess is unhistorical, Cambyses's demand for one is highly unlikely.

From a historiographical point of view, there is a striking similarity between these stories of Cambyses's link with the conquered kingdom of Egypt and those we observed in Cyrus's alleged link with the royal house of Media. In the versions told by Herodotus and Xenophon, Cyrus was the son of Cambyses I and Mandane. Ctesias's version claimed that Cyrus II was no relation of Astyages and only married his daughter Amytis following the conquest of Media. In the case of both kings, these stories aim to present them to their new subjects as the legitimate kings – Cyrus either as grandson or son-in-law of Astyages, and likewise Cambyses as grandson or in-law of Ahmose.

Not satisfied with the conquest of Egypt, Cambyses next led his army to the oasis of Siwa with its sanctuary of the god Amun. The purpose for this undertaking is not evident. The oasis lay about 500 km west of the royal capital Memphis; the sanctuary for the Libyan deity Amun was well respected, and even had been given sacrifices by the Lydian king Croesus. But it is his campaign against Nubia that marks Cambyses as a king who transgresses beyond the known world at the cost of his men. The Nubian expedition was judged disastrous and badly led and caused considerable loss of life amongst the Persian troops, most of whom died of hunger and thirst in the desert. The campaign was one of the many atrocities committed by Cambyses, serving as proof of his ineptness as a military leader, his failure as a king and his insanity. Yet against this alleged failure stands the fact that Nubia is listed as one of the lands of the empire in two inscriptions of Cambyses's successor Darius I (ruled 522–486), and a Nubian delegation is depicted on the Apadana reliefs in Persepolis, built by Darius I as a visual presentation of the lands (Figure 4.2). Thus, Cambyses's expedition must have had a level of success, conquering, if not all, at least part of Nubia.

Cambyses's invasion of Nubia was not the first one undertaken to attack the region south of the first cataract of the Nile, at Elephantine. Psamtek II (Gr. Psammetichus, ruled 595–589) had led a successful campaign against Nubia in 592 with the support

Figure 4.2   Nubian delegation from the Apadana reliefs, Persepolis. The Nubian delegates are seen bringing a jar, possibly with precious contents, an ivory tooth and an okapi. *Source*: Available at https://commons.wikimedia.org/wiki/Category:Nubian_delegation_Apadana_eastern_stairs.

of Greek mercenaries, who left their inscriptions on the colossal statue of Pharaoh Ramses II (ruled 1279–1213) at Abu Simbel: 'When king Psammetichus went to Elephantine, this was written by those who, with Psammetichus son of Theokles, sailed and came above Kerkis, as far as the river allowed. Potasimo led the foreign-speaking and Amasis the Egyptians. Archon son of Amoibichus and Pelequs son of Eudamus wrote us (= these lines)' (transl. after Fornara 1983: 28, no. 24).

4.4   The Apis Bull

The most detailed incident described in Herodotus's story about Cambyses is his killing of the sacred Apis bull, and it is in this instance that Egyptian sources enable us to counterbalance the negative image Cambyses receives in the Greek account. The Apis bull, the embodiment of the god Osiris, was conceived through a strike of lightning from heaven, and the cow would not conceive another calf afterwards. The animal bore distinctive marks. It was black, with a white diamond-shaped sign on its forehead, the image of an eagle on its back, the hairs under the tail double and a knot under its tongue (Hdt.III.28.3). When Cambyses returned to Egypt after his Nubian campaign, the festival in honour of the Apis bull was underway. Cambyses ridiculed the Egyptians' worship of an animal as a divine being and, to prove the bull's mortality, stabbed it with his dagger. The Apis bull, traditionally buried in great splendour in a funerary ceremony, had to be buried secretly by fearful priests. For the Egyptians, so Herodotus, Cambyses's sacrilegious act was final proof of his madness.

Yet Egyptian epigraphic sources tell a different story. An inscription written on the sarcophagus of the deceased Apis bull, which was laid to rest in a special burial complex for the sacred bulls in Memphis called the Serapeum, attests to the fact that this particular Apis bull had been born in the 27th year of Ahmose II, that is, in 543, and had died in November 524. The inscription, as well as an epitaph written on a stele, record that the Apis bull was buried with all due ceremony and honour, as was customary (Figure 4.3). The sarcophagus inscription bore Cambyses's name, and a royal cartouche represented him as Pharaoh Mesuti-Re, stating that the burial took place on the order of the king himself.

> Year 6, third month of Harvest, day 10(?) (= November 524), of his Majesty, King of Upper and Lower Egypt, [Mesu]ti-Re – may he live forever – the god was taken up pea[cefully to the West and was placed at rest in the necropolis, in] his [place], which is the place prepared for him by his majesty, [after] all [the ceremonies] of the embalming room [had been carried out for him]. [Offerings] were made for him, clothing, [his amulets and all his gold ornaments] and every kind of semi-precious stone [...] temple of Ptah, which is inside the Hemag [...] towards Memphis, saying: 'Take...'. All was done in accordance with the words of his Majesty [...] in Year 27[...] [Camby]ses – may he live [...] (Epitaph; transl. after Kuhrt 2010: 122, no. 12).

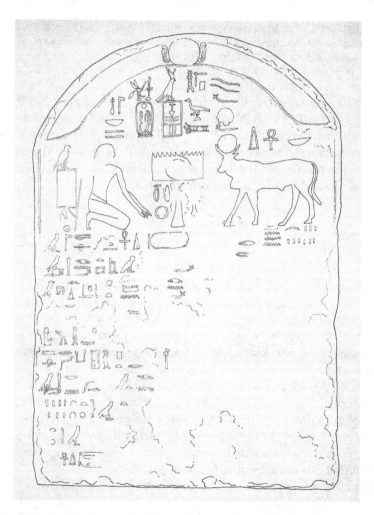

Figure 4.3 Cambyses's Stele for the Apis Bull. Cambyses is depicted as an Egyptian, kneeling before the sacred Apis bull. *Source*: Drawing by Marion Cox.

The Horus, Uniter of the Two Lands, King of Upper and Lower Egypt, Mesuti-Re, son of Re, Cambyses – may he live forever. He made a fine monument for his father, Apis-Osiris, with a great sarcophagus of granite, dedicated by the King of Upper and Lower Egypt, Mesuti-Re, son of Re, Cambyses – may he live forever, in perpetuity and prosperity, full of health and joy, appearing as King of Upper and Lower Egypt, forever. (Sarcophagus Inscription, transl. after Brosius 2000: 17, no. 22)

Both inscriptions are crucial evidence, not only because they demonstrate Cambyses's acceptance as king of Egypt in the dating formula and his royal name, but also because they testify that Cambyses was actively involved in overseeing the burial ceremonies and ensuring them to be carried out in the proper manner. There is no room for error, as the epitaph dedicated to the next Apis bull demonstrates. The new Apis bull had been born in May 525 and died in the fourth year of Darius I, that is, in 518. Recent doubts raised in regard to the date of death of the Apis bull and the instalment of the new Apis bull may consider the possibility that the priests always needed to have a bull ready to be presented as the successor, as the bull's lifespan could not be predicted, and a new calf would take about 10 months of gestation.

4.4.1 The Apis Bull and the Death of Cambyses

Herodotus himself points out the correlation between his account of Cambyses's killing of the Apis bull and that of Cambyses's death. According to him, Cambyses inflicted a mortal wound with his dagger on himself, and he points out explicitly that the manner of Cambyses's injury mirrored precisely the way the Persian king had wounded the sacred Apis bull. The implication is that fate or divine intervention ensured Cambyses's punishment for his sacrilege. An oracle had foretold Cambyses he would die in a place called Ecbatana. Having assumed the name to refer to the royal city in Media, and having decided to avoid it, the king learned that the place where he lay dying also bore the name Ecbatana, albeit located in Syria. 'As he (= Cambyses) was springing onto his horse, the cap slipped off the scabbard of his sword, and the naked blade struck his thigh, wounding him in the same part where he himself had once struck the Egyptian god Apis. Believing the blow to be mortal, Cambyses asked what was the name of the town where he was. They told him it was Ecbatana. He had already had a prophecy from Buto (= Imet) that he would end his life in Ecbatana. Cambyses had thought this meant that he would die in old age in Median Ecbatana, his capital city, but as events proved, the oracle prophesised his death in Ecbatana in Syria (= near Mt. Carmel)' (Hdt.III.64.3–4). Whether Cambyses indeed died in this manner, or whether the description of his death is subject to Herodotus's literary construct, remains an open question.

4.4.2 The Killing of His Sister-Wife

During his Egyptian campaign, Cambyses was accompanied by his (unnamed) wife. According to Herodotus, she was one of two full sisters whom he had married, ostensibly against Persian custom, as he sought, only to dismiss, the advice of the royal judges in the matter. This sister-wife had dared to criticise Cambyses's rulership, and he, enraged, killed his pregnant spouse. The immoral and outrageous behaviour in this brief remark touches several levels: Cambyses's failure as a ruler by being unable to allow any criticism, his lack of respect for moral boundaries by committing incest and his lack of self-control evidenced in the rash killing of his spouse and his unborn child. The fact that Cambyses produced no male offspring seems to be the punishment for his action. An afterstory completes the gruesome act: out of sheer wilfulness, Cambyses then killed his cup-bearer, the young son of Prexaspes (Hdt.III.35). When Croesus, the former king of Lydia, who apparently had been entrusted by Cyrus to guard Cambyses, criticised him for his deed, he himself got shot by an arrow but was saved by royal servants. This is a pure invention, considering that Croesus had already died shortly after the Lydian conquest, but a story that placed doubt on Cambyses's fitness to rule from the very beginning, being already mistrusted by his father. The historical truth of any of these stories therefore must be doubted.

4.4.3   Fratricide

We now need to turn to the story of the killing of his brother Bardiya, called Smerdis in Herodotus. This is a key story, not only for Cambyses but also for his successor Darius I. Smerdis and Cambyses were full brothers, meaning they descended from the same father and mother. Smerdis, according to Herodotus, had accompanied his brother to Egypt, but for a rather petty reason was ordered by Cambyses to return to Persia. In a subsequent dream, Cambyses saw his brother sitting on the Persian throne, an image that unmistakably symbolised Smerdis's claim to power. Cambyses therefore ordered the Persian Prexaspes to kill his sibling. Prexaspes fulfilled Cambyses's command and Smerdis died in Susa, either being killed during a hunt, or being drowned in the Persian Gulf. But, as Herodotus then uncovers, Cambyses had acted rashly because the person who had claimed the Persian throne was not his brother Smerdis but someone who only shared his brother's name. This false Smerdis had acted together with his brother Patizeithes.

Herodotus identifies the brothers as *magi*, a title given to priests. Patizeithes had put his brother on the throne and declared that he was the real Smerdis, who was to be regarded as king, and that the power was to be taken from Cambyses. Cambyses accused Prexaspes of having ignored his order to kill Smerdis, but was assured that his brother indeed had been killed. Realising his own error, and feeling remorseful, Cambyses set out towards Susa to confront the rebel but then died en route.

Once again, the story of Prexaspes is a historiographical construction, echoing the story of the Median king Astyages, his courtier Harpagus and the intended killing of Cyrus. We recall that Harpagus had been ordered to kill the child Cyrus. Astyages's reason for the killing is in fact the same one we find for Cambyses's killing of Smerdis, that is, a dream in which both males were regarded as threats to the respective ruling king. Unlike Prexaspes, Harpagus did not carry out that request but gave the child away to grow up hidden by foster parents. But like him, Harpagus suffered the loss of his son when Astyages killed him apparently in wilful revenge for Harpagus's failure to follow his command (Hdt.I.119). It may therefore be concluded that the story of Prexaspes and his son was introduced as a literary device following a previous pattern, and served to underline Cambyses's irrational behaviour, in this case, taking his dream about Smerdis as sufficient evidence to assume a threat to his rule.

FURTHER READING

On the palace site and the unfinished tomb see Kleiss, W. (1980). Zur Entwicklung der achaemenidischen Palastarchitektur. *Iraniqua Antiqua* 15: 199–211; the case for locating Cambyses's resting place in Narezzash is made by Henkelman, W. (2003). An Elamite memorial. The Šumar of Cambyses and Hystaspes. *AchHist* 13: 101–172.Bessac, J.-C. and Boucharlat, R. (2010). Le monument de Takht-e Rustam, près de Persépolis dit 'tombeau inachevé de Cambyses': note technique et reconsidérations. *ARTA* 2010 (3): 1–39. The date of the conquest of Egypt is discussed by Quak, J.F. (2011). Zum Datum der persischen Eroberung Ägyptens unter Kambyses. *Journal of Egyptian History* 4: 228–246. On Egypt and the Apis bull see Depuydt, L. (1995). Murder in Memphis. The story of Cambyses' mortal wounding of the Apis bull (ca.523 BCE). *Journal of Near Eastern Studies* 54: 119–126. On the killing of his sister-wife: Drew, G.R. (2009). Honeymoon salad. Cambyses' Uxoricide according to the Egyptians (Hdt.3.32.34). *Historia* 58: 131–140.

5

From Bardiya to Darius I

5.1 The Succession of Darius I

The deaths of Cambyses II and his brother Bardiya resulted in the vacancy of the Persian throne, as none of the brothers had left any male offspring and thus no heir to the throne. Technically this made Cyrus's daughters Atossa and Artystone the next members of the royal family to claim the kingship, but female succession was not an option in Persian kingship. Still, the importance of royal daughters as securers of the throne was a concept the Persians may have been familiar with through their Elamite predecessors. Therefore, the best measure a candidate could take at that point to legitimise his succession to the Persian throne was to marry one or both of these daughters. Essentially, this is what Darius I did in 522 following the deaths of Cambyses and Bardiya. But it is the question as to how and when these two kings died that has been vexing scholars to this day. The problem lies in the different accounts provided in our sources, the primary one being the inscription carved by Darius I at Mt. Bisitun in Media, and the variant account being that given in Herodotus, and both must be considered in our discussion.

5.1.1 Herodotus's Version of Events

As we noted in the previous chapter, Smerdis, the name Herodotus knows for Bardiya, was in Persis when the Persian courtier Prexaspes killed him on Cambyses's order, although his death was kept secret. Not, apparently, secret enough, for two *magi*, called Patizeithes and Smerdis, the latter named just like the king's deceased brother, seized the opportunity, with Patizeithes placing his brother on the throne pretending to be the real Smerdis. This false Smerdis not only shared the same name with Cambyses's sibling, he also resembled him and thus was regarded as the real Smerdis at the Persian court. After Cambyses's death, the false Smerdis reigned for

A History of Ancient Persia: The Achaemenid Empire, First Edition. Maria Brosius.
© 2021 John Wiley & Sons, Inc. Published 2021 by John Wiley & Sons, Inc.

seven months, apparently favoured by all the peoples of the empire, except the Persians, that is, the people living in Persis, for he declared that no tribute needed to be paid for three years, and that the men were exempt from military duty (Hdt.III.67). But in due course, the false Smerdis was uncovered and killed in a palace coup led by seven Persian nobles. Apparently, the Persian Otanes, the son of Pharnaspes and a member of the Achaemenid clan, began to doubt Smerdis's identity. He asked his daughter Phaidyme, the widow of Cambyses living at the royal court, to find out whether Smerdis was indeed the king or an imposter. Gaining access to the king's chamber, she discovered him to be an impostor, and the plan was hatched to overthrow the false Smerdis (Hdt.III.69). Otanes called upon the two Persian nobles Aspathines and Gobryas, and together they enlisted the help of Intaphernes, Megabyxus and Hydarnes. The last one to join this group was Darius, son of Hystaspes and Otanes's cousin. They soon agreed to Darius's plan to approach the supposed king under the pretext of wanting to convey a message from Darius's father and, having gained access to the royal chambers, overcame the imposter. In the meantime, the two *magi* had forced Prexaspes to proclaim that the false Smerdis was in fact the 'real' one in order to avoid a major upheaval. Rather than giving in to the rebels, Prexaspes announced that the real Smerdis was dead and that the Persians were ruled by an impostor. He then took his own life, throwing himself off the palace tower. Thereupon the seven nobles forced their way into the royal chambers, stabbing the eunuchs and guards in the hallways. Patizeithes was taken instantly while the other, the false Smerdis, was confronted by Gobryas and Darius. It was up to Darius to risk shooting the right person in the complete darkness of the closed room while Gobryas seized the *magus*, but his arrow struck the right man. In accordance with the punishment for a rebel, the false Smerdis was beheaded.

5.1.2 Darius's Version: The Inscription of Bisitun

Turning to the account written by Darius himself, we discover similarities with, but also some key differences compared to, Herodotus's version. Darius's inscription was carved at a height of c.70 m on the smoothed rock face of Mt. Bisitun in Media. Mt. Bisitun, or Bagastana in Old Persian, which translates as the 'Mountain of the Gods', is located close to a village bearing the same name and rises along the Persian Royal Road, which led from Susa via Babylon to Ecbatana and continued east via Ragae towards Bactra. Significantly, and in its scale unprecedented in the Ancient Near East, the text was carved in three languages, Elamite, Babylonian and Old Persian (Figure 5.1). But beyond commemorating the events leading to his accession to the throne with this monumental inscription and accompanying relief, Darius also ensured that his version of events was disseminated across the empire. This not only is his claim made in paragraph 70 of the inscription, but also is evidenced in fragments of a Babylonian version recovered in Babylon alongside part of the relief, and in an Aramaic copy which was discovered in Egyptian Elephantine and which is dated to the late fifth century.

The trilingual inscription was placed alongside a relief showing king Darius standing before nine men, the rebel leaders he defeated in the year following his accession to the throne in 522. Darius has one foot placed on the body of

Figure 5.1   The Bisitun relief shows king Darius wearing a crown, the left hand holding his bow, the right hand raised up. He appears to be in direct communication with the figure in the winged disc hovering above the entire scene. This figure also wears Persian clothing, and he, too, holds up his hand. Behind the king are his bow-bearer and his axe-bearer. Darius's right foot is holding down the defeated Gaumata, who has both hands raised in surrender. Before the king stand nine rebels, their hands bound behind their backs, they themselves roped together at their necks. The last figure is that of Skunkha, the Scythian rebel with the pointed hat. As his figure was added after the inscriptions had been completed, it had to be carved into the Elamite inscription to the right of the relief. Below the relief are the Babylonian and the Old Persian versions. A second Elamite inscription was then carved to the left of the relief. The inscriptions in the relief itself identify the rebels. *Source*: Author photograph.

Gaumata, who is lying on the ground, his hands raised in submission. Gaumata is the name given by Darius to the imposter who gained the throne by impersonating Bardiya. The remaining rebels stand before the king, a long robe tied at their necks holding them together. Each one is identified by an inscription. Behind the king stand two of his closest courtiers, his bow-bearer and his axe-bearer. Towering above this scene is the bust of a male figure wearing Persian dress and emerging from of a winged disc. This figure most likely represents the principal god of the Persians, Auramazda.

5.2   The Death of Bardiya

The crucial section regarding the death of Cambyses and the killing of his brother Bardiya is Paragraph 10 of the Darius's inscription of Bisitun (hereafter DB). The passage explicitly states that Cambyses, son of Cyrus, king of Persia, king of lands, and Bardiya were full brothers. Darius also implicates Cambyses in his brother's murder, killing him prior to the Egyptian campaign: 'Cambyses had a brother, Bardiya

Sources in Translation 5.1

Darius's Inscription of Bisitun (DB)

The inscription can be divided into five sections. Paragraphs 1–9 serve as an introduction of Darius himself, Section Two includes paragraphs 10–15 and deals with the revolt of Gaumata. The longest is Section Three, covering paragraphs 16–50, recounting the revolts against Darius and the battles fought to supress them. Section Four with paragraphs 51–70 was the original final statement of the inscription, in which Darius expressed blessings for those who upheld his beliefs, and cursed those who did not. Section Five with paragraphs 71–76 were added later on account of the fact that two more rebellions occurred after the completion of the original inscription and thus had to be added to the account. The recording of the additional rebellions caused a problem for the original design of the relief. Since Darius was eager to add the figure of the Scythian rebel Skunkha to the line of defeated rebels, a space had to be smoothed on the rock, thereby deleting part of the original Elamite inscription to the right of the relief. In consequence, the Elamite version had to be carved a second time on the rock face.

Column I

§1. I (am) Darius, the Great King, king of kings, king in Persia, king of the lands, the son of Hystaspes (OP Vihtaspa, Elam. Mishtashpa), the grandson of Arsames, an Achaemenid.

§2. Darius the king says: 'My father (is) Hystaspes; the father of Hystaspes (is) Arsames; the father of Arsames (is) Ariaramnes; the father of Ariaramnes (is) Teispes (OP Cishpish, Elam. Shishpish), the father of Teispes (is) Achaemenes (OP Haxamanish, Elam. Hakkamannush).'

§3. Darius the king says: 'For that reason we are called Achaemenids. From ancient times we are noble men. From ancient times our family has been royal.'

§4. Darius the king says: '(There are) eight in my family who formerly have been kings. I (am) the ninth (king). Thus we are nine kings in succession.'

§5. Darius the king says: 'By the favour of Auramazda I am king. Auramazda bestowed kingship upon me.'

§6. Darius the king says: 'These (are) the countries which belong to me. By the favour of Auramazda I was their king: Persia, Elam, Babylonia, Assyria, Arabia, Egypt, (the People)-by-the-Sea, Lydia, Ionia, Media, Armenia, Cappadocia, Parthia, Drangiana, Aria, Chorasmia, Bactria, Sogdiana, Gandara, Scythia, Sattagydia, Arachosia, and Maka, altogether twenty-three countries.'

§7. Darius the king says: 'These (are) the countries which belong to me. By the favour of Auramazda they were my subjects; they brought tribute (OP baji, Elam. bazish) to me. What I said to them, either by night or by day, that they used to do.'

§8. Darius the king says: 'In these countries, the man who was loyal, I treated well, who was disloyal, I punished severely. By the favour of Auramazda, these countries obeyed my law. As I said to them, thus they used to do.'

§9. Darius the king says: 'Auramazda bestowed this kingdom upon me. Auramazda brought me aid until I had held together this kingdom. By the favour of Auramazda I hold this kingship.'

§10. Cambyses had a brother, Bardiya by name, of the same mother and the same father as Cambyses. Afterwards Cambyses slew Bardiya. When Cambyses had slain Bardiya, it did not become known to the people that Bardiya had been slain. Afterwards Cambyses went to Egypt. When Cambyses had set out for Egypt, the people became disloyal. The Lie grew greatly in the land, in Persia, Media, and the other countries.

§11. Darius the king says: 'Afterwards there was one man, a *magus*, Gaumata by name. He rose up from Paishiyauvada – from a mountain called Arakadri. In the month Viyaxna (Bab. Addar) 14 days had passed when he rose up (= 11 March 522). He lied to the people thus: 'I am Bardiya the son of Cyrus, the brother of Cambyses.' Afterwards all the people rebelled against Cambyses and went over to him, both Persia and Media, and the other countries. He seized the kingship. In the month Garmapada (Bab. Du'z) nine days had passed (= 1 July 522), and then he seized the kingship. Afterwards Cambyses died his own death.

§12. Darius the king says: 'The kingship, which Gaumata the *magus* had seized from Cambyses, had from ancient times belonged to our family. Then Gaumata the *magus* took from Cambyses both Persia and Media and the other countries. He took (them) and made them his own property. He became king.'

§13. Darius the king says: 'There was no man, neither a Persian nor a Mede nor anyone of our family, who might have taken the kingship from that Gaumata the *magus*. The people feared him greatly, since he used to slay in great number the people who previously had known Bardiya. For this reason he used to slay the people: 'That they may not know me, that I am not Bardiya, the son of Cyrus.' No one dared say anything about Gaumata the *magus* until I came. Afterwards I prayed to Auramazda. Auramazda brought me aid. In the month Bagayadish (Bab. Tashit) 10 days had passed (= 29 September 522), then I with a few men slew Gaumata the *magus* and the men who were his foremost followers. A fortress Sikayuvatish by name and a district Nisaya by name, in Media – there I slew him. I took the kingship from him. By the favour of Auramazda I became king. Auramazda bestowed the kingship upon me.'

§14. Darius the king says: 'I restored the kingship, which had been taken away from our family, that I restored. I re-installed it in its proper place. Just as they had been previously, so I restored the sanctuaries which Gaumata the *magus* had destroyed. I restored to the people the farmsteads, the livestock, the servants and the houses which Gaumata the *magus* had taken away from them. I re-installed the people in their proper places. I restored Persia, Media and the other lands that had been taken away, just as they were previously. By the favour of Auramazda I did this. I strove until I had restored our royal house to its proper place, as it was previously. So I strove by the favour of Auramazda, so that Gaumata the *magus* did not take away our royal house.'

§15. Darius the king says: 'This (is) what I have done after becoming king.'

§16. Darius the king says: 'When I had slain Gaumata the *magus*, (there was) one man, Açina by name, the son of Upadarama; he rose up in Elam. He said to the people: "I am king in Elam." Afterwards the Elamites became rebellious (and) went (over) to Açina. He became king in Elam. And there was one man, a Babylonian, Nidintu-Bel by name, the son of Ainaira. He rose up in Babylonia. He lied to the people thus: "I am Nebuchadnezzar son of Nabonidus." Afterwards all the Babylonian people went (over) to Nidintu-Bel. Babylonia became rebellious, (and) he seized the kingship in Babylonia.'

§17. Darius the king says: 'Afterwards I sent (a messenger) to Elam. Açina was led to me bound. I slew him.'

§18. Darius the king says: 'Afterwards I went to Babylonia against Nidintu-Bel who called himself Nebuchadnezzar. The army of Nidintu-Bel held (the bank of) the Tigris. There it took its stand, and because of the waters (the river) was unpassable. Afterwards I embarked (part of) my army upon (rafts of) skin, another (part) I made ride on camels, and for another part I brought up horses. Auramazda brought me aid. By the favour of Auramazda we crossed the Tigris. There I defeated that army of Nidintu-Bel utterly; in the month Açiyadiya (Bab. Kislim), 26 days had passed (= 13 December 522), then we fought the battle.'

§19. Darius the king says: 'Afterwards I went to Babylon. When I had not yet reached Babylon – (there is) a place, Zazana by name, on the Euphrates – there that Nidintu-Bel who called himself Nebuchadnezzar came with an army against me to fight a battle. Afterwards we fought the battle. Auramazda brought me aid. By the favour of Auramazda I defeated the army of Nidintu-Bel utterly. The rest (of the army) was thrown into the water, (and) the water carried it away. In the month Anamaka (Bab. Tebet) two days had passed (= 18 December 522), then we fought the battle.'

Column II

§20. Darius the king says: 'Afterwards Nidintu-Bel fled with a few horsemen (and) went to Babylon. After that I went to Babylon. By the favour of Auramazda I seized Babylon and captured Nidintu-Bel. Afterwards I slew that Nidintu-Bel in Babylon (*Babylonian text continues* [thereafter: *Bab. cont.*] and the nobles who were with him. I executed 49. This is what I did in Babylon.)'

§21. Darius the king says: 'While I was in Babylon, these (are) the countries which became rebellious from me: Persia, Elam, Media, Assyria, Egypt, Parthia, Margiana, Sattagydia, (and) Scythia.'

§22. Darius the king says: '(There was) one man, Martiya by name, the son of Cincakhri, (and there is) a place Kuganaka by name, in Persia – there he lived. He rose up in Elam. He said to the people thus: "I am Imanish, king of Elam."'

§23. Darius the king says: 'At that time I was near to Elam; afterwards the Elamites were afraid of me. They captured that Martiya who was their chief and slew him.'

§24. Darius the king says: '(There was) one man, Phraortes by name, a Mede, who rose up in Media. He said to the people thus: "I am Khshathrita, of the family of Cyaxares." After that the Median army that was in the palace, that became rebellious against me (and) went (over) to Phraortes. He became king in Media.'

§25. Darius the king says: 'The Persian and Median army which was under my control was a small force. After that I sent forth an army. (There was) a Persian, Hydarnes (OP Vidarna, Elam. Mitarna) by name, my subject – him I made their chief. I said to them: "Go forth, defeat that Median army which does not call itself mine!" Afterwards Hydarnes marched off with the army. When he had come to Media, there is a place, Maru by name, in Media – there he fought a battle with the Medes. He who was chief among the Medes was not there at the time. Auramazda brought me aid. By the favour of Auramazda my army defeated that rebellious army utterly. In the month Anamaka 27 days had passed (= 12 January 521), then the battle was fought by them. (*Bab. cont.:* They killed [3827] among them and took prisoner 4329. Then Hydarnes did not undertake another campaign against Media.) Afterwards that army of mine waited for me in a district of Media called Kampanda until I came to Media. (*Bab. cont.:* Then they came to me at Ecbatana.)'

§26. Darius the king says: 'I sent an Armenian subject of mine, Dadarshish by name, to Armenia. I said to him: "Go forth, defeat the rebellious army which does not call itself mine – defeat that!" Afterwards Dadarshish marched off. When he arrived in Armenia, the rebels assembled (and) went forth to fight a battle against Dadarshish. (There is) a village, Zuzahya by name, in Armenia – there they fought the battle. Auramazda brought me aid. By the favour of Auramazda my army defeated that rebellious army utterly. In the month Thuravahara (Bab. Ayyaru) eight days had passed (= 20 May 521), then the battle was fought by them.'

§27. Darius the king says: 'For the second time the rebels assembled and went forth to fight a battle against Dadarshish. (There is) a fortress, Tigra by name, in Armenia – there they fought the battle. Auramazda brought me aid. By the favour of Auramazda my army defeated the rebellious army utterly. In the month Thuravahara 18 days had passed (= 30 May 521), then the battle was fought by them. (*Bab. cont.*: They killed 546 among them and took prisoner 520.)'

§28. Darius the king says: 'For the third time the rebels assembled (and) went forth to fight a battle against Dadarshish. (There is) a fortress, Uyava by name, in Armenia – there they fought the battle. Auramazda brought me aid. By the favour of Auramazda my army defeated that rebellious army utterly. In the month Thaigracish (Bab. Simann) nine days had passed (= 20 June 521), then the battle was fought by them. (*Bab. cont.:* They killed 472 of them and took prisoner 525(?) Then Dadarshish did not undertake another expedition.) After that Dadarshish waited for me until I came to Media.'

§29. Darius the king proclaims: '(There is) a Persian, Omises (OP Vaumisa, Elam. Maumishsha) by name, my subject – him I sent to Armenia. Thus I said to him: "Go forth, there is an army which is rebellious and does not call itself mine – defeat it!" Afterwards Omises marched off. When he had come to Armenia, the rebels assembled (and) went forth to fight a battle against Omises. (There is) a district, Izala by name, in Assyria – there they fought the battle. Auramazda brought me aid. By the favour of Auramazda my army defeated that rebellious army utterly. In the month Anamaka 15 days had passed (= 31 December 522), then the battle was fought by them. (*Bab. cont.*: They killed 2034 of them.)'

§30. Darius the king says: 'For the second time the rebels assembled (and) went forth to fight a battle against Omises. (There is) a district Autiyara by name, in Armenia – there they fought the battle. Auramazda brought me aid. By the favour of Auramazda my army defeated that rebellious army utterly. In the month Thuravahara, on the last day (= 11 June 521), the battle was fought by them. (*Bab. cont.*: They killed 2045 among them and took prisoner 1558. Then Omises did not undertake another expedition.) After that Omises waited for me in Armenia, until I came to Media.'

§31. Darius the king says: 'Afterwards I went away from Babylon (and) went to Media. When I had come to Media, (there is) a place, Kunduru by name, in Media – there that Phraortes who called himself king in Media came with an army to fight a battle against me. Afterwards we fought the battle. Auramazda brought me aid. By the favour of Auramazda I defeated the army of Phraortes utterly. In the month Adukani 25 days had passed (= 8 May 521), then we fought the battle. (*Bab. cont.*: We killed ⌈34 425?⌉ of them and took prisoner (...).)'

§32. Darius the king says: 'Afterwards that Phraortes fled with a few horsemen. (There is) a district in Media, Raga by name, there he went. After that I sent an army in pursuit. Phraortes was seized (and) led to me. I cut off his nose, ears and tongue, and I put out one of his eyes. At my gate he was kept bound (and) all the people looked at him. After that I impaled him at Ecbatana. And in the fortress at Ecbatana I hanged the men who were his foremost followers. (*Bab. cont.*: I executed his nobles, a total of ⌈47⌉. I hung their heads inside Ecbatana from the battlements of the fortress.)'

§33. Darius the king says: '(There was) one man, Tritantaechmes (OP Ciçan-taxma, Elam. Zishshantakma) by name, a Sagartian, who became rebellious against me. He said to the people thus: "I am king of Sagartia, of the family of Cyarxares." After that I sent forth a Persian and Median army. (There was) a Mede, Takhmaspada by name, my subject – him I made their chief. I said to them: "Go forth, defeat the rebellious army which will not call itself mine!" Afterwards Takhmaspada marched off with the army, and he fought a battle with Tritantaechmes. Auramazda brought me aid. By the favour of Auramazda my army defeated the rebellious army and it captured Tritan-taechmes (and) led (him) to me. After that I cut off his nose and ears, and I put out one of his eyes. At my gate he was kept bound (and) all the people looked at him. Afterwards I impaled him at Arbela. (*Bab. cont.*: The total dead and surviving of the rebel force was ⌈447?⌉.)'

§34. Darius the king says: 'This (is) what I have done in Media.'

§35. Darius the king says: 'Parthia and Hyrcania rebelled against me. They called themselves supporters of Phraortes. My father Hystaspes was in Parthia – the people had abandoned him; they had become rebellious. After that Hystaspes marched off with the army which was faithful to him. (There is) a place, Vishpauzatish by name, in Parthia – there he fought a battle with the Parthians. Auramazda brought me aid. By the favour of Auramazda Hystaspes defeated that rebellious army utterly. In the month Viyaxna 22 days had passed (= 8 March 521), then the battle was fought by them. (*Bab. cont.*: They killed ⌈6346⌉ of them and took prisoner ⌈4346?⌉.)'

Column III

§36. Darius the king says: 'Afterwards I sent forth a Persian army to Hystaspes from Raga. When that army had reached Hystaspes, he took it (under his command and) marched off. (There is) a place, Patigrabana by name, in Parthia – there he fought a battle with the rebels. Auramazda brought me aid. By the favour of Auramazda Hystaspes defeated the rebellious army utterly. In the month Garmapada one day had passed (= 11 July 521), then the battle was fought by them. (*Bab. cont.*: They killed 6570 of them and took prisoner 4192. Then he executed their leader and the nobles who were with him, a total of 80.)'

§37. Darius the king says: 'After that the country became mine. This (is) what I have done in Parthia.'

§38. Darius the king says: '(There is) a country, Margiana by name, that rebelled against me. There was one man, Frada by name, a Margian – they made him their chief. After that I sent a Persian, Dadarshish by name, my subject, satrap of Bactria, against him. I said to him: "Go forth, defeat the army which does not call itself mine!" Afterwards Dadarshish with the army marched off, and he fought a battle with the Margians. Auramazda brought me aid. By the favour of Auramazda my army defeated that rebellious army utterly. In the month Açiyadiya 23 days had passed (= 28 December 521), then the battle was fought by them. (*Bab. cont.*: He executed Frada and the nobles who were with him, a total of ⌈46?⌉. He killed ⌈55 2xx?⌉ and took prisoner 6572.)'

§39. Darius the king says: 'After that the country became mine. This (is) what I have done in Bactria.'

§40. Darius the king says: '(There was) one man, Vahyazdata by name, and (at) a place, Tarava by name, (and) a district, Yutiya by name, in Persia – there he lived. He rose up in Persia a second time. He said to the people: "I am Bardiya son of Cyrus." After that, the Persian army, which was in the palace, (and which had come up) from Anshan previously, rebelled against me (and) went (over) to that Vahyazdata. He became king in Persia.'

§41. Darius the king says: 'Afterwards I sent forth the Persian and Median army which was under (my control). (There was) a Persian, Artavardiya by name, my subject – I made him their commander. The rest of the Persian army went after me to Media. Afterwards Artavardiya went with the army to Persia.

When he arrived in Persia – there is a place named Rakha, in Persia – there that Vahyazdata who called himself Bardiya came with an army to fight a battle against Artavardiya. Afterwards they fought the battle. Auramazda brought me aid. By the favour of Auramazda my army defeated that army of Vahyazdata utterly. In the month Thuravahara 12 days had passed (= 24 May 521), then the battle was fought by them. (*Bab. cont.*: They killed 4404 of them and took prisoner (...).)'

§42. Darius the king says: 'Afterwards Vahyazdata fled with a few horsemen (and) went to Paishiyauvada. From there he took an army to himself. Once more he marched to fight a battle against Artavardiya. There is a mountain, Parga by name – there they fought the battle. Auramazda brought me aid. By the favour of Auramazda my army defeated that army of Vahyazdata utterly. In the month Garmapada five days had passed (= 15 July 521), then the battle was fought by them. (*Bab. cont.*: They killed [6246] of them and took prisoner [4464].) And (my army) captured Vahyazdata, and they captured the men who were his foremost followers.'

§43. Darius the king says: 'Afterwards I (impaled) Vahyzadata and the men who were his foremost followers – (there is) a place, Uvadaicaya by name, in Persia – there I impaled them.'

§44. Darius the king says: 'This (is) what I have done in Persia.'

§45. Darius the king says: 'That Vahyazdata who called himself Bardiya had sent forth an army to Arachosia against a Persian, Vivana by name, my subject, satrap of Arachosia, and he (= Vahyazdata) had made one man their commander. He (= Vahyazdata) had said to them: "Go forth and defeat Vivana and the army which calls itself (that) of Darius the king!" Afterwards the army which Vahyazdata had sent forth against Vivana marched off to fight a battle. (There is) a fortress, Kapishakanish by name – there they fought the battle. Auramazda brought me aid. By the favour of Auramazda my army defeated that rebellious army utterly. In the month Anamaka 13 days had passed (= 22 December 522), then the battle was fought by them. (*Bab. cont.*: The total dead and surviving of the troops whom Vahyazdata had sent was [...].)'

§46. Darius the king says: 'Once more the rebels assembled and went forth to fight a battle against Vivana. (There is) a district, Gandutava by name – there they fought the battle. Auramazda brought me aid. By the favour of Auramazda my army defeated that rebellious army utterly. In the month Viyaxna seven days had passed (= 21 February 521), then the battle was fought by them. (*Bab. cont.*: The total dead and surviving of the troops whom Vahyazdata had sent was 4579.)'

§47. Darius the king says: 'Afterwards the commander of the army which Vahyazdata had sent forth against Vivana fled with a few horsemen and went off. (There is) a fortress, Arshada by name, in Arachosia – past that he went. Afterwards Vivana marched off with the army in pursuit of them. There he captured him, and he slew the men who were his foremost followers. (*Bab. cont.*: The total dead and surviving of the troops of Vivana was (...).)'

§48. Darius the king says: 'After that the country became mine. This (is) what I have done in Arachosia.'

§49. Darius the king says: 'Whilst I was in Persia and Media, for the second time the Babylonians rebelled against me. (There was) one man, Arakha by name, an Armenian, the son of Haldita, who rose up in Babylonia – from a district called Dubala. He lied to the people thus: "I am Nebuchadnezzar son of Nabonidus." Afterwards the Babylonian people rebelled against me (and) went (over) to that Arakha. He seized Babylon. He was king in Babylon.'

§50. Darius the king says: 'Afterwards I sent forth an army to Babylon. (There was) a Persian, Intaphernes (OP Vindafarna, Elam. Mindaparna) by name, my subject – him I made their chief. I said to them: "Go forth, defeat that Babylonian army which will not call itself mine!" Afterwards Intaphernes went to Babylon with the army. Auramazda brought me aid. By the favour of Auramazda Intaphernes slew the Babylonians and led (them) in fetters. In the month Varkazana 22 days had passed (= 27 November 521), then he captured that Arakha who falsely called himself Nebuchadnezzar, and the men who were his foremost followers. I gave orders that Arakha and the men who were his foremost followers were impaled at Babylon. (*Bab. cont.*: The total dead and surviving of the army of Arakha was 2497.)'.

Column IV

§51. Darius the king says: 'This (is) what I have done in Babylon.'

§52. Darius the king says: 'This (is) what I have done by the favour of Auramazda in one and the same year, after I became king: I have fought 19 battles. By the favour of Auramazda I defeated them and captured nine kings. One (was) a *magus*, Gaumata by name; he lied, saying: "I am Bardiya, the son of Cyrus." He made Persia rebellious. One (was) an Elamite, Açina by name, he lied, saying: "I am king in Elam." He made Elam rebellious. One (was) a Babylonian, Nidintu-Bel by name. He lied, saying: "I am Nebuchadnezzar son of Nabonidus." He made Babylonia rebellious. One (was) a Persian, Martiya by name. He lied, saying: "I am Imanish, king in *Elam.*" *He* made Elam rebellious. One (was) a Mede, Phraortes by name; he lied, saying: "I am Khshathrita, of the family of Cyaxares." He made Media rebellious. One (was) a Sagartian, Tritantaechmes by name. He lied, saying: "I am king in Sagartia, of the family of Cyarxares." He made Sagartia rebellious. One (was) a Margian, Frada by name. He lied, saying: "I am king in Margiana." He made Margiana rebellious. One (was) a Persian, Vahyazdata by name. He lied, saying: "I am Bardiya son of Cyrus." He made Persia rebellious. One (was) an Armenian, Arakha by name. He lied, saying: "I am Nebuchadnezzar son of Nabonidus." He made Babylonia rebellious.'

§53. Darius the king says: 'These (are) the nine kings whom I have captured in these battles.'

§54. Darius the king says: 'These (are) the countries which became rebellious. The Lie made them rebellious, because these men lied to the people. Afterwards Auramazda gave them into my hand. As (was) my desire, so I treated them.'

§55. Darius the king says: 'You who shall be king hereafter, protect yourself vigorously from the Lie. The man who follows the Lie, punish him severely, if you shall think thus: "Let my country be secure!"'

§56. Darius the king says: 'This is what I did. By the favour of Auramazda in one and the same year I have done it. You who shall read this inscription hereafter, let what (has been) done by me convince you, do not consider it a lie.'

§57. Darius the king says: 'I will take Auramazda's anger upon myself that I did this truly, and not falsely, in one and the same year.'

§58. Darius the king says: 'By the favour of Auramazda also I have done much more that (has) not (been) written down in this inscription; for this reason (it has) not (been) written down, lest – what I have done should seem (too) much to him who will read this inscription hereafter, (and) this should not convince him, (but) he regard it (as) false.'

§59. Darius the king says: 'In their entire lives, previous kings have not done so much as I, by the favour of Auramazda I have done in one and the same year.'

§60. Darius the king says: 'Now let what I have done convince you! Thus make (it) known to the people, do not conceal (it)! If you shall not conceal this record, (but) make (it) known to the people, may Auramazda be a friend to you. May your offspring be numerous, and may you live long!'

§61. Darius the king says: 'If you shall conceal this record (and) not make (it) known to the people, may Auramazda be your destroyer and may you have no offspring!'

§62. Darius the king says: 'I did this what I did in one and the same year. By the favour of Auramazda I did (it). Auramazda and the other gods who are brought me aid.'

§63. Darius the king says: 'For this reason Auramazda and the other gods who are brought me aid because I was not disloyal, I was not a follower of the Lie. I was no evil-doer, neither I nor my family, (but) I acted according to righteousness. Neither to the powerless nor to the powerful did I do wrong, and the man who supported my (royal) house, him I treated well, the man who did it harm, him I punished severely.'

§64. Darius the king says: 'You who shall be king hereafter – the man who shall be a follower of the Lie, or (the man) who shall be an evil-doer, may you not be his friend, (but) punish him severely.'

§65. Darius the king says: 'You who shall hereafter look at this inscription which I have written down, and these sculptures, do not destroy (them). As long as you have strength, protect them!'

§66. Darius the king says: 'If you look at this inscription or these sculptures (and) do not destroy them and, as long as there is strength in you, protect them, may Auramazda be your friend, and may your offspring be numerous, and may you live long! And may Auramazda make what you shall do successful for you!'

§67. Darius the king says: 'If you look at this inscription or these sculptures (and) destroy them and do not, as long as there is strength in you, protect them, may Auramazda be your destroyer, and may you have no offspring! And may Auramazda let what you shall do go wrong for you!'

§68. Darius the king says: 'These (are) the men who at that time were there, when I slew Gaumata the *magus* who called himself Bardiya. At that time these men co-operated as my followers: Intaphernes by name, the son of Vahyasparuva, a Persian; Otanes (OP Utana, Elam. Huttana) by name, son of Thukhra (Elam. Tukkura), a Persian; Gobryas (OP Gaubaruva, Elam. Kambarna) by name, the son of Mardonius (OP Marduniya, Elam. Marduniya), a Persian; Hydarnes (OP Vidarna, Elam. Mitarna) by name, the son of Bagabigna, a Persian; Megabyxus (OP, Elam. Bagabuxsha) by name, the son of Datavahya (Elam. Daddumaniya), a Persian; Ardumanish (Elam. Hardumannush) by name, the son of Vahuka (Elam. Maukka, (= Gr. Ochus)), a Persian.'

§69. Darius the king says: 'You who shall be king hereafter, protect well the offspring of these men!'

§70. Darius the king says: 'By the favour of Auramazda this (is) the inscription which I have made besides in Aryan. It has been written both on clay tablets and on parchment. I also wrote down my name and my lineage, and it was written down and was read (aloud) before me. Afterwards I have sent this inscription in all directions among the lands. The people strove (to use it).'

Column V

§71. Darius the king says: 'This (is) what I did in the second and the third year, after I became king. (There is) a country called Elam that became rebellious. (There was) one man, Athamaita by name, an Elamite. They made him (their) chief. After that I sent forth an army. (There was) one man, Gobryas by name, a Persian, my subject – I made him their chief. Afterwards Gobryas went with the army to Elam and fought a battle with the Elamites. Afterwards Gobryas defeated the Elamites and crushed (them); he captured their chief and led him to me. After that I slew him. After that the country became mine.'

§72. Darius the king says: 'Those Elamites were disloyal, and Auramazda was not worshipped by them. I worshipped Auramazda. By the favour of Auramazda, as (was) my desire, so I treated them.'

§73. Darius the king says: 'He who worships Auramazda, his shall be the (fulfilment of his) prayer, both (while he is) living and (when he is) dead.'

§74. Darius the king says: 'Afterwards I went with an army against Scythia. After that the Scythians who wear the pointed cap came against me, when I arrived at the sea. By means of rafts (of skin) I crossed it with the whole army. Afterwards I defeated those Scythians utterly. They (the army) captured another part of them (= Scythians); that (part) was led to me bound. And they captured their chief, Skunkha by name, (and) led him to me bound. There I made another (their) chief, as was my desire. After that the country became mine.'

§75. Darius the king says: 'Those Scythians were disloyal, and Auramazda was not worshipped by them. I, however, worshipped Auramazda. By the favour of Auramazda, as (was) my desire, so I treated them.'

§76. Darius the king says: 'He who worships Auramazda, his shall be the (fulfilment of his) prayer, both (while he is) living and (when he is) dead.'

by name, of the same mother and the same father as Cambyses. Afterwards Cambyses slew Bardiya. When Cambyses had slain Bardiya, it did not become known to the people that Bardiya had been slain. Afterwards Cambyses went to Egypt. When Cambyses had set out for Egypt, the people became disloyal. The Lie grew greatly in the land, in Persia, Media, and the other countries.' At this point the impostor called Gaumata appears on the scene, claiming to be Bardiya and calling the people to rebel against Cambyses: 'Afterwards there was one man, a *magus*, Gaumata by name. He rose up from Paishiyauvada – from a mountain called Arakadri. In the month Viyaxna (Bab. Addar) 14 days had passed when he rose up (= 11 March 522). He lied to the people thus: "I am Bardiya the son of Cyrus, the brother of Cambyses." Afterwards all the people rebelled against Cambyses and went over to him, both Persia and Media, and the other countries. He seized the kingship. In the month Garmapada (Bab. Du'z) nine days had passed (= 1 July 522), and then he seized the kingship. Afterwards Cambyses died his own death.' In other words, Gaumata, the false Bardiya, caused a rebellion of the lands of the Persian empire while Cambyses was away in Egypt, and rose to kingship. The text makes no mention of any attempt on the part of Cambyses to quash that rebellion, but merely states that he died. The ambiguous wording leaves it open whether Cambyses died of a self-inflicted injury or committed suicide.

5.2.1 Herodotus and the Bisitun Inscription: A Comparison

The name Gaumata is not known to Herodotus, but it appears in a corrupted form in a later Roman source, Justin (lived c. second century CE), as Cometes, indicating that Darius's version, or at least a part of it, was somehow transmitted to the Greek and Roman world alongside Herodotus's one. This Gaumata is identified both as a Mede and as a *magus*. But only Herodotus mentions the involvement of two brothers in the plot, and this remains a problem, as opinions differ as to whether there were indeed two *magi* staging the plot, or whether the name Patizeithes is merely a title deriving from an Old Persian word *pati-xshāyaθiya*, which may be translated as 'viceroy', and thus could identify Bardiya. The name Oropastes, given in Justin as the name of the second brother, likewise may not be a personal name but an epithet deriving from *ahura – upasta*, meaning '(he who has) Aura's support'. Equally difficult is the question of what relevance to place on the fact that Gaumata/Smerdis was a *magus*. It has sparked the debate that his was a religious rebellion, but it is difficult to find any grounds for it. Darius describes Gaumata's reign as a reign of terror, violating sanctuaries as well as people. The issue becomes even more complicated when considering that the Babylonian version of DB identifies the impostor only as a Mede, not a *magus*. More important might be the fact that the coup began in Media, and that therefore it could be assumed that the Medes took the opportunity in 522 to try to break from the Persian empire. But the case of Gaumata differs from that of all other rebels. They, too, claimed to be the rightful claimant to the thrones of Media, Elam or Babylon, but they had the support of an army and were defeated in open battles. The overthrow of Gaumata, in contrast, remained a hidden event, inside a fortress, or, following Herodotus, inside the palace. In addition, in DB col. IV §52, Darius explicitly states that Gaumata's revolt took place in Persia, not Media. Considering all these issues, it is highly likely that there was only one rebel, Bardiya, or, as Darius claims, Gaumata, whose brief rule was marked by harshness and sacrilege – accusations we are familiar with as being used by kings and conquerors who want to malign their predecessor in order to make their own rule appear as a liberation.

5.2.2   A Murder Mystery

The question remains how Bardiya came to his death. If we follow the chronology given in the Bisitun Inscription, Bardiya had died in 525 before to Cambyses's Egyptian campaign, but Gaumata only appeared in March 522. This discrepancy is inexplicable unless we admit that Darius's claim of Bardiya's death in or before 525 cannot be correct. Bardiya must have still been alive in the spring of 522. So one wonders whether Bardiya was killed on Cambyses's order sometime in the spring/summer of 522, as Herodotus states, or whether this is a false accusation which requires us to consider a completely different scenario. The alternative view posits that there never was a false Bardiya, and that in fact the real Bardiya was killed in September 522. Babylonian documents register the reign of Bardiya as 'king of Babylon, king of lands' from the spring of 522, the earliest being dated to 14 April. Yet according to the Bisitun Inscription, Cambyses's death occurred only after 1 July 522. It is therefore possible to reconstruct the following scenario: Bardiya acted as regent in Persis during Cambyses's absence in Egypt, but then claimed the Persian throne in March 522. His rule was recognised in Babylon a month later. After Cambyses's death, Bardiya reigned for a further three months before he was killed as the false Bardiya on 29 September at the hands of Darius. The opportunity for such a coup was ideal: Cambyses had died in summer 522 without leaving a son and heir; accordingly, the kingship passed to his brother Bardiya. He, too, had no male offspring, only a daughter named Parmys (Elam. Uparmiya). If Bardiya also were to die, there was no direct heir to claim the Persian throne. Thus, Bardiya's death provided Darius with a unique opportunity to claim the kingship. Quite possibly Darius disguised the regicide of Bardiya by inventing the figure of Gaumata as the false Bardiya, which allowed him to present himself as the saviour of the Persian throne.

5.2.3   Darius the Achaemenid

Several reasons support the idea that Darius usurped the throne and went to some lengths to justify his actions and to legitimise his claim to the throne. The first issue is his claim to the kingship, the second his extraordinary marriage policy pursued shortly after assuming the throne. Calling himself an Achaemenid, Darius claimed to be of royal descent, with eight of his family having been kings before him. The Achaemenid clan belonged to the Persian tribe of the Pasargadae, and links between the two families were established when Cyrus II married Pharnaspes's daughter Cassandane. As a son of Hystaspes and nephew of Pharnaspes Darius was a member of the Achaemenid clan, but he was far removed from claiming the throne of the Pasargadae:

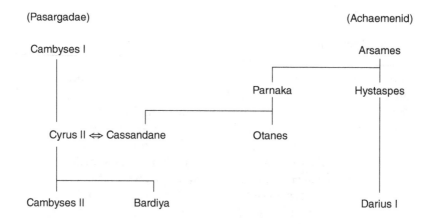

The genealogy links Darius to the line of Cyrus II through his uncle Parnaka/ Pharnaspes and the marriage between Cyrus II and Parnaka's daughter Cassandane, Darius's cousin, yet his claim to kingship remains a remote one nevertheless. This makes Darius's need to legitimise his claim to kingship obvious, as does the elaborate construction of the Bisitun Inscription and relief, and his goal to distribute copies of the text across the empire. The Inscription of Bisitun was an instrument of power and a unique piece of propaganda. No previous king had had the need to stress his right to succession in this way. To make such an effort and to go to such lengths to explain his position does imply a strong need to legitimise the kingship.

There are further issues related to Darius's claim to royalty. Cyrus's title 'king of Anshan' was discarded and replaced by a new title, in which Darius first identified himself as 'Darius the king, son of Hystaspes, an Achaemenid, king of kings, a Persian, king of Persia', and then added the titles 'Great King, king of kings, king of lands'. This was the beginning of a new royal tradition which created a break between the kings of the line of Teispes and Cyrus I and those of Darius's own family, which included Hystaspes, his grandfather Arsames and his great-grandfather Ariaramnes, with Teipses as the common ancestor between the two family lines, and with Achaemenes as the oldest ancestor. He is a figure first introduced here, and, though his historicity is disputed, his name became the eponym for the Achaemenid Dynasty. The main reason for doubting the existence of Achaemenes is the fact that all available evidence, from the seal of Cyrus I to the inscriptions of Cyrus II, names Teispes as the earliest ancestor. He is the common link between these 'two lines' of kings, if, for a moment, we follow Darius's claim, allowing for the following genealogy:

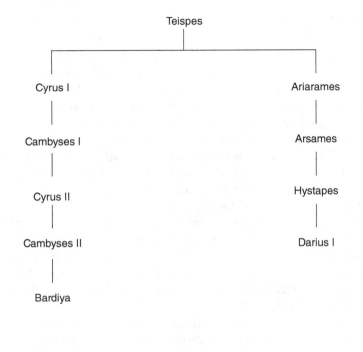

5.2.4   Teispes

But the introduction of the Achaemenid ancestry is not the only novelty. Darius I was also the first king to identify himself by his ethnicity as a Persian. With this, he abandoned the Elamite tradition followed by his predecessors and introduced a new people ruling of their own accord. As we shall see, it was a means to create a Persian identity amongst the Persian noble class, which was supported through the introduction of Persian as a written language and the establishment of the Persian cult of Auramazda.

5.2.5   The Royal Line of Kings

A puzzling issue of the inscription is Darius's claim to descend from a line of kings, being the ninth in succession. There is no evidence to suggest that his father and grandfather were in fact kings. According to DB col. II §35, Darius's father, Hystaspes, was the governor of Parthia, while Herodotus claims he served as a courtier under Cyrus II and acted as *hyparchos*, governor, of Parsa, at the time of Bardiya's reign. As for Darius himself, he served as a spear-bearer of Cambyses II in Egypt. No information exists about the status of Arsames and Ariaramnes. Due to the lack of any factual evidence, scholars have dismissed the idea of a dual kingship of the line of the Pasargadae and that of the Achaemenids. Furthermore, Darius makes no mention of any of the Pasargadae kings in his claim to be the ninth king in the royal line. If they were included, we would arrive at a figure of 11 kings; or, assuming Darius only counted the kings of the Achaemenid line, he would be the sixth king, not the ninth. His number only makes sense if we complete his list of kings with the names of Cyrus II, Cambyses II and Bardiya. Yet the contradiction between his claim and Cyrus's statement that both Cambyses I and Cyrus I were kings of Anshan, remains.

5.2.6   Dynastic Marriages

The strongest indicator for Darius's need to legitimise his reign is his marriage policy. Darius established a dynastic policy not only through his own multiple marriages but also by creating an intricate system of alliances which bound both the family of Otanes and that of Gobryas to him. Prior to becoming king, Darius had married a daughter of Gobryas, whose name is not recorded, though it has recently been suggested she may be identified with Irdabama, also known as Abbamush, in texts from Persepolis, and as Apame in Babylonian documents dated to 503/2 and 502/1. In these texts she bears the title *sha ekalli*, which translates as 'woman of the palace'. This marriage produced three sons, Artobarzanes, the first born, Ariabignes and Arsamenes. Sisters of Darius were married to Gobryas and Otanes, respectively. The children of these unions were married to offspring of Darius. Mardonius, the son of Gobryas, married Darius's daughter Artazostre (Hdt.VI.43.1, PFa 5), and Amestris, a daughter of Otanes, was wed to Darius's son and heir to the throne, Xerxes. This intricate web of marriage alliances involving three families over two generations was a purposeful construction of loyalty ties between two noble Persian families and the king, and reflected their exalted status among the remaining nobles.

Yet it is Darius's marriages to the royal princesses which stand out as an exceptional dynastic act. Upon his accession to the throne, Darius married the daughters of Cyrus and sisters of Cambyses, Atossa and Artystone, and Otanes's daughter Phaidyme, who was the widow of both Cambyses and Bardiya, as well as Bardiya's daughter Parmys. In addition, he married his niece Phratagune, daughter of Artanes. The reason for this string of royal marriages is obvious. With the exception of Phaidyme, any male offspring resulting from the marriage of the royal daughters with other Persian nobles could claim a direct descent from the line of Cyrus II and therefore would have a more legitimate claim to the throne of the Teispids. That possibility Darius had to prevent from happening.

5.3   The Consolidation of Empire

With Darius's kingship secured, the years following his accession to the throne were spent on the internal and external consolidation of the empire. Internally, Darius focused on a monumental building programme, evidenced in the completion of Cyrus's palace at Pasargadae, the building of an Achaemenid palace in Susa and the start of his own palace complex at Persepolis, which became the representational centre of the empire throughout Achaemenid rule and the embodiment of Achaemenid power. He took measures to document the existing law codes of the lands of the empire, established a standard Persian weight, undertook a reform of the satrapies and their tributes and introduced Persian coinage. The *daric*, the name perhaps reflecting his own name, weighed 8.4 g and was 98% pure gold and equalled one shekel. It shows the king as archer, in a half-kneeling, half-running position with bow and arrow. Silver coins were known as '*sigloi*' (sg. *siglos*) and weighed 11.2 g and consisted of more than 90% silver. Herodotus suggests that the minting of coinage was restricted to the king and any attempts at striking coins at local level were regarded as a satrap's striving for independent power, exemplified in the case of Aryandes the satrap of Egypt

(Hdt.IV.166). When Darius I learned about Aryandes's minting of silver coins, he was immediately removed from office and received the punishment typical for a rebel. In line with his predecessors, he cared for the maintenance and restoration of temples and sanctuaries across the empire, from Egypt to Asia Minor.

Darius also ordered the collection of the existing laws of the imperial lands to establish the legal guidelines for each satrapy. One such decree is preserved in a fourth-century copy from Egypt, written in Demotic. The text documents that the laws had been written down in two different languages, one in Aramaic, the other in Demotic:

> The matters that occurred following what was written in the book of decrees from Year 44 of the Pharaoh – life, prosperity, health – Amasis – life, prosperity, health – until Cambyses was in command of Egypt. He died ...(?) before regaining his country.
>
> Darius made [the chiefs?] of the whole earth obey him because of his greatness of heart. He wrote (to) his satrap in Egypt in Year 3, saying: 'Have them bring to me the scholars [...] among the soldiers, priests and scribes of Egypt [...]. They are to write the law of Egypt from the olden days until Year 44 of Pharaoh – life, prosperity, health – Amasis – life, prosperity, health!
>
> The law ... [...] of the temples and the people, have been brought here ... (?) a papyrus until Year 19 [...] Egypt. They were ... [...] (in) Year 27. He wrote matters [...] in the manner(?) of the law of Egypt. They wrote a copy on papyrus in Assyrian writing (= Aramaic) and in documentary writing (= Demotic). It was completed before him. They wrote in his presence; nothing was left out. (Demotic papyrus BN 215, transl. Kuhrt 2010: 125, no. 14c)

Sources in Translation 5.2

Darius's Inscription on a Stele from Red Sea Canal (DZc)

Construction of the Red Sea Canal

As part of his endeavours to secure and improve the overland and naval routes, in 517 Darius ordered the building of a canal leading from the eastern Delta of the Nile to the Red Sea. This project had previously been attempted under the Egyptian king Nekau II (Gr. Nechos, ruled 610–595), but had been abandoned under an extreme loss of the lives of 120 000 men. Working conditions were hard in this arid and barely populated desert region, but Darius succeeded in completing the task. The canal allowed ships to sail directly from Memphis through the Red Sea and the Persian Gulf to the coastal regions of the southern Persian empire and beyond to the mouth of the Indus River. It guaranteed swifter trade and better communication between the empire's satrapies. The canal was about 45 m wide and 5 m deep, covering a distance of 84 km. To commemorate this engineering feat, the canal was lined with at least 12 stelae, each one over 3 m high and inscribed in three cuneiform scripts as well as in Egyptian Hieroglyphic, with a text that included lists of the lands of the empire. Four stelae have been found. Of these, three are now in the Egyptian Museum in Cairo; the other one, the stele from Shalluf, is housed in the Louvre in Paris (Figure 5.2). The Old

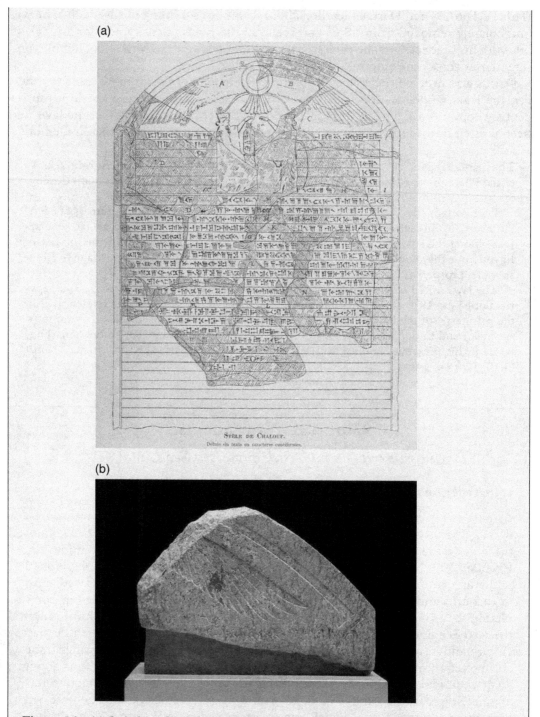

Figure 5.2 (a) Stele from Shalluf (drawing). The stele shows two male figures in Persian dress, wearing Persian-style hair and a crown, beneath the winged sun-disc. *Source*: After Menant 1887). (b) Fragment of the stele from Shallouf showing part of the left wing of the sun disc. *Source*: Louvre AO2251. Photo © Musée du Louvre Dist. RMN-Grand Palais/ Franck Raux.

Persian inscription states Darius's claim to have seized Egypt, clearly denying Cambyses's conquest.

§1.   Auramazda is a great god, who created that sky, who created this earth, who created man, who created happiness for man, who made Darius king, who gave to king Darius a kingdom which is great, which possesses good horses and good men.

§2.   I am Darius, the Great King, king of kings, king of lands, king of this great earth, son of Hystaspes, the Achaemenid.

§3.   Darius the king says: 'I am a Persian. From Persia I seized Egypt. I ordered the digging of this canal from a river called Nile, which flows in Egypt, to the sea which begins in Persia. Afterwards this canal was dug just as I ordered, and ships passed through this canal from Egypt to Persia, as I had wished.' (DZc)

5.3.1   Royal Cities

5.3.1.1   Pasargadae

Under Darius several major building projects were underway, all of which served to establish and consolidate the empire. Among these, the completion of the palace site of Pasargadae entailed a slight dilemma. As a usurper to the throne, Darius I may have had every desire to downplay the importance of Cyrus II and Cambyses II, yet he could not totally subject these kings to a *damnatio memoriae*, a condemnation of memory. It has been suggested that this conundrum was the reason why Darius I decided to complete the construction of Pasargadae; it is the only way we can account for the very different architectural styles found here, a pre-Achaemenid style evident in the layout of the palace building, the winged genius of the Entrance Gate reminiscent of Assyrian winged genii, the Assyrianising reliefs on the doorposts of the Audience Palace depicting Assyrian bull-men and fish-men, in contrast to the figures carved in the Achaemenid royal style found in parts of Cyrus's Residential Palace (Figure 5.3). Darius also added trilingual inscriptions in the Audience Palace and Residential Palace declaring Cyrus as an Achaemenid. They served to demonstrate the link between Cyrus and Darius, legitimising his claim to the throne even more, yet the inscriptions use the Old Persian script which Darius himself claims to have invented, and thus, they can only have been set up by him and not by Cyrus. Similarly, the palace sites of Sang-e Siah and Bardak-e Siah, both located near Borazjan in southwestern Fars, may have been completed by Darius. At both sites we find palace structures with black and white column bases reminiscent of those found at Cyrus's palace at Pasagadae while at the same time bearing architectural features of Achaemenid palaces. These mixed features may point to earlier Persian building projects which were then completed by Darius, or else may be regarded as early examples of Achaemenid palace architecture.

5.3.1.2   Susa

The building of the palace at Susa may also have been due to a highly political motive. Susa had been one of the capitals of the Elamite kings, and had enjoyed a brief revival

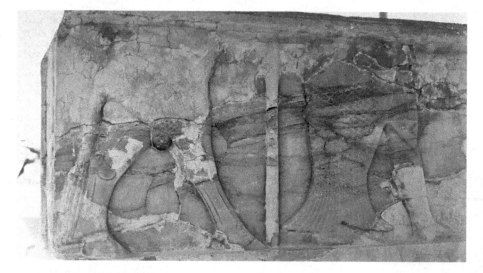

Figure 5.3 Relief from Palace S, Pasargadae showing the lower bodies of a bull-man and a fish-man. These figures are known from Neo-Assyrian palaces and seem to have been an artistic feature adopted by Cyrus II. *Source*: Author photograph.

under Neo-Elamite kings from the second half of the seventh century. Susa had been 'quietly' incorporated into the Persian empire, most likely as part of Cyrus II's march towards Babylon. But the Elamite population of Susa and its hinterland was a potential hotbed for revolt; after all, the Elamites, in two separate rebellions led by Açina and Imanish, respectively, had tried to oppose Darius I in 522/1. One way to prevent further resistance was to manifest Persian presence in Susa and rank it amongst other Persian royal capitals such as Ecbatana, Babylon and Bactra. The Audience Hall from Susa was built on the same square ground plan as that of Persepolis (Figure 5.4). The site was accessed through an entrance gate where an over-life-size statue of Darius was found during the French excavations in 1972 (Figure 5.5). Both the statue and the statue base bear inscriptions in Hieroglyphic and cuneiform. Their emphasis lies in the Persian control over Egypt and the king's acceptance of – and by – Egyptian gods.

5.3.2 Parsa – City of the Persians

Parsa, known as Persepolis in the Greek sources, is located in the plain of Marv Dasht in Persis, about 50 km distance from Pasargadae (Figure 5.6). Persepolis came to symbolise the Persian empire as well as Achaemenid power. The building process of the magnificent palace complex of Persepolis, which measures about 455 m × 300 m, began here a few years after Darius's succession to the throne, in c.518. As we have seen in Chapter 4, the site itself may have been identified by Cambyses II. But the location also has historical significance. About 5 km to the north lies Naqsh-e Rustam, probably to be identified with ancient Nupishtas, which features a rock formation sacred to the Elamites and still bears the remains of an Elamite relief depicting a king and his queen framing a religious scene. Darius chose the rock face of Naqsh-e Rustam as his final resting place, carving a tomb chamber and sarcophagi-shaped spaces inside the

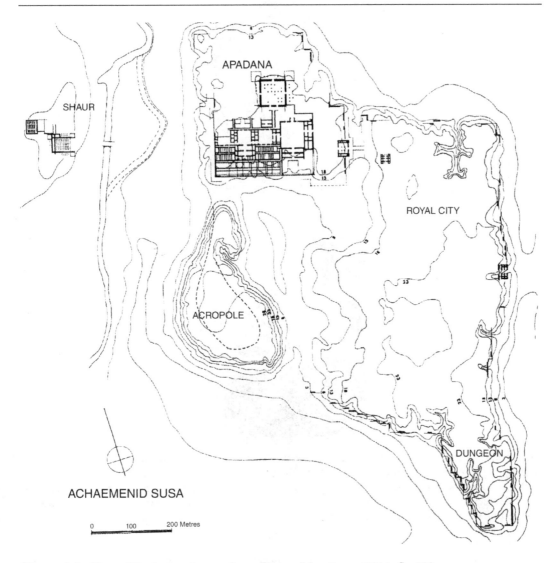

SHAUR

APADANA

ROYAL CITY

ACROPOLE

DUNGEON

ACHAEMENID SUSA

0   100   200 Metres

Figure 5.4   Plan of Darius's palace at Susa. *Source*: After Perrot 2013, fig.100.

rock and finishing the rock surface with an elaborate cross-shaped façade with a relief in its upper section (Figure 5.7). Three of his successors were to follow his example to build their tombs there, though only Darius's can be identified due to inscriptions carved alongside the relief.

The earliest ceremonial buildings on the Persepolis terrace, which itself was elevated 8 m from the ground, were a magnificent Audience Hall, called Apadana, the adjacent palace of Darius, and the Treasury. The Audience Hall, measuring 60 × 60 m, featured 36 stone columns 19.5 m high, its bases carved to resemble Egyptian lotus flowers turned upside down. The fluted columns were crafted by Ionian stonemasons, and the capitals featured double-headed bulls carved in the distinctive Achaemenid style. These capitals held a ceiling built of cedar wood. The hall was raised 3 m from the ground, and was accessed by two staircases, one on the north side, the other on

Figure 5.5 Statue of Darius from Susa. The statue was crafted in Egypt. Although the figure is wearing Persian dress, the stiff stance points to Egyptian craftsmen executing the work. The sides of the base depict the people of the empire, each one in a kneeling position and identified by their ethnikon carved in Hieroglyphics. The statue is now housed in the National Museum of Iran, Tehran. *Source*: Photograph courtesy of the National Museum, Tehran. Photo © Amir Farzad.

the east side. They feature Persian courtiers and bodyguards on one side, and the delegations of 23 lands on the other. It is the most splendid display of empire, with the delegations bringing gifts to the king in the form of livestock, mostly horses, but also sheep, a lioness with cups and an okapi, and precious objects used for banqueting, such as jars and beakers, as well as weapons, jewellery and cloth.

Darius's private palace, called *tacara*, was built just to the south of the Apadana and was also based on a square ground plan. Initially, the complex was accessed from a staircase at the southern fortification wall, where Darius carved two of his inscriptions (DPe and DPd). In the course of its long building process, which is still attested in the reign of Artaxerxes III (ruled 359–338), Persepolis was built by hundreds of workers, men, women and children, and included a variety of ethnic groups from across the empire, all of them working in their trained profession. Texts from the Persepolis archive refer to the labourers as *kurtash* and include stonemasons, irrigation workers, painters, goldsmiths, weavers, bakers and brewers. Work groups consisted of an almost even number of male and female workers and their children, often amounting to several

Sources in Translation 5.3

Darius's Foundation Inscription from Susa (DSf)

The building inscription from Susa shows how much pride Darius I took in having assembled the best resources from the lands of the empire to construct the palace. The so-called Foundation Charter was first published in 1929. The trilingual inscription is written in Elamite, Babylonian and Old Persian. Copies of this text were found written on clay and on marble tablets, as well as on the glazed tiles of the frieze of the Great Hall. The inscription is now in the Louvre; fragments are in the Archaeological Museum in Susa. Two further foundation charters, one written in Elamite (DSz) and one in Babylonian (DSaa), were found in the Apadana, the Throne-Hall, of Darius I during the excavation season of 1969/70, and are thought to be variants of the text. Recounting the different peoples and materials brought from across the empire, the text is testament to the fact that Darius regarded the palaces as a conglomeration of elements taken from the entire realm, and being worked into one magnificent building, effectively resulting in a microcosm of the empire.

Darius's Foundation Inscription from Susa

§1. Auramazda is a great god, who created this earth, who created the sky, who created man, who created happiness for man, who made Darius king, one king among many, one lord among many.

§2. I am Darius, the Great King, king of kings, king of the lands, king of this earth, son of Hystaspes, an Achaemenid. And Darius the king says: 'Auramazda, who is the greatest of the gods, has created me, has made me king, he has given me this kingdom, which is great, and which has good horses and good men. By the favour of Auramazda, my father Hystaspes and Arsames, my grandfather, were both alive when Auramazda made me king on this earth. Thus it was the desire of Auramazda to choose me as his man on this entire earth, he made me king on this earth. I worshipped Auramazda. Auramazda brought me aid. What I ordered (to be done), this he accomplished for me. I achieved all of what I did by the grace of Auramazda.

§3. This palace which I built at Susa: its materials were brought from afar. The earth was dug down deep, until the rock was reached in the earth. When the excavation had been made, then rubble was packed down, some 40 cubits (= c.20 m) deep, another (part) 20 cubits deep. On that rubble the palace was constructed. And that earth, which was dug deep, and that rubble, which was packed down, and the sun-dried bricks, which were moulded, the Babylonian people – they performed (these tasks).

§4. The cedar timber was brought from a mountain called Lebanon. The Assyrian people brought it to Babylon. From Babylon the Carians and Ionians brought it to Susa. The *sissoo*-timber was brought from Gandara and from Carmania. The gold which was worked here was brought from Sardis and from Bactria. The precious stone lapis lazuli and carnelian which was worked here was brought from Sogdiana. The precious stone turquoise, which was worked here, this was brought from Chorasmia. The silver and the ebony were brought from Egypt. The ornamentation with which the wall was adorned was brought from Ionia. The ivory which was worked here was brought from Ethiopia (= Nubia), and from India and from Arachosia. The stone columns which were worked here were brought from a village called Abiradu, in Elam. The stone-cutters who worked the stone were Ionians and Sardians. The goldsmiths who worked the gold were Medes and Egyptians. The men who worked the wood were Sardians and Egyptians. The men who worked the baked brick were Babylonians. The men who adorned the wall were Medes and Egyptians.'

§5.   Darius the king says: 'At Susa a very excellent work was ordered, a very excellent work was brought to completion. May Auramazda protect me, and Hystaspes my father and my country.'

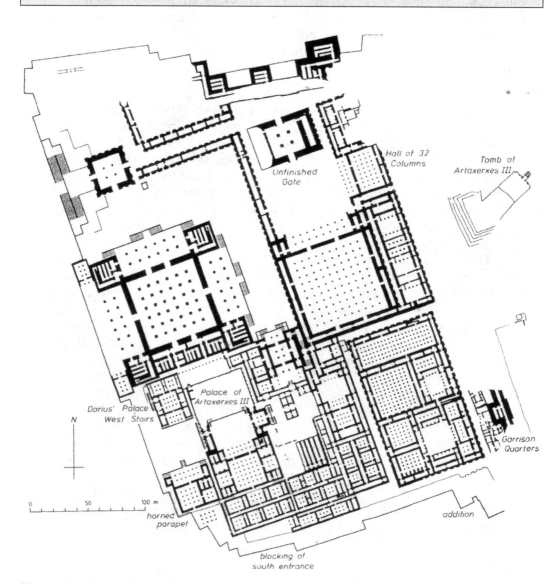

Figure 5.6   Plan of Persepolis. *Source*: After Schmidt 1953, fig.35b.

Figure 5.7   Naqsh-e Rustam. The tomb of Darius I is the second on the left, identified by its inscriptions. It is thought that the tomb facing the viewer is that of Xerxes, while the first tomb on the left might be that of Artaxerxes I. In the foreground is a tower-like structure known as the Ka'aba-e Zardusht, almost identical to the Zendan-e Suleiman at Pasargadae. Better preserved, the Ka'aba-e Zardusht shows a long staircase leading up to a single chamber inside the tower. *Source*: Photograph courtesy of Michael Alram.

hundred people in total. They lived in villages in the vicinity of Persepolis and in the wider region of Persis, working in different royal dwellings. The Persepolis archives have documented their reimbursement for their labour, being paid in different kinds of grain, flour, wine, beer and sheep, or in silver.

5.4   Foreign Policy

Militarily, Darius secured the borders of the Persian empire in the north and east. Although we lack a detailed account of these campaigns, Darius confirmed the border with India, securing the eastern front as far as the Indus River. The admiral of the fleet in charge of the expedition was Scylax of Caryanda. In the west, Darius's campaigns led to the conquest of Samos and the securing of the north African coast between 519 and 513/2. Thrace and Macedon also accepted Persian sovereignty. The Hellespontine region was secured by Megabazus, as were the islands off the coast of Asia Minor.

Herodotus recalls the story of Oroites, the satrap of Sardis, who acted without the king's authority when he planned to conquer Samos, at the time ruled by Polycrates. Using Polycrates's ambition to expand his power to the whole of Ionia, Oroites invited him to Sardis to offer his support, thus getting Polycrates to leave the island. Oroites claimed that he was no longer loyal to Cambyses II. If Polycrates saved Oroites's life, he would help him to gain control of Ionia. Polycrates sent his scribe Maeandrius to Oroites to assess his trustworthiness, and, being persuaded, he informed Polycrates

Box Text 5.1

The Persepolis Archives

Clay tablets recording administrative procedures were found at two separate locations on the Persepolis terrace during excavations in 1933/4 and 1936/7 led by Ernst Herzfeld. About 30 000 clay tablets and fragments were found in one room on the north side of the fortification wall, and over 200 were found in Room 33 of the Treasury and adjacent areas. Most of the Persepolis Tablets were written in Elamite, but there are also about 500 clay tablets written in Aramaic. Few tablets were written in Phrygian, Old Persian or Greek. The Fortification Tablets date to the reign of Darius I, beginning in 506 and down to 497, the Treasury Tablets to the reigns of Darius I, Xerxes I and Artaxerxes I, from 492 to 458. Of the Fortification texts about 2200 have been published by Richard T. Hallock in 1969 and 1978; the remaining corpus is still unpublished, including the Aramaic texts. George G. Cameron began publication of the Treasury texts in 1948. The Treasury texts in particular focus on expenses for workers at Persepolis, listing builders, sculptors, makers of inlays, goldsmiths and stonemasons, as well as wine makers. The following texts exemplify ration payments for workers at Persepolis from both the Fortification archive and the Treasury archive.

Text 1:

Tell Irshena, the chief of workers, Parnaka spoke as follows:

150 quarts of flour from Persepolis issued as ration to Addarnurish the Assyrian who handles cedar(?) (wood at) Persepolis, (as rations for) months III, IV, V, VI, VII, for a total period of 5 months, Year 24 (of Darius I). Monthly he receives 30 quarts.
Shamanda wrote. He received the *dumme* from Yauna.
In Year 24, month V (= July/August 498), the sealed document was delivered. (PF 1799)

Text 2:

5 karsha, 2 shekels (of) silver, supplied by Shakka, (which) the workmen making sculptures (of) stone and wood at Parsa received, (for whom) Vahush is responsible. Sheep (are) the equivalent of (silver), 1 (sheep for) 3 shekels (as the rate has been) set by edict.
Month Bagayadi, Varkazana, Aciyadiya, Year 10 (of Xerxes) (= September/ October to November/December 476).
7 men (receive) 1 ½ shekels each, 5 men ¾ of a shekel each, 6 men ½ shekels. (PT 26)

Text 3:

Tell Vahush, the Treasurer, Artatakma speaks as follows:

3 karsha, 6 shekels, and ¾ of a shekel (of) silver from the Treasury of the king, give it to them – (to) makers of inlay(s), makers of relief(s), (for) whom you are responsible, (as) silver which is to go to them. The equivalent (of) the

> wage (in) money (is) in sheep (as the) wage of the months Samiamantash: 1;
> Viyaxna, the former: 1; Viyaxna the later (= intercalendrial month): 1. A total
> of 3 months in Year 12 (of Xerxes).
> In Hiamasika(?) they made [...]
> 1 man receives 1 ½ shekels per month, 5 men each receive ¾ of a shekel per
> month, 14 men each receive ½ a shekel per month. Total 20 men.
> As set by edict, 1 sheep (is the) equivalent (of) 3 shekels (of) silver. (For) this
> silver, Pi(pi)kadabarma (and) the 'helpers' have rendered an accounting (for)
> the people (as required) by the edict.
> Month Karbashiya, Year 13 (of Xerxes (= August/September 452)). A sealed
> document has been given. Tetukka wrote (the document), from Akkushuna(?)
> (he got a receipt). (PT 27)

that a journey to Sardis was safe. Once in Sardis, Polycrates was killed, though the accompanying Samians were granted a safe passage home. Only the non-Samians were to stay behind. Among them was a physician from Croton called Democedes, who later was to serve at Darius's court.

Oroites, according to Herodotus, continued to hold his office at Sardis through the reign of Bardiya and apparently tried to expand his power when he killed the satrap of Dascyleium, Mitrobates, as well as his son Cranaspes. When Darius sent a messenger to make inquiries about Oroites's actions, Oroites killed him on his return journey. In light of Oroites's disloyal behaviour, Darius announced that he was to be eliminated. Rather than sending an army, which could alarm Oroites in advance and allow him to prepare an opposition, Darius chose a subtler way. Bagaeus, son of Artontes, was sent to Sardis with several letters written by Darius and sealed with his royal seal. Arriving at the satrapal palace, the letters were read out by the royal scribes one by one to the armed guards, thereby testing their loyalty to the king. The final letter then demanded; 'King Darius charges the Persians in Sardis to kill Oroites' (Hdt.III.128), and so they did. After Oroites's death, Maeandrius took over his office in Samos, but eventually handed the power to Polycrates's brother Syloson.

Whether this transition was peaceful or not is difficult to say. Maeandrius initially seemed to have agreed to the treaty with the Persians, but then became ambitious and was determined to stay in power; in consequence, some Persian envoys were murdered. Otanes, who had been instructed to carry out a peaceful transition of rule in Samos, was now forced to attack the Samians. Maeandrius fled to Sparta and tried to bribe king Cleomenes with cups made of precious metal. Cleomenes, however, did not accept the gift and, fearing that Maeandrius would try to corrupt others, ordered his expulsion from Sparta. Herodotus's intentions in telling this story are far from clear. What could have been a possible motive for Maeandrius to bribe the Spartan king? Perhaps the Spartans, knowing that Maeandrius had disobeyed the Persian king, did not want to be victims of a potential Persian revenge for granting Maeandrius asylum.

5.4.1 The Scythian Campaign

In 513, Darius undertook a campaign against the Scythians of the Black Sea region, and this marked the advance of Persian troops and ships into northern Europe. The architect Mandrocles of Samos was the mastermind for the construction of a bridge over the Bosporus, built, ingeniously, by lining up the Persian fleet to allow the army to cross over. Darius then advanced through Thrace to the River Tearus, where he apparently set up an inscription (Hdt.IV.91); the Ionian fleet sailed as far as the Danube to await the arrival of the infantry. With the exception of the Getae, the Thracian tribes surrendered to Persian power without apparent resistance, offering Earth and Water to the king, thus formally accepting his supremacy. The Thracians joined the Persian army and Darius pursued his march towards the Danube to meet up with the Ionian fleet. The Ionians safeguarded the bridge over the Danube for 60 days while awaiting Darius's return.

Herodotus describes the following campaign against the Scythians in great detail, pointing out the failure of the enterprise due to the Scythians refusing to meet the Persians in battle and instead leading them far into unknown territory. It was made particularly difficult since the Scythians, a non-settled, nomadic or semi-nomadic tribe, possessed no cities and did not farm land, points of potential weakness of any settled group as these could be destroyed by the enemy. Instead, Herodotus recounts Darius's increasing frustration with the fruitless pursuit of the Scythians, eventually leaving him to give up and return to the Hellespont. Yet, contrary to Herodotus's view, two inscriptions of Darius, from Susa and from his tomb at Naqsh-e Rustam, list the European Scythians among the peoples of the empire. Thus, control over the Black Sea region must have been achieved at least to some extent. Recent research proposed that rather than conducting a one-sided attack west of the Black Sea, Darius may in fact have opted for a two-pronged attack, approaching the Scythians from both western and eastern coasts of the Black Sea, and accordingly securing the borders at the Danube River and the Sal River.

5.4.2 The Athenian-Persian Alliance of 508/7

The end of the sixth century witnessed the first encounter between Persia and mainland Greece, initiated by Athens on account of the political turmoil the city was experiencing. Therefore, in 508/7, an Athenian delegation acting on behalf of Cleisthenes's government made its way to the Persian court. They were instructed to seek the king's support in order to quell the internal political turmoil which had erupted between the democratic and oligarchic factions in Athens, the latter being supported by Sparta in their aim to topple the democrats in favour of Isagoras as ruler of Athens. The mission of the Athenian delegation to Persia was successful: Darius agreed to enter an alliance with Athens. It meant that (democratic) Athens could be certain of Persian protection in case of a political and military attack which threatened its current government – a protection which presumably was to materialise in the form of financial aid, though it was feasible that military support could also be provided, considering that Persian garrisons were stationed in Thrace and Macedon. In addition, it may be supposed that the Thracian and Macedonian forces themselves could be commanded to support Athens since both regions were under Persian sovereignty at the time. As for naval support, that, too, could potentially be supplied by Ionian or Cypriote ships under Persian command.

The condition for securing the Persian alliance was Athenian recognition of the supremacy of the Persian king. Accordingly, the delegates submitted Earth and Water, the symbolic tokens of submission to the king's authority. Yet, by the time the Greek ambassadors returned to Athens, the political threat had ceased: Isagoras's coup had been foiled and the democratic faction was re-affirmed. In consequence, according to Herodotus, the delegates were blamed by Athens for having entered the alliance with Persia. But Herodotus's story does not add up. Why would the delegates be accused of forming an alliance with Persia by the same political faction that had sent them on this mission in the first place? Is it feasible that the democratic faction was so fickle that they changed their mind as soon as the imminent danger of Isagoras's coup was averted? Could the alliance the Athenian government sought with Persia have been anything but a long-term undertaking, and not just a short-term measure to address the immediate threat at hand? The latter simply does not seem likely: Athens could in no way be certain that a further coup would threaten Athens, given that it was acutely aware that the Spartan hoplites formed the superior military power in Greece, and that accordingly Sparta posed a constant threat as a potential support for a next political coup. By the same token, it seems politically highly naïve to assume that the Persian king would consider an alliance with Athens on a short-term basis and for a one-off event. If that had been the case, the delegates surely would have been expected to return to Athens with Persian money and/or military forces in tow to deal with the immediate danger the city was facing. The alliance of 508/7, then, must have been considered by both sides as a long-term arrangement. Thrace and Macedon had submitted Earth and Water in c.513, and it is reasonable to expect that this news had found its way to central Greece. Unless we assume that the Athenians were the first European state to recognise the potential benefits of an alliance with Persia, the idea must have originated somewhere else, as must have the knowledge that, in return for having its sovereignty recognised, Persia would protect the interests of local regions and cities without much interference. The developments in Thrace and Macedon after 513 may well have given Athens the impetus to turn to Persia for help five years later. If anything, the acceptance of Persian sovereignty promised economic prosperity, as it gave a city access to the trading network of Persian Asia Minor and beyond. For all we know, Athens and Persia entered an alliance in 508/7 in which Athens recognised Persian sovereignty. This alliance obligated Persia to aid Athens in a political (and possibly military) conflict, while at the same time it committed Athens to loyalty to the king.

5.4.3 The Ionian Revolt

In 499/8, a rebellion broke out in Ionia led by Aristagoras of Miletus. Miletus, like many other Ionian cities of Asia Minor, was governed by a city-ruler who had accepted the overlordship of Cyrus II following the conquest of Lydia, paying taxes and tribute to the Persian satrap in Sardis. In 513/2 these city-kings had proved their loyalty to Darius when they maintained the bridge over the Danube River to safeguard Darius's return from Scythia. The wealth and prosperity of the Ionian cities were based on commerce and trade. Miletus itself had been one of the most formidable cities in the archaic period and had not only prospered commercially but also had become a centre for famous scientists and philosophers of the time. Because of their geographical location, the city-states here already controlled trade routes and had the support of the maritime industry, which built trading ships as well as war ships. Their economic stability was secured through the Persian king, whose policy it was to maintain each local power in its present state if it was to the advantage of the political ambitions of the empire. Compared to the political tendencies of the city-states on mainland Greece, the Ionian Greeks clearly had more in common with the political structure of Cypriote and Phoenician city-kingship than with the concept of democratic rule.

5.4.4   The Sequence of Events

Our only source for the events relating to the Ionian Revolt of 499/8 to 493/2 is Herodotus. The overall impression of his account is that the motives for the revolt lay in the personal ambition and animosity of a tyrant and a satrap, namely Aristagoras of Miletus and Artaphernes, satrap of Sardis. Herodotus himself displays a rather negative attitude towards the revolt, while the form of his account makes a secure chronology for the sequence of events rather impossible.

Three major points can be distinguished: firstly, the Persian expedition to the island of Naxos, secondly, the importance of Histaeus and his alleged involvement in the revolt, and thirdly, the role of Aristagoras, including the reaction of Athens and Sparta when Aristagoras asked for their support. According to Herodotus, a group of political exiles from Naxos arrived in Miletus in 500/499 and asked Aristagoras for support to reinstate them on the island. Aristagoras sought the council of his Persian satrap, Artaphernes, in Sardis, and ultimately king Darius approved of the expedition to Naxos, which was commanded by the Achaemenid Megabates. A successful undertaking would give the Persians a stronghold on Naxos, as well as on the islands of Paros and Andros, which were dependent on Naxos. The Persians also would gain entry to the Cyclades.

In 499, the Persian fleet sailed off to Chios and from there returned to take the route towards Naxos. During this sail a quarrel began between Aristagoras and Megabates over Scylax. Scylax commanded the ships from Myndus, but on discovering that one of the ships had been left unguarded, Megabates held him responsible for the neglect and punished him. Aristagoras, however, freed Scylax from his bond and thus enraged Megabates, who, in reaction, betrayed the expedition to the people of Naxos. The Persians were unable to take the city and, after a siege of four months, they returned to the coast of Asia Minor. Aristagoras, concerned about his unfulfilled promise to Darius guaranteeing the success of the expedition, about the cost of the military undertaking and about the possible consequences for his failure, decided to rebel against the Persian king. His decision, according to Herodotus, apparently coincided with a message from Histaeus commanding Aristagoras to revolt against the king.

Aristagoras gathered other Ionian tyrants to plan the revolt. One of them, Hecataeus of Miletus, voted against any undertaking against the Persian king in respect of the king's power and support of all the other nations (Hdt.V.36), but he was outvoted. Among the other city-rulers who refused to participate in the revolt were Oliatus of Mylasa, Histiaeus of Termera and Coes of Mytilene. They were seized and forced to return to their cities. To win the support of the Milesians, Aristagoras is said to have introduced *isonomia*, equal (political) rights, in the city and used this strategy throughout Ionia. But why should other city-rulers agree to hand over their power to gain independence from the Persian king when effectively they had to concede their own position and power?

In a next step, Aristagoras sought the support of king Cleomenes of Sparta, probably in the winter of 499/8. The proposed plan suggests that Aristagoras's ambition went far beyond his initial aim to seize Naxos and the Cyclades, because he tried to convince Cleomenes to use his army in Asia Minor and then advance to take Susa and become master of all the lands of Persia. But Cleomenes lost interest in such an undertaking when he learned that an overland journey from Sardis to Susa would take three months. An attempt to bribe the Spartan king into the revolt subsequently failed as well. Aristagoras next tried to win over Athens to support the revolt. The city agreed to send 20 ships under the command of Melanthius. The Eretrians in addition sent five triremes. This fleet arrived at Miletus in the spring of 498. The first military operation was directed towards Sardis, which the Ionians approached from Ephesus. During the attack, a fire broke out in the city and destroyed most of its houses and the temple of the city-goddess Cybele. Lydians and Persians of the city nevertheless made an attempt to defend themselves, and the Ionians retreated to their ships. Other Persians from the surrounding lands came to the aid of the Persians and Lydians, and a battle near Ephesus forced the Ionians to abandon the revolt. While they fled to their respective cities, the Athenians and Eretrians abandoned the revolt and returned home.

The rebellion now took on its own dynamics and spread from Miletus to the Hellespont, Caria and Cyprus. Some Ionians moved towards the Propontis and took Byzantium and tried to win the support of the cities of the Hellespontine region. In the south, Caria was said to have joined the revolt, but the date of this rebellion is far from certain. The Persians first had to concentrate their forces on Cyprus, where Onesilus revolted in Salamis. Onesilus's brother, Gorgus, the king of Salamis, and the city of Amathus opposed the revolt (Hdt.V.105). Regardless, Onesilus expelled his brother from Salamis and attacked Amathus. A Persian army under Artybius and the Phoenician fleet set off towards Salamis, and Onesilus was killed, perhaps in the summer of 497. The Phoenician cities on Cyprus aided the Persians to restore control over the island.

In a next step, Persian focus turned to the Hellespont and Caria. Daurises, Darius's son-in-law, took Dardanus, Abydus, Percote, Lampsacus and Paesus. He advanced to Caria and successfully fought a battle against the Carians at the Marsyas River. When Daurises died in battle, Hymaees took over his command and moved first towards the Propontis, then via the Hellespont to the Troad. In Caria, Artaphernes and Otanes started a counter-attack, taking Clazomenae and Cyme, perhaps in 496. During the entire period, the Ionians could not account for a single military success. Cyprus and the Hellespontine region were back under Persian control; Aristagoras and his remaining supporters fled to Myrcinus in Thrace. Here Aristagoras was killed in c.497/6 (Thuc. IV.102.2–3).

In 494, the Persians launched an offensive by land and sea against Miletus. The fleet, consisting of Cypriote, Phoenician, Cilician and Egyptian ships, amounted to a total of 600 vessels. They faced an Ionian navy of 350 ships under the command of Dionysius of Phocaea. When the Persian fleet approached, most of the Samian ships deserted the front line, causing many others to follow. On land, the Persians successfully attacked Miletus and took the city. Some of the inhabitants were taken hostage and brought to Susa only to be resettled near the Red Sea.

Histaeus himself, according to Herodotus, was allowed to leave Susa for Ionia in order to explore the reasons for revolt in Ionia, where the satrap Artaphernes rightly suspected Histaeus's connection with Aristagoras and the revolt. Miletus, the city Histaeus had governed before Aristagoras, refused him entry, and Chios ceased to support him. Histaeus then launched an attack on Chios, supported by a small fleet from Lesbos. He may have hoped to use the island as a base for further attacks on the mainland. He also besieged Miletus and attacked Thasos, which had stayed neutral during the revolt. But at this point, Histaeus was attacked by the Phoenician fleet and was forced to abandon his undertaking. There were very few places he could seek refuge, but his army needed food supplies. Probably in spring 493, he arrived at Atarneus, and finally met the Persian Harpagus in battle. He was taken prisoner, brought to Sardis and brought before Artaphernes, who sentenced him to death.

The aftermath of the revolt consisted of serious measures against the rebelling cities, with girls and boys – most likely belonging to families implicated in the rebellion – being taken to the royal court. After wintering in Miletus in 494/3, the Persians subjected the islands Chios, Lesbos and Tenedos. The Chersonnese was secured by the Phoenician fleet and Cyzicus offered her submission to the king. The Persian Oebares, son of Megabazus, was appointed satrap of Dascyleium. In 493, Artaphernes began the reorganisation of Ionia, and in the following spring, Mardonius was dispatched to oversee the implementation of political changes imposed on some cities of Asia Minor.

5.4.5 Problems in the Historical Account

Herodotus's narrative of the Ionian Revolt bears some inconsistencies, such as in his account of Naxos. The Persian Megabates was put in charge of the expedition to Naxos by Darius himself. Therefore, the entire enterprise was authorised by the king and not by Aristagoras. He and the exiled Naxians may have been responsible for the fleet, but Aristagoras still was under Darius's command. It is unlikely that Megabates would betray the purpose of the expedition to the Naxians for the sole reason of spoiling matters for Aristagoras, considering that his own position was at risk if he betrayed Darius's order. There is also the issue of Aristagoras's request for support from Sparta and, upon being denied Spartan aid, from Athens. There is a striking parallel between the episode of Aristagoras's mission to Cleomenes and the story of Oroites and Polycrates of Samos. Aristagoras promised Cleomenes the rule of Asia Minor if not the whole of Persia in advancing to take Susa. Likewise, the former Sardian satrap Oroites promised Polycrates of Samos hegemony over Asia Minor if he supported Oroites against the Persian king (Hdt.III.126). This should alert us once again that Herodotus favoured literary construct over historical reality.

As for Sparta as a possible ally in the revolt, it seems that any promise of Spartan rule in Asia Minor was an extremely ambitious, not to say impossible, claim, especially considering the Spartans' inability to leave their country for any length of time due to their fear of a revolt by the helots, the unfree population of Sparta. Athens did send 20 ships but never engaged in the fight, returning to mainland Greece after the first battle. Neither Sparta nor Athens was committed to the Ionians and their revolt during the six-year period.

The argument that economic pressures from Persia triggered the revolt, that is, the payment of 400 talents of annual tribute and further contributions to local garrisons and governors, as well as gifts for the king or the satrap, is also difficult to uphold. The Ionian cities had previously paid tribute to the Lydian kings, while evidence from

Box Text 5.2

Earth and Water

Greek sources frequently refer to the Persian demand of Earth and Water. This request is understood to have been a symbolic gesture of submission to the king and of recognition of the king's sovereignty, as well as an expression of the subject's commitment and loyalty to the king. Yet only the Greek sources mention such a gesture as a characteristic of Persian diplomacy, and only in connection with European regions, first being mentioned to have been performed by Thrace and Macedon, then, in 508/7, by Athens. Darius is said to have sent embassies to Greece to demand these tokens again from the Greek states before the punitive campaign in 490, and so did Xerxes prior to his campaign of 480/479. In both these cases, this gesture might have been understood as a non-aggression pact between a Greek city-state and Persia. Still, no sources allude to such a procedure for any other land on the borders of the Persian empire with which diplomatic contacts were established or which came under Persian domination.

> Arriving at Sardis he (= Xerxes) first of all sent messengers to Greece to ask for Earth and Water and to order the preparations of meals for the king; he sent messengers everywhere except Athens and Sparta. He sent for the second time to ask for Earth and Water because he was quite sure that those who had not given them earlier when Darius had asked now would be terrorised and give them; anyway, he wished to find this out and so sent the messengers. (Hdt.VII.32)

> Of those who gave Earth and Water there were the following: Thessalians, Dolopians, Ainianes, Perraibians, Lokrians, Magnetes, Malians, Achaians of Phthiotis, and Thebens, and the other Boiotians except for the Thespians and Plataeans. The Greeks who were proposing to make war on the barbarians swore an oath against them, that any Greeks who gave themselves up to the Persians without being compelled to should be required to give up a tenth of their property to the god of Delphi, if things went well for the Greeks. (Hdt.VII.132)

the fifth century suggests that Athens demanded the same sum of payment as *phoros* after 433, a sum which was later increased to 460 talents (Meiggs and Lewis 1988: 87–88).

5.4.6 *The Punitive Campaign of 490*

As a consequence of Athens's and Eretria's involvement in the Ionian Revolt, however passive it may have been, Darius planned to punish both cities. In 491, he ordered the construction of warships and transport vessels for horses by the people at the coast. At the same time, Darius sent an embassy to Greece demanding Earth and Water from Athens, but was refused. The island of Aegina, however, long-term enemy of Athens, accepted Persian sovereignty. Mardonius crossed the Hellespont and marched west. Thasos, apparently equipped with a strong naval force, offered no resistance and

Macedonia reconfirmed their acceptance of Persian domination, offered in c.513. The tribe of the Brygi in Thrace tried to resist Persian control but eventually had to succumb. The expedition then continued by sea, but the navy suffered heavy losses due to a storm at Mt. Athos, forcing Mardonius to abandon his naval campaign.

In 490, a Persian expedition of c.20 000 men set off from Cilicia towards Greece under the command of Datis, a Mede, and Artaphernes, son of Artaphernes of Sardis (Hdt.VI.94). From Samos, they sailed around the islands towards Naxos, where they landed and destroyed the temple of the city. The reason for this is unclear, unless it was a renewed attack after the initial attempt to take the island. It cannot be regarded as a Persian attempt to attack Greek religious sites, because during his onward journey, Datis anchored off the island of Delos to make offerings to Apollo. Eretria suffered the first military blow, falling after a seven-day siege. The Persians then made for Athens, and on the advice of Hippias, the exiled Athenian tyrant who had found refuge in the empire, landed at the Bay of Marathon. The Athenians' decision was to meet the Persians well outside their city and march directly against them. The Plataeans supported the battle with 600 troops, while the runner Phidippides was sent to Sparta to ask for their support.

In principle willing to support Athens, the Spartans had to delay their march to mainland Greece for religious reasons. It was only the ninth day of the month, and they had to await the time of the full moon before they could move. When the Spartans finally reached Attica on the eighteenth day, they learned that the battle had been fought the previous day. The battle itself was lost for the Persians when the Athenians first attacked the wings of the battle line and then, instead of pursuing the soldiers, turned to the centre. The Persians fled from the plain through the marshland back to their ships and made for Phalerum. Presumably, they hoped to arrive there before the Athenians troops could gather in Athens and start their defence. But it appears that the Athenians reached the city before the Persians, who decided to abandon the attack and return to Asia Minor. Herodotus's casualty figures are highly exaggerated: the Persians are said to have lost 6400 men, the Athenians a mere 192.

The story itself appears to contain a strong historiographical element, as the enmity between Athens and Persia shows a remarkable parallel to the story of Naxos and Persia (Hdt.V.30–37), as well as to the events surrounding Hippias and Aristagoras of Miletus. Both Aristagoras and Hippias were labelled tyrants, both appealed to Artaphernes to undertake a military action against a Greek city and in both cases the incentive used was the promise to increase Persian influence over Naxos and Athens, respectively. Hippias was a political exile wanting to return, Aristagoras acted on behalf of exiled Naxians wanting to return to power; both Hippias and Aristagoras expected a continuation of their own power, should the Persian enterprise be successful. Equally, for both Aristagoras and Hippias the attacks that happened on their initiatives ended in a failure for Persia. The siege of Naxos had to be abandoned and led Aristagoras to unite most of the Ionian cities to rebel against the king. Likewise, the Persian attack on Athens at Marathon ended in a defeat and eventually led to the establishment of the Hellenic League against Persia. It is quite possible that Herodotus created a narrative construct in which Hippias's story served to foreshadow the events of the Ionian Revolt. The fact that he placed it just before the beginning of the revolt strongly indicates this intention, as does placing the second passage at the eve of Marathon. Taking into account Herodotus's penchant for mirroring events, this may be how we have to read and interpret these two passages, concluding that these are historiographical constructs rather than a reflection of historical reality.

Yet there is an even more important point to address, namely the motive for the campaign of 490. Herodotus's claim that the Persian king wanted to reinstall Hippias as a pro-Persian tyrant in Athens in order to facilitate governance over a Persian-controlled city only works if we accept that the conquest of Athens, symbolically standing for the conquest of all of Greece, was the reason for the 490 campaign. This argument is still being upheld in modern scholarship, which regards the Persian campaign as a clear indicator for the Persian expansion to Greece. Yet the Persian diplomatic mission to the Greek states meant to exclude other cities from the planned attack and to concentrate on those two cities that had played a role in the Ionian Revolt. None of the city-states on the Peloponnese were targets. The key issue for Persia was the fact that Athens had interfered in Persian politics by having offered support – active or not – to the rebelling Ionian cities. From a Persian perspective, and in light of the Athenian-Persian alliance of 508/7, Athens had violated the treaty and had interfered in imperial matters.

Thus it may be concluded that the Persian campaign of 490 was a punitive one, and that it was the direct result of Athenian and Eretrian interference in Persian politics in Ionia. As it was a limited campaign, the Persian king left the military command to two of his generals, Artaphernes and Datis, rather than leading it himself. After the sacking of Eretria, no Persian governor or pro-Persian government was installed there; similarly, there were no plans to do so in Athens. It is unlikely, therefore, that the Persians intended to install Hippias, who by now was rather advanced in years, as tyrant in Athens.

The Persian commander Megabazus was left in charge with continuing the conquest of those people of the Hellespont who had not yet accepted Persian sovereignty. Among those were the Paeonians, many of whom seem to have been deported to Persia after the conquest of their cities. Next, messengers were sent to the Macedonian king Amyntas demanding Earth and Water. Herodotus's story that Amyntas had his own way of handling the ambassadors, namely, killing them after a banquet, must be dismissed as fictional, since this does not square with the evidence that Thrace and Macedon did indeed ally with the Persian king, renewing this alliance before Xerxes's invasion, and even contributed contingents to Xerxes's invasion of Greece.

Megabazus, meanwhile, was on his journey home, bringing with him the Paeonian prisoners. Having seen the location where Histaeus was building his new city, Myrcinus, he warned Darius that Histaeus had the means to start a revolt against the king, for the region would give him plenty of wood for shipbuilding and the silver mines guaranteed the financial side for any undertaking. As the region was settled with a mixed population of Greeks and foreigners, these could be easily united under Histaeus's command. Darius ordered Histaeus to his palace at Susa, praising him as a loyal counsellor of the king and making him a member of the King's Table. In this way, Histaeus was under Darius's control, and any danger of revolt in Thrace was averted.

Not satisfied with the partial success of the punitive campaign, Darius planned a renewed attack on Athens and began preparations for this military attack shortly after the Persian defeat at Marathon. Then, in 486, a rebellion in Egypt led, probably, by Psammetichus IV, turned Persia's focus to Egypt. But Darius died before he could quash the revolt, in December 486, and it was left to his son and successor, Xerxes I, to carry out his father's plans.

FURTHER READING

For the Old Persian inscriptions see Schmitt, R. (2009). *Die altpersischen Inschriften der Achämeniden*. Wiesbaden: Reichert. Lecoq, P. (1997). *Les inscriptions de la Perse achéménide*. Paris: Gallimard. For the different language versions of the Bisitun Inscription see Vallat, F. (1977). *Corpus des inscriptions royales en élamite achéménide* Unpublished PhD. dissertation. https:// archive.org/details/CorpusInscriptionsRoyalesElamiteAchemenid/mode/2up; von Voigtlander, E. (1978). *The Bisitun Inscription of Darius the Great: Babylonian Version*. London: School of Oriental and African Studies. Greenfield, J.C. and Porten, B. (1982). *The Aramaic Version of the Inscription of Bisitun*. London: School of Oriental and African Studies. Schmitt, R. (1991). *The Bisitun Inscriptions of Darius the Great: Old Persian Text*. London: School of Oriental and African Studies. The revolt of Gaumata has been thoroughly analysed by Wiesehöfer, J. (1978). *Der Aufstand Gaumatas und die Anfänge Dareios' I*. Bonn: Habelt (Reihe Alte Geschichte 13). Balcer, J.M. (1987). *Herodotus and Bisitun*. Stuttgart: Steiner (Historia Einzelschriften 49).

The Achaemenid palaces are discussed by Stronach, D. (2001). From Cyrus to Darius: notes on art and architecture in early Achaemenid palaces. In: *The Royal Palace Institution in the First Millennium BC* (ed. I. Nielsen), 95–122. Aarhus: Aarhus University Press (Monographs of the Danish Institute at Athens 4). Kleiss, W. (2000). Zur Planung von Persepolis. In: *Variatio Delectat. Iran und der Westen. Gedenkschrift für Peter Calmeyer* (eds. R. Dittman, B. Hrouda, U. Löw, et al.), 355–368. Münster: Ugarit (AOAT 272). Naser, E. (2013). Persian splendours. Ancient palaces in Iran. *World Archaeology* 49: 42–49. Yaghmaee, E. (2010). Excavations in Dashtestan (Borazjan, Iran) (abstract). In: *The World of Achaemenid Persia. History, Art and Society in Iran and the Ancient Near East* (ed. J. Curtis and St. J. Simpson), 317. London: Tauris; Sarfaraz, A. (1971). Un pavillion de l'époque de Cyrus le Grand à Borazdjan. *Bastan Chanassi* 7–8: 22–25. For the archive texts from Persepolis see Hallock, R.T. (1969). *Persepolis Fortifications Tablets*. Chicago: University of Chicago Press (Oriental Institute Publications 92). Cameron, G.G. (1948). *Persepolis Treasury Tablets*. Chicago: University of Chicago Press (Oriental Institute Publications 65).

For the Scythian campaign see Jacobs, B. (2000). Achaimenidenherrschaft in der Kaukasus-Region und in Cis-Kaukasien. *Archäologische Mitteilungen aus Iran und Turan* 32: 93–102. Hartog, J. (1988). *The Mirror of Herodotus*. Berkeley: University of California Press.

6

The Face of Empire

6.1 Achaemenid Kingship

No image encapsulates the idea of Achaemenid kingship more emphatically than the audience relief from Persepolis (Figure 6.1). Originally the central relief of the Northern and Eastern staircases leading up to the Throne Hall, the *Apadana*, of Persepolis, it shows the enthroned king wearing a long-sleeved Persian dress, a many-folded robe held by a belt. The king wears a crenellated crown and in his hands holds the symbols of power, the staff and a lotus flower. His feet rest on a footstool. Behind the king, but sharing the same elevated platform, stands the heir to the throne at equal height with the seated king. The king is approached by a bearded male wearing a tunic and trousers, his head covered with round cap made of felt or leather. His body bows slightly and one hand is held before his lower face in a gesture of respect. This stance may be the act of showing obeisance to the king. Two incense burners are placed between the two figures, assuring that the air surrounding the king is fragrantly scented. The king and heir depicted here most likely are Darius I and Xerxes, the 'Second-after-the-king' (OP maθista-), as he calls himself in an inscription. Behind the royal figures are two court officials, one wearing the king's weapons, bow and arrow, as well as an axe, and a dagger, called *akinakes*, at the waist. The second courtier is wearing a long robe and a soft headcover, which also covers part of his lower face. His right hand holds what appears to be a towel or another object, which has been folded over, the left hand resting on the wrist of the right. His function is difficult to discern. He may be a royal attendant, although he looks rather different from those depicted in the doorways of the adjacent Hundred Column Hall. Here the servants accompanying the king hold fly-whisks or parasols, ointment flasks or towels, and are dressed in Persian robes, but their faces are clearly visible. Perhaps the second courtier has a religious function, comparable to the men depicted in sacred scenes on seals from Persepolis or on a relief from Dascyleium showing two priest-like figures in the process of performing an animal sacrifice. Behind the courtiers are two standard-bearers, while two Persian guards are standing on the opposite side behind the visitor. The entire audience scene

A History of Ancient Persia: The Achaemenid Empire, First Edition. Maria Brosius.
© 2021 John Wiley & Sons, Inc. Published 2021 by John Wiley & Sons, Inc.

Figure 6.1 The audience relief from Persepolis shows the king enthroned, holding a staff and a lotus flower in his hands. His feet are resting on a footstool. Behind the king stands the heir to the throne. They have been identified as Darius I and Xerxes I, or, alternatively, as Xerxes I and the designated heir to the throne, Darius. There are two courtiers, one of whom holds the king's axe. The king is receiving a visitor dressed in tunic and trousers. He is bowing slightly, his hand held before his mouth in a gesture of respect. Between the king and his visitor stands an incense burner. Two pairs of Persian guards frame the scene. The audience relief was originally placed in the centre of the Apadana staircases to the north and the east of the Audience Hall. At a later date, they were moved to the Treasury. One of the reliefs is now in the National Museum of Iran, Tehran. *Source*: Photograph courtesy of the National Museum, Tehran. Photo © Amir Farzad.

is set under an elaborate baldachin, which shows rows of striding lions and rosettes. Above the scene appears the Persian figure in the winged disc holding a ring, most likely the symbol of Auramazda (see 6.3 Persian Religion).

The central position of the king within the relief reflects his position in the royal court, and so does the central position of this panel within the reliefs of the staircase, which show the delegations of the gift-bearing peoples of the empire on the one side and members of the court and Persian guards on the other. The latter may represent the Immortals, a corps of 10 000 guardsmen, and so called because their number always remained constant. The king presents himself as the absolute monarch, loyally followed by his heir, his courtiers and his subjects. The calmness exuded by the enthroned king expresses dignity, order and peace. The respect for the hierarchical structure establishes the stability of the kingship; this, in turn, signals the stability of the empire. It is a royal image which has no known predecessors in Assyrian or Babylonian royal art, but appears to be an innovation we first observe in Achaemenid monumental design. Quite in contrast to the Assyrian palace reliefs, which emphasise the king as a victorious warrior in battle or in a hunt, the image of the enthroned king holding an audience aims to convey a very specific message: the empire of the Persian king is an empire at peace, an empire in which there is no need to fight wars but in which the king ensures the stability of the realm. The idea of the Persian Peace, or *pax persica*, was most strongly expressed in the inscriptions and the art created under

Darius I. It finds further support in the reliefs inside the staircases leading to the Audience Hall which depict royal courtiers ascending the staircase in relaxed poses, at ease with one another and in joyous anticipation of entering the Audience Hall to meet the king. The reliefs show them chatting to one another, shaking hands or touching shoulders, gestures which reflect a relaxed atmosphere and comfortable familiarity.

6.1.1 The Power of Royal Imagery

Within Persepolis, the audience scene of the Apadana reliefs reappears in variant forms – a reduced scene showing only the enthroned king, or the enthroned king with a visitor standing before him – in the doorways of the Hundred-Column-Hall built by Xerxes I and completed by Artaxerxes I. But these doorways add another, highly symbolic aspect. In these scenes the king's throne stands on a massive platform divided into four tiers. This platform is borne by rows of men, each wearing distinctive clothing that allows us to identify their ethnicity; their arms are raised to support the tier above them. The male figures represent the peoples of the empire, amounting to a total of 28 men, counting both sides of the doorway. The image serves as a symbol which states that the king, enthroned in all his splendour on top of the platform, enjoys the support of the people of the lands of the empire. Each one of them contributes to the stability of the throne, that is to say, the kingship. They are united in their endeavour to uphold the kingship and safeguard the king (Figure 6.2).

The image of the people of the empire as throne-bearers also appears on the tomb reliefs of Naqsh-e Rustam. In this image, the king, standing on a tiered platform supported by the peoples of the empire, stands before a fire altar, with his hands raised in prayer; the winged disc with the figure of Auramazda hovers above the scene, the sun-and-moon motif carved at the side of the relief. The accompanying inscription comments on the image:

> (…) look at the sculptures (of those) who bear the throne, then shall you know, then shall it become known to you: the spear of a Persian man has gone far; then shall it become known to you: a Persian man has delivered battle far indeed from Persia. Says Darius the king: 'This which has been done, all that by the will of Auramazda I did. Auramazda bore me aid until I did the work. May Auramazda protect me from harm, and my royal house and this land. This I pray of Auramazda, this Auramazda may give to me. O man, that which is the command of Auramazda let this not seem repugnant to you; do not leave the right path; do not rise in rebellion.' (DNa §§4–6)

That the image of the enthroned king has a key role in conveying the ideology of an empire at peace becomes evident in its application on seals used by Persian officials and administrators in Persepolis and beyond. Several examples have been recovered from the Persepolis archive, but perhaps most striking is the imprint of the audience scene on *bullae* from Dascyleium in Phrygia, all that remains of the parchment documents they once sealed (Figure 6.3). The scene on the Dascyleium *bullae* showing the enthroned king and his visitor is a reduced scene of the great audience scene, but clearly a reminder in the satrapal centre of the way the king wanted to be perceived.

Figure 6.2 Detail of the upper section of a royal tomb showing the throne-bearers. First introduced by Darius I, the image of the king on a platform held by peoples of the empire became a motif that was used not only for the royal tombs, but also in the doorjambs of the Hundred-Column-Hall. Each figure is distinct by its ethnic clothing, headdress and shoes, their number amounting to 28, representing the provinces of the Persian empire. This image, taken from the tomb of Artaxerxes II at Persepolis, shows the king standing before a fire altar in the same gesture we already observed in the Bisitun relief. The figure of Auramazda hovers above the scene and both the king and Auramazda have their hand raised. In the top right corner is the carving of what appears to be the sun and a half-moon. *Source*: Photograph courtesy of Michael Alram.

Figure 6.3 *Bulla* from Dascyleium. The *bulla* depicts a variant of the Persepolis audience scene. Here the enthroned king welcomes a visitor wearing tunic and trousers, as well as a round cap, his hand raised in front of his mouth. Between the king and the visitor stand two incense burners. Behind the king a courtier holds a fly-whisk, while a second courtier holds a large object at his side. Two guards stand behind the visitor. The scene is completed with a winged disc. *Source*: Photograph with kind permission of Deniz Kaptan.

Casting its influence even wider, we find adaptations of this image in the art of local dynasts within the Persian empire. The so-called Harpy tomb from Xanthos, dated to the first half of the fifth century, depicts variants of the audience scene, with one side (east) perhaps the most expressive version of a male figure seated on a throne, holding a staff and a pomegranate, and receiving the gift of a cock from an attendant. Behind this figure stands the actual visitor, who also holds a long staff and is accompanied by a dog. A marble slab belonging to the funerary monument of Erbinna/Arbinas, the ruler of Xanthos, also echoes a Persian audience scene. Though the setting is Greco-Lycian, the enthroned figure wears a Persian soft cap, the tiara, while an attendant holds a parasol above the ruler. A further audience scene is depicted on one side of the tomb of Payava, a Lycian dynast who died around 360 (Figure 6.4). The audience scene is thought to show the satrap Autophradates receiving an embassy.

Satraps and local rulers alike emulated royal representations, expressing their affinity with the king and their loyalty, and using the scene as the model of the expression of power. Its latest application is found in an extraordinary place: the inside of a soldier's shield in a battle scene carved on a sarcophagus from Sidon. This sarcophagus depicts a battle scene with Alexander III and the Persians, and is therefore known as the Alexander Sarcophagus. The Persians are depicted as a defeated group, slain or hopelessly defending themselves against Alexander and the Macedonian soldiers, their short swords ineffective, their shields raised above them, no longer useful to defend their bodies. It is on the inside of one of these raised shields that the image of the royal audience scene has been detected, and it is a powerful reminder how far down the hierarchical ranks this image must have reached that the stonemason sculpting the

Figure 6.4 The Payava Sarcophagus (BM 1848, 1020.142). It shows a seated ruler in Persian dress, including a soft headdress and *kandys*, receiving several dignitaries standing in front of him. Payava was a ruler in Xanthos, Lycia in the mid-fourth century. The audience scene may depict the Persian satrap Autophradates receiving Payava. *Source*: Photograph courtesy of the Trustees of the British Museum.

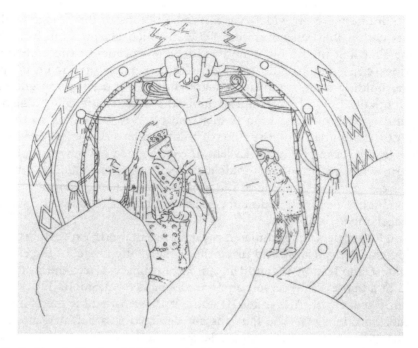

Figure 6.5   Inside of a Persian shield from the Alexander Sarcophagus The shield depicts a variant of the Persepolis audience scene. Before the king a visitor is bowing respectfully, while a courtier stands behind the king, holding a fly-whisk. *Source*: Drawing by Marion Cox.

sarcophagus possessed information about this scene and its function on the inside of a soldier's shield (Figure 6.5). To the soldier himself, the image served as a permanent reminder that this was what he fought for – the king, and the stability of the empire. Darius I and his successors knew the power of visual imagery, and they used it to best effect on the variety of media available to them. This image reached administrative officials as well as military troops; it was a way of binding individuals to the king, of allowing them to identify with the centre of power.

6.2   Royal Ideology

Darius's idea of kingship and his royal ideology found strong visual and written expression. As king, he ruled with the support of the principal god of the Persians, Auramazda. The god ensured that the king and the empire upheld Order (OP *arta-*) and resisted the Lie (OP *drauga-*). The dualism between Order and Lie extended to refer to good and evil, to peace and rebellion. The king, guided by Auramazda, would only follow the Order, do good and secure peace. Those who opposed him followed the Lie, which meant disrupting order and rising in rebellion. With these sentiments, Darius created a direct link between kingship and religion, sanctioning the deeds of the king as the intended wish of the god, while those acting against the king also acted against the god. He struck a fine balance here, not claiming to be divine himself, but being the worldly representative of Auramazda's power.

Sources in Translation 6.1

Darius's Inscriptions from Susa (DSe), Persepolis (DPd) and Naqsh-e Rustam (DNa)

In his inscription from Susa, Darius emphasised his endeavours to achieve peace in the empire, to establish an equilibrium between the strong and the weak. He appeared as the wise ruler whose judgement is rational and balanced. A second inscription declared the values and wishes of his empire. Almost written as a prayer, he exclaimed that the gods may avert bad fate from his country, to avoid wars, famine and rebellion. But there is also a subtle hint at a less peaceful side to Darius: stating the presence of good horses and good men or soldiers, he left no doubt that, if at all necessary, he would be ready to defend his values and go to war. But it is the second inscription of his tomb at Naqsh-e Rustam in which Darius outlined his kingship most clearly. As a king who upheld the Order, he dispersed justice for man, acting as an even-handed judge with a firm mind and a controlled temperament. Guided by his fairness, he punished those who did harm and honoured those who did good. He dispensed justice with skill and fairness. In the same way he ruled the empire justly, he excelled as a military leader, both as a soldier and as a cavalryman. There is no doubt that he was the first to defend the realm, the first to fight against anyone who threatened the peace of the empire.

Darius's Inscription from Susa (DSe)

§3. Darius the king says: 'By the favour of Auramazda these are the countries which I seized outside Persia. I ruled over them, they brought me tribute. They did what I told them. My law held them firm. Media, Elam, Parthia, Aria, Bactria, Sogdiana, Chorasmia, Drangiana, Arachosia, Sattagydia, Gandara, Sind, Amyrgian Scythians, Scythians with pointed caps, Babylonia, Assyria, Arabia, Egypt, Armenia, Cappadocia, Sardis, Ionia, Scythians from Across-the-Sea (= the Black Sea), Skudra, *petasos*-wearing Ionians, Libyans, Ethiopians, men from Maka, Carians.'

§4. Darius the king says: 'I changed many bad things that had been done to good things. By the favour of Auramazda I dealt with the countries which fought against each other, so that their people do not kill each other anymore, and I returned everyone to his place. And in the face of my decisions, they respected them in such a way that the strong neither beats nor deprives the weak.'

§5. Darius the king says: 'By the favour of Auramazda I completed many building projects which previously had been abandoned. I saw the fortification walls (of Susa), which had been built previously, had fallen into disrepair from age, and I rebuilt them. These are the fortification walls which I rebuilt.'

§6. Darius the king says: 'May Auramazda together with the (other) gods protect me, and my royal house, and what has been inscribed by me.'

Darius's Inscription from Persepolis (DPd)

§1.   Auramazda (is) great, the greatest of gods. He created Darius the king, he bestowed the kingdom on him. By the favour of Auramazda, Darius is king.

§2.   Darius the king proclaims: 'This country, Persia, which Auramazda bestowed upon me, is good, and possesses good horses and possesses good soldiers. By the favour of Auramazda, and of me, Darius the king, it does not feel fear of any other.'

§3.   Darius the king proclaims: 'May Auramazda bring me aid, together with all the gods; and may Auramazda protect this country from a (hostile) army, from famine, from the Lie! Upon this country may there not come an army, or famine, or the Lie. This I pray as a blessing from Auramazda, together with all the gods. May Auramazda together with the other gods grant me this blessing.'

Second Inscription of Naqsh-e Rustam (DNb)

§1.   Auramazda is a great god, who created this excellent work which is seen, who created happiness for man, who bestowed wisdom and courage upon Darius the king.

§2.   Darius the king says: 'By the favour of Auramazda I am of such a kind that I am a friend of the Right, and not a friend of the Wrong; it is not my desire that the weak man should suffer injustice at the hands of the strong, it is not my desire that the strong man should suffer injustice from the weak.

§3.   I desire what is Right. I am not a friend of the man who follows the Lie. I am not hot-tempered; the things that develop in me during a dispute I hold firmly under control through my mind, I am firmly in control of myself.

§4.   I reward the man who seeks to contribute according to his efforts; I punish him who does harm, according to the harm done; I do not wish that a man should do harm; nor do I wish that, if he should do harm, he should not be punished.

§5.   What a man says against a man does not convince me, until I hear the testimony of both.

§6.   I am content with what a man does or brings (as tribute) (for me) according to his abilities, my pleasure is great and I am well disposed towards him.

§7.   Of such a kind is my understanding and my judgement: when you shall see or hear of what I have done in the palace and on the battlefield, this is my courage which I possess over my mind and my understanding.

§8.   This indeed is my courage as far as my body possesses the strength; as a commander I am a good commander; immediately, the right decision is taken according to my understanding when I meet a rebel, and when I meet (someone who is) not a rebel, at this moment, due to my understanding and judgement, I know that I am above panic when I see a rebel as well as when I see (someone who is) not a rebel.

§9.   I am trained in my hands and in my feet; as a horseman, I am a good horseman; as a bowman, I am a good bowman, both on foot and on horseback; as a spearman, I am a good spearman, both on foot and on horseback.

§10. These are the skills which Auramazda has bestowed upon me, and which I have been strong enough to exercise. By the favour of Auramazda, what I have done, I have achieved with the skills which Auramazda has bestowed upon me.

§11. O man, proclaim loud and clear of what kind you are, and of what sort your abilities are, and of what kind your loyalty is. Let that which has been heard by your ears not seem false to you; hear that which has been said to you!

§12. O man, let that which I have done not seem to you to be false; observe what the weak man has done. O man, see what I have done [...] not to overstep [...] and do not be ill disposed towards happiness [...].'

6.3 Persian Religion

Intertwined with royal ideology is the subject of Persian religion. Yet this is probably the most difficult topic in the field of Achaemenid studies, not only due to the limited corpus of sources available to us but also due to our lack of detailed knowledge about the early phases of development of Persian religious customs. At the time of the first Persian empire, the religion that will come to be known as Zoroastrianism by the time of the Sasanian empire (224–651 CE) was still evolving and few of its aspects were tangible. While it is known how Cyrus II regarded foreign religions, we have very little idea which god or gods he worshipped as a Persian. The Persians regarded mountains, rivers, water and fire as sacred, but we know little about how rituals were performed to honour them. It is only with Darius I and the Achaemenid royal inscriptions that Auramazda emerges as the principal god of the Persians, though he is often mentioned together with other, unnamed gods.

The Persepolis texts tell us that non-Persian gods were recognised in Persis, including the Assyrian god Adad, and the Elamite god Humban. 'Turkama the priest received 57 quarts of wine supplied by Ushaya and used them for the gods: 7 quarts for Auramazda, 20 quarts for the (Elamite) god Humban, 10 quarts for the river Huputish, 10 quarts for the river Rannakarra, 10 quarts for the river Shaushaunush' (PF 339). There were two kinds of priests, *shatins* and *magi*, the latter often being mentioned in connection with a religious ceremony called *lan*.

A key issue in the discussion about Achaemenid religion is the question of whether the Persians depicted their god(s). The scene of religious worship on the tomb façades of Naqsh-e Rustam, where the king is seen standing before a fire altar in a gesture of prayer, has been interpreted to mean that their god was worshipped in the abstract. But the crux of the matter is the figure of a Persian in a winged disc, overarching the scene (Figure 6.6). This figure is holding one hand up in a gesture of prayer, while the other holds a ring. The artistic image itself has Assyrian predecessors in which the god Ashur appears in the winged disc. In the Persepolis reliefs, the winged disc with the half-figure of a Persian holding a ring features prominently, and likewise is prevalent on seals, though these mostly depict the winged disc without the male figure. Scholars of Achaemenid history have been reluctant to recognise Auramazda in this figure, suggesting that this may be Achaemenes, the eponymous founder of the empire, or a manifestation of *khvarnah*, the 'good fortune' which accompanies Persian kingship. Neither of these

Figure 6.6   Winged disc with Auramazda. This figure is prevalent in Persepolis. The winged sun disc is a motif already found in Egypt, where it represents the god Horus. In Assyria, the winged disc with the bust of a male divine figure representing the god Assur features on Neo-Assyrian reliefs. The figure here wears Persian dress and a crown. His hairstyle and beard adhere to Persian style. His right hand is raised; in his left hand he holds the ring of power. The figure most likely represents the Persian god Auramazda. *Source*: Drawing by Marion Cox.

suggestions convince: the depiction of Darius's alleged ancestor Achaemenes as a semi-divine figure is untypical and without comparison prior to or after the Achaemenid empire, while the idea of the good fortune of the Persian kings is attested only for the later Sasanian empire. It seems much more apt to identify the figure in the winged disc with Auramazda, who, in his gesture of prayer, seems in direct communication with the praying king below, while the ring symbolises the ring of power, amply attested in Mesopotamian art, in which a deity passes the ring, the symbol of power, to the king, who thus gains divine authority. A striking example of such an investiture scene is that carved on a rock face at Sar-e Pol-e Zahab. Dating to the end of the third millennium BCE, it shows Anubanini, king of the Lullubi tribe, receiving the ring of power from the goddess Ishtar (Figure 6.7). The king has one foot placed on the body of a slain enemy, while below the scene we find a row of captured enemies bound by a rope. The scene, which may have served as a model for Darius's relief at Bisitun, combines military prowess and divine sanctioning to express Anubanini's political rule.

Auramazda, 'the good, or wise, lord', is evoked as the creator of the universe, of mankind and of man's good fortune, but there is no evidence yet of his counterpart, Ahriman, who represents evil and only becomes tangible in the Sasanian period. The dualism expressed in royal ideology of Order and Lie, of Good and Evil, depicts ideological and moral entities which originate in Persian religious thought, yet there is no hint that the latter was already fully developed in the Achaemenid period. For these reasons, scholars tend to refer to this early form as Mazdaism in order to convey the recognition of the highest god of the Persians; the term also signals that this religion was still in its early stages of development. It was promoted by the prophet Zoroaster and eventually came to bear his name as Zoroastrianism. A considerably divided and ongoing scholarly debate surrounds Zoroaster and his religion, beginning with questions concerning the prophet's life and the problem of written religions documents.

Figure 6.7   The relief of Anubanini from Sar-e Pol-e Zahab dates to the end of the third millennium BCE and shows Anubanini, king of the Lullubi tribe, being installed as king by the goddess Ishtar. The goddess holds the ring of power in one hand; in the other she holds a rope with which two prisoners have been bound. The king himself, equipped with his axe and bow, stands with one foot on a defeated enemy. Beneath the scene are six more prisoners, their hands bound behind their backs. *Source*: Photograph with kind permission of Gian Petro Basello.

Several royal inscriptions make a point of mentioning Auramazda as the first among several gods: 'Auramazda and the other gods that are'. Who these gods were, and how many, we simply do not know. Artaxerxes II is the first Achaemenid king to mention the god Mithra, the god of treaties, and the goddess Anahita, goddess of water and fertility, in his inscriptions, though the name Mithra appears already as part of personal names in the Persepolis texts. Thus, the first mention of his name in inscriptions from Artaxerxes II allows no conclusions about the introduction of his cult, or that of Anahita, in his reign, but only the suggestion of a possible elevation of these two deities.

> This palace Darius my great-great-grand-father built; later under Artaxerxes, my grandfather, it was burnt; by the favour of Auramazda, Anaitis and Mithras, this palace I built. May Auramazda, Anaitis and Mithras protect me from all evil and that which I have built may they not shatter or harm. (A²Sa)

6.3.1 Funerary Customs

The king and members of the royal family were buried in an official funerary ceremony. Wherever the king died, his body had to be returned to Persis and laid to rest in his designated tomb in Naqsh-e Rustam, and, in the later empire, in Persepolis, where two tombs were cut into the Kuh-e Rahmat and an unfinished tomb built south of the palace complex. At the announcement of the king's death, a mourning period across the empire had to be observed and may have been similar to the 40-day mourning period that was held in Babylonia for the king and other members of the royal family. Eternal fires, which burned at sacred sites across the empire, were extinguished and relit only at the coronation of the new king. The tombs of the Persian king contain sarcophagus-like coffins cut out of the rock, hinting at the fact that the body of the deceased was not allowed to touch earthy ground.

The closest example of such a burial that has come down to us is that of the Achaemenid tomb from the Acropole of Susa, dated to the end of the Achaemenid period on the basis of two coins found at the burial site. The bronze sarcophagus contained a skeleton richly decked out with gold jewellery and semi-precious stones. In addition, there were two vases made of alabaster and a silver bowl (Figure 6.8). Archaeologists assume that the coffin had been placed in a vaulted tomb. The deceased's gender is not clear; both males and females would be wearing jewellery, but perhaps the fact that no weapons were included in the burial allows the assumption that this was a female.

Funerary stelae and inscriptions from Egypt and western Asia Minor provide us with some idea of the burial customs of Persians, or rather those of members of the local elite who wanted to emulate Persian funerary customs. Thus, for example, a stele from

Figure 6.8   The sarcophagus from Susa. The sarcophagus was discovered on 6 February, 1901 by the French geologist and archaeologist Jacques de Morgan. The tomb contained a human skeleton richly decorated with jewellery, including gold bracelets, earrings, a gold torque and a three-strand necklace. It also included two alabaster jars and a silver bowl. The absence of weapons points to a female having been buried in the bronze coffin. The find of two coins allowed a dating to the late Achaemenid period. *Source*: After Morgan 1905.

Dascyleium depicts a funerary banquet, showing the deceased *en couchant*, reclining on a couch, while his wife is seated on a high-backed chair next to him. Both hold Achaemenid-style bowls in their hands. A similar banquet scene is depicted on a wall painting from Karaburun, in which a male figure, also *en couchant*, is surrounded by servants. He, too, holds an Achaemenid-style bowl in his hand. The funerary stele of a Persian-Egyptian from Saqqara dated between 525 and 404 depicts the deceased celebrating a funerary banquet (Figure 6.9). He wears the long robe of the Persians and is seated on a high-backed chair, holding a bowl in one hand, a lotus flower in the other. The accompanying inscription, written in Hieroglyphic and Demotic, identifies the deceased as 'Djerbherbes son of Artam, born of the lady Tanofrether' (transl. Brosius 2000: 91, no. 197).

Figure 6.9 Stele from Saqqara. Divided into two tiers, the stele depicts the mummification of the dead person in accordance with Egyptian custom in the upper tier, and a funerary banquet of the deceased in the lower tier. While the servants are Egyptians, the deceased is depicted as a Persian, wearing the many-folded Persian dress and a diadem. In one hand he balances a shallow bowl in characteristic Persian manner on three fingers; in the other he holds a lotus flower. *Source*: Drawing by Marion Cox.

6.4   Persepolis: The Microcosm of Empire

Persepolis was the representational centre of the Persian empire. With its Audience Hall, the private palaces of Darius I and his successors Xerxes I and Artaxerxes I, the Treasury, the Tripylon or Central Palace, the Hundred-Column-Hall and the administrative offices all placed on the raised platform built against a hillside known by its modern name, Kuh-e Rahmat, it encapsulated the power of the Persians. It presented a microcosm of the empire, a deliberate attempt to reflect the diversity of the realm, its different peoples and its many artistic styles. Architecturally, Persepolis combined features from across the empire, yet the merging of the different artistic elements resulted in the creation of a distinctive Achaemenid style.

The depiction of the gift-bearing peoples of the empire grouped into ethnic units, each of them led by a Persian courtier to be taken to meet the king, added to the idea that this was the centre of empire where the different peoples found themselves represented. Their specific gifts included a lioness with her cups, an okapi, horses, sheep and zebus, cups, bowls and jars, daggers, jewellery, including bracelets, bails of cloth and gold from India (Figure 6.10).

Most of all it was an expression of the way the Achaemenid kings wanted to present their kingship. The doorways of the Tripylon and the Hundred Column Hall show the king enthroned on a platform borne by the peoples of his empire. Others depict him striding along in almost private scenes, accompanied by a parasol-bearer or a servant carrying a flask or what appears to be a towel. Yet a third theme shows the king as the royal hero, seemingly in a fight with a lion or a mythical beast, but his dagger already plunged into the beast's chest, certain of victory. The message conveyed in these images is that of harmony and peace, of any possible danger already averted by the king, who enjoys the support of his peoples.

Figure 6.10   The Elamite Delegation of the Apadana, Persepolis (by A. Davey at https://commons.wikimedia.org/w/index.php?curid=30191538).

Box Text 6.1

Persepolis – A Ceremonial Centre?

An ongoing and seemingly insoluble debate divides scholars on the question of the function of Persepolis. The opinion voiced strongly in past debates posits that Persepolis was the imperial centre where the Persians celebrated the ancient festival of the New Year, Nouruz. This view has met with increasing scepticism which doubts the city's ceremonial function. Reasons for the former suggestion are based on the interpretation of the gift-bearing peoples of the lands of the empire on the Apadana reliefs and the lines of servants carrying foodstuffs up the stairs of the private palaces of the kings. Two texts from the Persepolis archive seem to give this interpretation support. They record the withdrawal of huge food resources for Darius's wife Artystone at a date in March 503, including almost 2000 litres of wine and 100 sheep, implying that these were to be used for the New Year celebrations.

What is missing, however, is any hard evidence for such a New Year celebration in Persepolis. By all accounts, Persepolis was a palace complex, albeit on a grander scale than its counterparts in other royal cities, but in which, nevertheless, day-to-day activities took place, from keeping accounts to collecting taxes and paying workers, seemingly throughout the year, with no indication of any enhanced activities in early March that could be interpreted as preparations for a feast on a magnificent scale. Rather, recent scholarship has revealed that, as is attested for the reign of Darius I, the king spent the spring period in Susa and that Babylonian visitors seem to join the king during that period. Perhaps we might be advised to look at Persepolis in the context of other palace sites. As a city-foundation, Persepolis stands in a long tradition of new palace sites built by Mesopotamian kings. Cyrus's foundation of Pasargadae belongs to this tradition, as does the unfinished palace at Dasht-e Gohar. The gift-bearing theme of the Apadana reliefs undoubtedly points to a special occasion, perhaps one on which the peoples of the lands brought their gifts to the king, but it does not necessarily point to New Year celebrations.

6.4.1 The Royal Court

The Persians were the prominent people in a multi-ethnic empire and formed a distinctive class, not only through their ethnicity, but also through their common language and religion, headed by the god Auramazda. Darius I himself stressed in his tomb inscription that he was 'a Persian man', and with that, cast a line to his fellow Persians who fitted this description as well. The figure of the royal hero, a crowned male dressed in a short Persian dress, about to kill a lion or a mythical beast, represents an image that dominates the Persepolis seals used by the Persian administrators of Parsa. This figure may not necessarily represent the king himself but the common, ordinary Persian who defends Order against upheaval, Good against Evil. It is these Persians who shape the core of the Persian court, members not only of the king's family but also of the Persian noble houses.

The term 'court' designates the physical space of the palace, as well as those people who surround the king. These are, in the first instance, the king's family, his wife, or rather, wives, sons and daughters, and also includes members of his extended family, his brothers, sisters, uncles and aunts, nephews and nieces, as well as their in-laws. Many of these will have been away from the court, residing in the satrapal palaces across the empire, so that we may differentiate between an inner court of those who were constantly around the king, and an outer court consisting of those who resided in the satrapal centres of the empire. Members of the Persian nobility, many of whom were bound to the king through marriage alliances, counted among the permanent members of the court. They could take high administrative offices, as, for example, Darius's uncle Parnaka did as the head of the Persepolis administration and possibly governor of the city and its province. Younger members will have worked their way up the ranks, serving as junior administrators or as attendants of the king. Far from regarding their position as menial, the attendants worked close to the person of the king and therefore needed to be trusted absolutely. Being the king's cup-bearer or the king's wine steward meant that this person was closer to the king than most, and there could not be any doubt as to their loyalty to the sovereign. The sons of the Persian aristocracy were educated at court to be prepared for future high office. The nobility was made up of the different Persian families, representing different tribes and clans which followed a long-established hierarchy. In addition, they were distinguished from another through their relative closeness to the king, which could be achieved, as we have seen, through a marriage alliance with a member of the king's family, or indeed the king himself.

6.4.2   Gift-Giving

The hierarchy of the Persian court was determined by an elaborate system of meritocracy, expressed, in part, through a system of gift-giving in which members of the nobility were awarded special gifts from the king. The kind of gift and its quality elevated one courtier above another and expressed favour and good standing with the king. Gifts were offered in return for services rendered to the king. The result of this meritocratic system no doubt kept members of the nobility in competition with one another, constantly vying for a better position within the hierarchy. All the while, one has to bear in mind that the privileges bestowed by the king were by no means permanent but could be revoked at any time. Thus continuous efforts had to be made by the nobility to demonstrate the worthiness of their position within the ranking order. Both individuals and groups of peoples were honoured by the king with royal gifts. These included horses with golden bridles, jewellery, such as bracelets and necklaces, weapons, bowls, jars and beakers made of precious metal, and royal robes. The latter ranked among the most precious ones that could be bestowed by the king upon a noble. Otanes is said to have been an annual recipient of such a robe in recognition of his declining the kingship.

The most highly prized gift was to be given a king's daughter in marriage, and our sources attest to this practice throughout Achaemenid rule. Several daughters of Darius were married to Persian nobles, including Daurises and Hymaees, who both died in Asia Minor in the early fifth century, and to Artokhmes, the commander of the

Phrygians in Xerxes's army. A princess called Ishtin was married to Bakeya (probably Gr. Bagaios), and Xerxes's daughter Amytis was married to Megabyxus, the son of Zopyrus. Atossa, the daughter of Artaxerxes II, was to marry Tiribazus, but the alliance was never concluded, most likely because Tiribazus fell out of favour with the king. The Sardian satrap Tissaphernes married a princess shortly after 401, having proved himself in his support against the rebelling Cyrus the Younger, and Orontes, satrap of Armenia and later Mysia, was honoured with a marriage to a royal princess, Rhodogune, as was Pharnabazus, who married Apame, probably after 388. One of the daughters of Darius III was married to Mithrodates and another to Spithridates, the satrap of Ionia.

Royal gifts were not exclusively reserved for the Persian nobility but could be made to visitors to the king. 'As for the gifts made by the Great King to ambassadors, who came to him from Greece and elsewhere, this is what they were: he gave to each one Babylonian talent of coined silver, and two silver cups of one talent (the Babylonian talent is worth 62 Attic minas). He also presented them with bracelets, a curved sword and a torque – a total value of one thousand darics – and further, a Median robe. The name of this robe is *dorophoric* ("presented as a gift")' (Ael.*var.hist.*I.22). Cambyses is said to have presented the Nubians with gifts presented by a people called Fish-eaters: 'When the Fish-eaters arrived from Elephantine at Cambyses's summons, he sent them to Ethiopia with orders what to say, and bearing as gifts a red cloak and a twisted gold necklace and bracelets and an alabaster box of incense and an earthenware jar of palm wine.' (Hdt.III.20.1). Cyrus the Younger gave the ruler of Cilicia gifts as tokens of honour, including a horse with a gold-mounted bridle, a gold necklace and bracelets, a gold dagger and a Persian robe. It is intriguing to note that the gifts for the king, borne by the foreign delegations on the Apadana staircase, resemble precisely the gifts the king presented to others, including bails of cloth, cups, bowls and beakers, jewellery and daggers crafted in Achaemenid royal style. Perhaps, what we may deduce from this observation is a system of redistribution of precious goods, collected by the king as gifts from the lands of the empire, to be redistributed as gifts to individuals in the king's service.

6.4.3   Rhyta

There is a striking omission from the list of royal gifts, both those given to and those given by the king. It is the *rhyton*, a drinking horn ending in an animal protome, which usually has an opening for the liquid to spurt out (Figure 6.11). Achaemenid *rhyta* were crafted in precious metal, gold and silver, as well as in bronze and clay. These vessels were used in a ceremonial context, at banquets and perhaps during religious ceremonies. Their style was unique, showing a fluted body and a distinctive protome crafted as an animal head, such as that of a bull, a lion or a horse. Those *rhyta* that have been recovered were found outside the Persian heartland on the fringes of the empire. They were clearly valuable objects, as their form was adopted and adapted at local level, as we can see on funerary stelae from western Asia Minor and from archaeological finds belonging to the Odrysian kings in Thrace. Curiously, adaptations of the *rhyta* were even recovered in Athens; they were made of clay and their protomes adapted to local taste, depicting, for example, the head of a dog or that of a foreigner.

Figure 6.11 *Rhyton* (BM 116411). The *rhyton* is made of silver with a bull protome made of gold. *Source*: Photograph courtesy of the Trustees of the British Museum.

6.4.4 The Women of the Court

Both the king's mother and the king's wife held exalted positions at the court. Achaemenid kings were polygamous, and not all women of the king were wives. Greek sources are quick to label them as concubines, but we must consider that some of these women were brought to the court from the lands of the empire, and some of these will have been members of the local, non-Persian nobility. As the mother of the king, and certainly as the mother of the heir to the throne, the king's mother and the king's wife took the most important positions close to the king, and Greek writers noted this fact when pointing out that the king dined alone, save for the company of his wife and his mother. No specific title is attested for them, but their status in close relation to the king sufficed to mark their position. The Persepolis texts tell us that any female member of the royal family was referred to as *dukshish*, meaning 'princess'.

Royal women were a visible feature of the king's entourage, accompanying him on hunts, on visits to the royal capitals and on campaigns. According to Curtius Rufus, royal women appear alongside the female relatives of the Persian nobles in the army train of Darius III. According to his description, a fire was carried on two silver altars in front, followed by the *magi*, 365 men in purple robes, white horses pulling the chariot of Auramazda, one horse of the sun, 10 chariots, horsemen of 12 nations, 10 000 Immortals, 15 000 king's kindred, spear-bearers, the king's chariot, 10 000 lancers, 200 king's relatives on the right and left, 30 000 infantry, 400 king's horses, the chariot of the king's mother, and one of the king's wife, the women of the queen's household on horseback, the king's *harmamaxa* for children and eunuchs, 365 concubines, 600 mules, 300 camels, the wives of the King's relatives and friends, the troops of sutlers and batmen, the band of light-armed troops (Curt.Ruf.III.3.8–16).

Apart from their representational function to appear in the king's company, women also travelled on their own, accompanied by their own attendants and servants. An accounting document dated to 500/499 records wine rations accorded to daughters of Hystaspes, that is, Darius's sisters: '210 (quarts of wine) Hihuddamana received and gave (it) to princesses, daughters of Hystaspes. They went from Media to Persepolis. He carried a sealed document of the king' (PFa 31: ll.13–16). A lady called Mizapir-zaka received a flour ration for a journey from Susa to Persepolis (PF 1546), and an unnamed woman went from Susa to Gandahar with the authorization of the king; she was accompanied by an elite guide (PF 1550). We know from Greek sources that Amytis, the daughter of Artaxerxes II, travelled to Syria to mediate between the king and her husband Megabyxus, and the king's mother, Parysatis, is said to have jour-neyed to Babylonia to recover the body of her son Cyrus the Younger in 401. Possibly, in their role as mediators, royal women appear to have held audiences in their own right, admitting other females to submit a petition, express a request or intervene for a family member.

Sources in Translation 6.2

The Persepolis Texts on the Economic Prosperity of Persian Royal Women

The Persepolis texts as well as several texts from Babylonia attest to estates of royal women in Parsa and Babylonia. The estates were run by their own staff, adminis-trators and bailiffs, who carried out the orders of these individual women. These orders were authorised using personal seals, a kind of signature, as the seal unde-niably identified its owner. Irtashduna/Artystone, Cyrus's daughter and one of Darius's wives, owned estates at Mirandu, Matannan and Kukkannakan in Persis.

Text 1

'Tell Datuka, Artystone spoke as follows:

"100(?) quarts of wine (are) to be issued to Ankama from my estate at Mirandu. Utar (is) their *hirakurra*."' (PF 1835)

Text 2

'Tell Shalamana, Artystone spoke as follows:

"From my estate (at) Kukkannakan 1000 quarts (of) wine (are) to be issued to Kamshabana the accountant. Irtima is the *hirakurra.*"
(In) Year 22 (the) sealed document (was delivered).' (PF 1837)

These orders were sealed with Artystone's own seal, attesting to the fact that these women could dispose of the products of their estates as they saw fit. As also becomes clear both from the Persepolis texts and from Babylonian docu-ments, these women employed their own administrative personnel. Babylonian texts from the bank house Murashu record that Parysatis (Bab. Purrushatu) let her land, with rent being collected by her bailiff Ea-bullitsu:

Text 3

'317 *kur* 2 PI, 3 *shatu* of barley, 5 *kur*, 2 PI, 3 *shatu* of wheat, (as) tax, part of the land of Parysatis and of the private domain of Ea-bullitsu, the administrator of Parysatis, (part) of Year 4 of Darius (II) the king who is at the service of Rimut-Ninurta, son of Murashu. Concerning the barley, 317 *kur* 2 PI, 3 *shatu*, concerning the wheat, 5 *kur*, 2 PI, 3 *shatu*, (as) tax, part of the lands of Year 4 of Darius (the) king, Nabu-iddin son of Bel-erib, and Bel-amat-usur, slave of Ea-bullitsu, on the order of Ea-bullitsu, administrator of Parysatis, (from) the hands of Rimut-Ninurta son of Murashu, have been received. They have been paid. Nabu-iddin and Bel-amat-usur shall draw up (the receipt) and, coming from Ea-bullitsu, administrator of Parysatis, to Rimut-Ninurta, they give (it).

(Written) in the presence of Ishtabuzana, judge of the Sin canal. (Written) in the presence of Nabu-mit-uballit, judge of the house of Parysatis, son of Mukin-apli.

(*List of six witnesses follows.*)

Nippur, day 11, month 6, Year 4 of Darius (II).' (TMHC 185; cf. Cardascia 1951: 95–96)

Text 4

'Xenophon knows of the villages owned by Parysatis near the Chalus River in Across-the-River, which had been given to her as a dowry, and later notes that she also owned villages in Media which had an abundance of grain, cattle and other unspecified property.' (Xen.*an*.1.4.9).

The royal woman Irdabama is not only attested as an estate owner, but also as the employer of several workforces, ranging for a group of just three to a large workforce located at Tirazzish (mod. Shiraz), of 480 workers. Comparisons and overlaps of workforces in different Persepolis texts allow the identification of Irdabama with Abbamush, a name which was rendered Apamu- in Babylonian and Apame in Greek texts. Irdabama may have been the daughter of Gobryas and Darius's first wife, as we have seen in Chapter 5. Irdabama dispensed large amounts of foodstuffs and wine from Susa, Hidali and Persepolis. Babylonian documents indicate that she also owned estates there. Being the senior wife, though not the mother of the heir to the throne, may have given her an extraordinary position amongst the royal women nevertheless, and entitled her to large estates and workforces. Her seal is carved in the Neo-Elamite style of the late period (Figure 6.12).

Text 5

'11 100 quarts of grain supplied by Kuntukka, workers of Irdabama received as rations, at Shiraz, their appointments being set by Rashda. Month 6, Year 22 (of Darius).

62 men 30 (quarts each), 8 boys 25, 34 boys 20, 26 boys 15, 19 boys 10, 22 boys 5. 190 women 30, 32 women 20, 11 girls 25, 20 girls 20, 24 girls 15, 17 girls 10, 25 girls 5. Total 480 workers.' (PF 1028)

Figure 6.12 Seal of Irdabama (PFS 51). The seal has been carved in Neo-Elamite style. It depicts a hunting scene featuring a Persian on horseback pursuing onagers with a long spear. Composite line drawing of impressions from the seal of Irdabama. *Source*: Courtesy of M.B. Garrison, M.C. Root and the Persepolis Seal Project.

6.4.5 The King's Friends and Benefactors

High up in the court hierarchy were the King's Friends and Benefactors. There may not have been a sharp distinction between the two titles, as they were bestowed both on individuals and on groups of people. Individuals who were appointed as King's Friend were admitted to dine with the king, to partake at the King's Table. These noblemen were not exclusively Persian, because a range of foreigners, including Greeks and Egyptians, count among them.

6.4.6 Courtiers

The Persepolis reliefs offer a valuable insight into those close to the king. Most prominently, they depict the Immortals, the king's bodyguard, as well as royal attendants, including the king's chariot driver, the king's carpet-bearer and the chair-bearer: '(...) whenever the king descended from his chariot (...) he never leaped down, although the distance to the ground was small, nor did he lean on anyone's arms; rather, a golden stool was always set in place for him, and he descended by stepping on this; and the king's stool-bearer attended him for that purpose'. (Dinon ap.Athen.XII.514). The head of the bodyguard was called *hazarapatish*; alongside him were the king's spear-bearer and the king's axe-bearer, as depicted on the audience relief. The title of the head of the administration is not known, but this office may have been held by a member of the king's family.

In addition to the head of the palace administration, there was a head of the royal treasury, a chief scribe, translators, a keeper of the gate and priests, as well as those members of the Persian nobility who acted as the King's Councillors, as Royal Judges and as the King's Eye. Gathering information about any issue that concerned the empire was paramount to ensuring inner stability and peace. Greek sources refer to these informants as the 'King's Eyes' and the 'King's Ears'. These men were active throughout the empire, observing anything within the satrapy or the satrap's palace that could potentially form a threat to the royal power. They probably reported back to a single court official who then passed the information to the king. 'Then he (= Cyrus II) assigned them to their tasks, some to the building of houses, some to be his bodyguard, one to be the King's Eye; to another he gave the right of bringing him his messages, to each he gave his proper work' (Hdt.I.114). And Pseudo-Aristotle writes: 'The king himself, they say, lived in Susa or Ecbatana, invisible to all, in a marvellous palace with a surrounding wall flashing with gold, electrum and ivory; it had a succession of many gate-towers, and the gateways, separated by many stades from one another, were fortified with brazened doors and high walls; outside these the leaders and most eminent men were drawn up in order, some as personal bodyguards and attendants to the king himself, some as guardians of each outer wall, called Guards and Listening-Watch, so that the king himself, who had the name of Master and God, might see everything and hear everything' (Ps.-Arist. *De Mundo* 398a). Access to the king was restricted, and few will have been permitted to approach him. Those seeking an audience were requested to wait at the palace gate, and while some, like Syloson of Samos, were allowed to speak to the king directly, others were not.

Separate from these were the royal physicians, who were required to be permanently on hand to attend to the king and his family, but who were of non-Persian descent. Hardly anything is known about the identity of the Royal Judges. Their jurisdiction will have been different from that of the satraps, who were able to pass judgement on land disputes and possibly other charges concerning satrapal politics. The Royal Judges were active in the courts across the empire, as can be gleaned from an example from Elephantine:

> On d[a]y 2 of the [m]onth Epeiph Year 27 of Darius the king (= 22 October 495), said Salluah, the daughter of Kenaiah, and Jethoma, her sister, to Jehour, daughter of Shelomam: 'We gave you half the sha[re] which the King's Judges and Rauaka the Troop Commander gave us, in exchange for half the share which came to you with Nehebeth. Tomorrow (or the) next day, we shall not be able to institute (suit) against you in (regard to) that share, [s]aying: "We did not give it to you." Brother or sister, son or daughter, near or far, shall not be able to institute (suit) against you. And whoever shall institute (suit) against you in (regard to) that share, which we gave you shall give you silver 5 karsh, and your share is yours furthermore.'
>
> The witnesses: [H]osea son of Hodaviah, Shelomam son of Azariah, Zephaniah son of Makki. (*six witnesses follow but the names are illegible*). (Cowley no. 1; transl. Porten 2011: 254–255)

6.4.7 Refugees and Foreigners

Among the many foreigners attested at the royal or satrapal courts, some came as refugees. Most notably we find Demaratus, the Spartan king who was exiled from his country, the former ruler of Athens, Hippias, who came to stay at Darius's court and, not without an element of irony, Themistocles, the strategist of the Battle of Salamis, who was ostracised in Athens in 469 and arrived in Persia by late 465. The Greek Onomacritus was oracle reader for Xerxes, while Zenon, Telephanes and Timokreon were artists attested at the courts of later Persian kings. Foreign physicians came from Egypt and Greece. Apparently, Amasis had sent an eye doctor to Cyrus II at his request; Democedes of Croton found himself at the court of Darius I and treated his wife Atossa, while Apollonides of Cos practised at the court of Artaxerxes I. The physician Ctesias of Cnidus claimed to have been at Artaxerxes II's court, where Polycritus of Mende also was attested.

The royal administration needed numerous scribes and translators, both at the royal court and in the satrapal residences. Among his many positions at the court of Cambyses II and Darius I, the Egyptian Udjahorresnet also served as a translator to the Persian king. Tissaphernes had his own Greek translator, as did Cyrus the Younger. The Greek Phalinus worked as a translator at the court of Artaxerxes II, and Melon at the court of Darius III.

Sources in Translation 6.3

Royal Pastimes: Banqueting and Hunting

Banqueting

Banqueting was an essential pastime at the royal court, as is attested in the reliefs of the staircases in Persepolis leading up to the king's private palaces (Figure 6.13). They depict rows of servants wearing Persian dress, carrying different foodstuffs on large trays and in bowls and jars, as well as sheep. They give the impression of preparing a grand meal for the king and his invited guests, offering a splendid reception following the gift-giving ceremony. The Greeks' fascination with Persian banquets has been captured in the following two texts:

Figure 6.13   Staircase of Darius's palace. *Source*: Author photograph.

Dining with the King

All who attend upon the Persian kings when they dine first bathe themselves and then serve in white clothes, and spend nearly half the day on preparations for dinner. Of those who are invited to eat with the king, some dine outdoors, in full sight of anyone who wishes to look on; others dine indoors in the king's company. Yet even those do not dine in his presence, for there are two rooms opposite each other, in one of which the king has his meal, in the other the invited guests. The king can see them through the curtain at the door, but they cannot see him. Sometimes, however, on the occasion of a public holiday, all dine in a single room with the king, in the great hall. And whenever the king commands a symposium (which he does often), he has about a dozen companions at the drinking. When they have finished dinner, that is, the king by himself, the guests in the other room, these fellow-drinkers are summoned by one of the eunuchs; and entering they drink with him, though even they do not have the same wine; moreover, they sit on the floor while he reclines on a couch supported by feet of gold; and they depart after having drunk to excess.

In most cases the king breakfasts and dines alone, but sometimes his wife and some of his sons dine with him. And throughout the dinner his concubines sing and play the lyre; one of them is the soloist, the others sing in chorus. (...) For one thousand animals are slaughtered daily for the king; these comprise horses, camels, oxen, asses, deer and most of the smaller animals; many birds are also consumed, including Arabian ostriches (...), geese and cocks. (Heracleides FGrH 689 F2, ap. Athen. *Deipnosophistae* IV.145)

The King's Dinner

400 artabai (hereafter a.) – a Median artabe is an Attic medimnos – of pure wheat flour,
300 a. of second-grade flour,
300 additional a. of third-grade flour
a total of 1000 a. of wheat flour for dinner.
200 a. of pure barley flour,
400 a. of second grade and
400 of third-grade,
a total of 1000 of barley flour.
200 a. of rye,
10 a. of the finest barley flour made for a drink,
x a. of ground cardamom, sifted fine,
10 a. of peeled barley,
1/3 a. of mustard seed.
400 male sheep,
100 oxen,
30 horses,
400 fatted geese,
300 turtle doves,
600 small birds of all kinds,
300 lambs,
100 young geese,

30 gazelles.

10 maries (*hereafter* m.) – a maris is 10 Attic choes – of fresh milk,

10 m. of sweetened whey.

A talent (*hereafter* t.) by weight of garlic,

½ t. by weight of pungent onions,

1 a. of Phyllon (silphium fruit?),

2 mnai of silphium juice,

1 a. of cumin,

1 t. by weight of posset from sour pomegranates,

¼ a. of oil of cumin,

3 t. of black raisins,

3 mnai of anise flowers,

1/3 a. of black cumin,

2 kapeties of seeds of *diarinon*,

10 a. of pure sesame,

5 m. of gleukos from wine,

5 m. of cooked round radishes in brine,

5 m. of capers in brine, from which they make sour sauce,

10 a. of salt,

6 m. of Ethiopian cumin,

30 mnai of dried anise,

4 k. of celery seed,

10 m. of sesame oil,

5 m. of cream,

5 m. of terebinth oil,

5 m. of acanthus oil,

3 m. of sweet almond oil,

3 a. of dried sweet almonds,

500 m. of wine.

When he was in Babylon or Susa, half was palm wine and half was grape wine. Two hundred waggon loads of green wood, 100 waggon loads of wood (*hule*), 100 square cakes of liquid honey, weighing 10 mnai. Whenever he was in Media, he distributed the following items: Three artabes of saffron seed, two mnai of saffron. These items were used for drinks and for breakfast.

He distributed 500 a. of pure wheat flour, 1000 a. of pure barley flour, 1000 a. of second-grade barley-meal; 500 a. of semidalis, 500 m. of *groats* made from *olyra*, 20 000 a. of barley for the animals, 10 000 waggons of chaff, 50 000 waggons of straw, 200 m. of sesame oil, 10 m. of vinegar, 30 a. of finely chopped cardamom. All these things listed he distributed to the soldiers (?). This is what the king consumes in a day, including his *ariston*, his *deipnon*, and what he distributes. (Poly.*Strat*.IV.3.31–32)

Hunting

The hunt was a royal activity which enabled the king and the Persian aristocracy to practise their riding skills and their ability to shoot. It was an opportunity for all to demonstrate Persian royal virtues: leadership, courage and military prowess. Most royal hunts were conducted on horseback, but chariot hunts are also attested. A famous seal of Darius I depicts him during a lion hunt, shooting his arrows from a two-wheeled chariot (Figure 6.14). Xerxes possessed a similar seal, but showing him killing a fantastical beast, a winged lion with horns and a bird's feet. The seal impression was found on clay *bullae* from Dascyleium and bears the inscription 'I am Xerxes the king'. (SXf; transl. Schmitt 1981). If we trust Ctesias, the king claimed the right to the first shoot, as the case of Megabyxus shows. Over-enthusiastically casting the first shot, his action during a hunt with Artaxerxes I was regarded as treason and he was sentenced to death. Only through the intervention of the king's mother, Amestris, was he allowed to live, though he was exiled from the Persian court. (Ctesias FGrH 688 F14 (40)). The hunts took place in the vast parks that surrounded the royal and satrapal palaces. Xenophon describes one such park for the satrapal palace of Celaenae in Greater Phrygia, stating that it was 'full of wild animals which he (= Cyrus the Younger) used to hunt on horseback whenever he wanted exercise for himself and his horses'. (Xen.*an.*I.2.8)

Hunting required the support of dogs, and we find a surprising number of them on seals depicting a hunting scene. Assyrian palace reliefs already depicted their key role in the hunting and pinning down of prey, but for Persia we have a unique token of the king's appreciation of his hunting dog in the form of a life-size bronze sculpture of a mastiff complete with his own collar (Figure 6.15).

Figure 6.14   Seal of Darius I (BM 89132). The seal is 3.3 cm high and was found in Egypt. The trilingual inscription reads '(I am) Darius the king'. The king is seen standing on a chariot hunting lions with bow and arrow. Above the scene, the god Auramazda appears in the winged disc. The scene is flanked by palm trees. *Source*: Drawing by Marion Cox.

Figure 6.15   The over-life-size statue of a mastiff was found in the southwest tower of the Apadana in Persepolis. It is made of black limestone. *Source*: After Curtis, Tallis and Salvini 2005, fig. 90.

FURTHER READING

The fundamental work on Achaemenid kingship is Root, M.C. (1979). *The King and Kingship in Achaemenid Art*. Leiden: Brill; For the audience scene on *bullae* from Dascyleium see Kaptan, D. (2002). *The Dascyleion Bullae. Seal Images from the Western Achaemenid Empire*. Leiden: Nederlands Instituut voor het Nabije Oosten. For Persepolis see Schmitt, E.F. (1953–1977). *Persepolis I–III*. Chicago: University of Chicago Press. A collection of royal audience scenes can be found in Brosius, M. (2010). The royal audience scene reconsidered. In: *The World of Achaemenid Persia* (eds. J. Curtis and J. St. Simpson), 141–152. London: Tauris; For Xerxes as "the greatest after the king" see Sancisi-Weerdenburg, H. (1983). Exit Atossa. Images of women in Greek historiography on Persia. In: *Images of Women in Antiquity* (eds. A. Cameron and A. Kuhrt), 22–33. London: Croom Helm.

On Achaemenid religion see Henkelman, W.F. and Redard, C. (2017). *Persian Religion in the Achaemenid Period / La réligion Perse á l'époque Achéménide*. Wiesbaden: Harrassowitz; Skjervø, P.O. (2014). Achaemenid religion. *Religious Compass* 8 (6): 175–187. Lincoln, B. (2012). *'Happiness for Mankind'. Achaemenid Religion and the Imperial Project*. Leuven: Peeters. Garrison, M. (2011). By the favour of Ahuramazda: kingship and the divine in the early Achaemenid period. In: *More than Men, Less than Gods. Studies on Royal Cult and Imperial Worship* (eds. P.P. Iossif, A.S. Chankowski and C.C. Lorber), 15–104. Leuven: Peeters. Finn, J. (2011). Gods, kings, men: trilingual inscriptions and symbolic visualizations in the Achaemenid empire. *Ars Orientalis* 41: 17–57. Henkelman, W. 2006, The other gods who are. Studies in Elamite-Iranian acculturation based on the Persepolis fortification texts. PhD. Diss. University of Leiden; Kellens, J. (2002). L'idéologie réligieuse des inscriptions achémenides. *Journal Asiatique* 290: 417–464. Kellens, J. (ed.) (1991). *La religion iranienne à l'époque achéménide*. Gent: Peeters; The Achaemenid tomb in Susa is discussed by Tallon, F. (1992). The Achaemenid tomb on the Acropole. In: *The Royal City of Susa. Ancient Near Eastern Treasures in the Louvre* (eds. P. Harper, J. Aruz and F. Tallon), 242–252. New York: The Metropolitan Museum of Art.

Aspects of the Achaemenid court are discussed in Jacobs, B. and Rollinger, R. (eds.) (2010). *Der Achämenidenhof / The Achaemenid Court*. Wiesbaden: Harrassowitz. Rollinger, R. and Wiesehöfer, J. (2009). Königlicher Haushalt, Residenz, und Hof. Der persische König und sein Palast. In: *Sprachen – Bilder – Klänge. Dimensionen der Theologie im Alten Testament und seinem Umfeld, Festschrift für S. R. Bartelmus* (ed. C. Karrer-Grube), 213–225. Münster: Ugarit. Brosius, M. (2007). New out of old: court and court ceremony in Achaemenid Persia. In: *The Court and Court Society in Ancient Monarchies* (ed. A.J.S. Spawforth), 17–57. Cambridge: Cambridge University Press.The importance of gift-giving has been addressed by Sancisi-Weerdenburg, H. (1989). Gifts in the Persian empire. In: *Le tribut dans l'empire achéménide* (eds. P. Briant and C. Herrenschmidt), 129–145. Paris: Peeters. For the King's Friends and Benefactors see Wiesehöfer, J. (1980). Die 'Freunde' und 'Wohltäter' des Grosskönigs. *Studia Iranica* 9: 7–21. The royal banquet has been analysed by Lewis, D.M. (1987). The king's dinner (Polyaenus IV.3,32). *AchHist* 2: 79–87; On Rytha see Ebbinghaus, S. (1999). Between Greece and Persia. *Rhyta* in Thrace from the late 5th to the early 3rd centuries BCE. In: *Ancient Greeks West and East* (ed. G.R. Tsetskhladze), 384–425. Leiden: Brill; On women and their economic activities at the Persian court see Brosius, M. (1996). *Women in Ancient Persia (559–331 BCE)*. Oxford: Oxford University Press.

7

The Organisation of Power

7.1 The Satraps

In order for such a vast and diverse empire to work effectively and successfully two things were essential: a well-functioning administration and a good system of contact between the king and the lands of the empire. Both relied on an excellent infrastructure to ensure communication, to collect taxes and tribute, to move people, armies and livestock, as and when required, and to enhance and secure overland commerce and trade. Each land of the Persian empire was governed by a satrap, a term which derives from the Old Persian word *khshçapavan*, 'protector of the realm'. Satraps were responsible for the collection of taxes within their satrapy, for overseeing local law and administration and for the levying of troops and naval forces. Cyrus II had adapted the system of satrapies from Babylonia, where the term *pihātu* signified the governors of Babylonian provinces. This term was still used under the Achaemenids to describe local governors in a satrapy.

> On the third day of the month Arahshamnu (= 29 October 539) Cyrus entered Babylon. [...] were filled with before him. There was peace in the city while Cyrus spoke (his) greeting to all of Babylon. Gubaru, his governor (Bab. *pihātu*), appointed the district officers in Babylon. (NCh col. II: ll.19–20)

In the Achaemenid empire, the Persian satraps were frequently appointed from members of the royal family, especially the brothers and sons of the king, but could also include sons-in-law. Satraps resided in the urban centre of a province. The satrapal palace emulated, on a smaller scale, the king's palace and, like it, was situated in a *para-daida*, a planned and landscaped garden which allowed for satrapal leisure pursuits such as hunting. Greek sources writing about Persia focus on the western part of the empire, and accordingly most of our information about the satrapies stems from western Asia Minor.

A History of Ancient Persia: The Achaemenid Empire, First Edition. Maria Brosius.
© 2021 John Wiley & Sons, Inc. Published 2021 by John Wiley & Sons, Inc.

7.1.1   The Satrapies

A frequently debated question relates to the number of the Persian satrapies and their relationship to, or identification with, the lists of lands given in our primary sources. These differ considerably from the list of satrapies mentioned by Herodotus. Darius's Bisitun Inscription lists 23 lands under Persian domination, beginning with those located in the centre of the empire (Persis, Elam, Babylonia), then naming the western lands (Assyria, Arabia, Egypt, (the People)-by-the-Sea), and those of the northwest (Sardis, Ionia). The northern lands include the provinces around the Black Sea and the Caspian Sea (Media, Urartu, Cappadocia, Parthia) and, finally, the eastern lands (Drangiana, Aria, Chorasmia, Bactria, Sogdiana, Paruparaesanna, Scythia, Sattagydia, Arachosia, Maka). The inscription at Naqsh-e Rustam adds six more lands, distinguishing three different tribes of Scythians, the Amyrgian Scythians, the Scythians with the pointed hats and the Scythians-beyond-the-Sea (= the Black Sea). Also added are Skudra, which refers to the lands of Thrace and Macedon, and Pat and Kush, that is, Libya and Nubia, and Caria. India is mentioned in an inscription from Persepolis, on the stele commemorating the digging of the canal from the Nile to the Red Sea, and on the statue of Darius from Susa.

Herodotus, in contrast, lists 20 satrapies, which name 70 different peoples and tribes, yet they appear in a rather haphazard order, with little reflection of geographic reality. He omits his own people, the Dorians of Asia Minor, though he records them as part of the Persian contingent in Xerxes's army. In the sixteenth satrapy, he fails to mention the Hyrcanians and the Arachosians. More confusing still is the fact that 12 lands in the Bisitun Inscription comprise five satrapies in Herodotus. Six other countries appear in the inscription as individual provinces, while they occur as parts of other satrapies in Herodotus. The Bisitun Inscription lists Arabia as one of the lands, but, according to Herodotus, this did not pay taxes. While Darius's list begins with the central lands of Persia, Herodotus's order starts with countries in the west, that is, Ionia, and then moves to the eastern provinces, ending with India. To explain the differences between Darius's list of lands and Herodotus's satrapy list, it has been suggested that there must have been a distinction between administrative districts and the tax-paying countries. This, however, would mean a confusing system and interference of different officials between combinations of provinces. It is unlikely that Herodotus had access to a primary source which was close to the information provided in the Bisitun Inscription. If he, thus, depended for his information on a list that existed in his own lifetime, it has to be considered that in a timespan of about 90 years, which will have passed since Darius's reign, the administration and organisation is likely to have undergone some, if not considerable, change.

Efforts to combine the two sets of information, the Persian primary sources and the list given in Herodotus as a secondary source, have failed due to the incompatibility of the order and the question of the status of the 'lands' of the empire versus the 'satrapies' of Herodotus. To make matters more complicated, other lists of lands, such as that from Darius's inscription at Naqsh-e Rustam (DNa), give 29 lands; a list from a Persepolis inscription (DPe) and two from Susa (DSe, DSaa) list 24 and 27/23, respectively. Finally, we have 32 lands listed in Xerxes's inscription from Persepolis (XPh). Because of these discrepancies, the lists of lands also have been regarded as

THE ORGANISATION OF POWER

incomplete or unreliable, as some omit, for example, Cilicia or Hellespontine Phrygia. Consequently, they been interpreted as ideological lists which bear no reflection of an administrative reality.

Recently, Bruno Jacobs offered an alternative approach to the problem, suggesting that they were structured hierarchically. 'To document the extent of the empire completely it would be quite sufficient to enumerate all provinces of one specific level of the administrative hierarchy' (Jacobs 2011). Jacobs differentiates between Great Satrapies, comprised of those lands which had been complex structures prior to their inclusion into the Persian empire, such as Media, Lydia, Babylonia, Egypt, Bactria and Arachosia, and Main Satrapies, which were larger units within the Great Satrapies, and included, for example, Assyria as part of Babylonia, Cappadocia as part of Lydia. A third level was then formed by Minor Satrapies. They were smaller regional units and can be identified for some, but not all, Great Satrapies, but they are evidenced in local political entities, such as Mysia as part of Hellespontine Phrygia, or Lycia as part of Caria. We also need to consider that the size and extent of the satrapies altered over the more than two centuries of Achaemenid rule. Thus, for example, the satrapy of Babylonia, which comprised Mesopotamia as well as the lands west of the Euphrates, was divided into the satrapies of Babylonia and that of Transeuphratene early in Xerxes's reign. As examples of the different formations and set-ups of the satrapies, the following sections discuss the eastern satrapy Bactria and the regions of the Caucasus and Thrace on the periphery of the empire.

7.1.2 The Great Satrapy of Bactria

Among the eastern provinces, Bactria, with its centre Bactra, or Zariaspa, stands out as a region which was already governed by a ruler before the Persian conquest. Bactria was an important eastern satrapy, its capital, Bactra (mod. Balkh), located on the crossroads between the western part of the empire and the east. A wealthy Great Satrapy, it boasted many cities. It encompassed Margiana, Sogdia, the Minor Satrapy of the Dyrbaeans, the Saka regions, the Dahae and Massagetae, and possibly Areia, reaching as far as the Hindukush and the Amu Darya River. Like other important satrapies, such as Hellespontine Phrygia and Egypt, the satrap of Bactria was a close kin of the king. Bardiya is said to have been appointed satrap there by his father, Cyrus II. Under Darius I, a Persian named Irtabanush (Gr. Artabanus) is attested as satrap there in an administrative document dated to 500/499 (PF 1287); he most likely was the brother of Darius. Xerxes's brother Masistes staged a revolt in his satrapy Bactria in 479/8, where he then seems to have been replaced by another brother, Hystaspes. He, in turn, was succeeded by another Persian named Irtabanush. The name implies that he, too, was a member of the royal family. In the later empire, an official named Akhvamazda worked under Artaxerxes III, most likely as the satrap of Bactra, while a man named Bagavant is mentioned as the governor of the city of Khulmi. The last satrap was the Achaemenid Bessus, who declared himself king as Artaxerxes V after the death of Darius III, and in defiance of Alexander's conquest of Persia. Together with Sogdiana, Bactria put up a strong resistance against Alexander III. The recent publication of Aramaic documents from Bactria dated to the late Achaemenid period, from Artaxerxes III to the end of the empire, provides evidence for a proper system of administration and a hierarchical structure of administrative command.

At Kalay Gyr in Chorasmia, the province bordering the northwest of Bactria and reaching as far as the Aral Sea, an Achaemenid palace has been uncovered featuring a hypostyle hall. The site may have been the residence of the Persian satrap there, though it is possible that it was the seat of a Chorasmian ruler whose palace emulated Achaemenid architecture (Francfort 1988: 179). In the satrapal centre of Drangiana, Zranka, identified with modern Dahan-e Golman, representational and administrative buildings of the Achaemenid period were excavated that most likely belonged to the local satrap.

7.1.3   The Status of the Caucasus Region and Thrace

Recent research on Thrace and archaeological excavations in the Caucasus region have shed light on the regions on the periphery of the empire (Map 7.1). Both came under Persian control under Darius I in the course of the Scythian campaign of 513/2. The current view holds that the Persians integrated the land as far as the Danube in the west and the Caucasus in the east. For a brief period, some areas beyond those natural borders were also included, but were relinquished after a period of time. Scholarly opinion varies in regard to the status of the Caucasus region, which includes Colchis and encompasses the entire region up to the

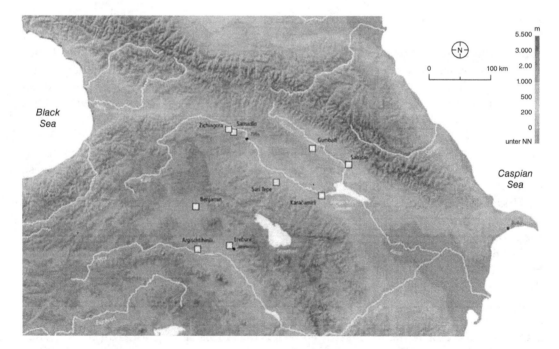

Map 7.1   Map of Achaemenid sites in the Caucasus. *Source*: With kind permission of Florian Knauss, Munich.

Caucasus Mountains. In contrast to Herodotus's assessment of an only loosely connected Colchis and her neighbours, Bruno Jacobs classified Colchis as a Minor Satrapy under the umbrella of the Main Satrapy of Armenia. As for Iberia, the Greek and mediaeval evidence for this region reveals that there is no evidence for the existence of an Iberian kingdom in the third century BCE. Whatever level of state formation existed there at the time, it must have been somewhat removed from a political system which supported a king. Thus it may be argued that, except for the Greek city-states in the Black Sea area, no strong form of indigenous government existed in the Caucasus region at the time of the Persian occupation. Archaeologically, Persian presence left a decisive mark on the region, especially on Iberia, leading us to assume that there must have been a considerable impact of Achaemenid political and cultural influence there. Continued Achaemenid control until the collapse of the empire meant that political directives came first and foremost from Persia. On the strength of the archaeological evidence, therefore, Herodotus's assessment cannot be accurate, yet the question of the political status of the Caucasus regions of Colchis and Iberia still remains open.

Recent excavations in the Caucasus region have dramatically added to our understanding of Achaemenid control in this area. At Karajamirli in Azerbaijan, remains of Achaemenid-style palaces or government buildings have been unearthed whose design matches that of Achaemenid columned halls. The bell-shaped column bases are sculpted with vertical leaves and a torus. Pottery finds and a glass bowl confirm the Achaemenid date of the site. At Ideal Tepe several Achaemenid buildings have been discovered, including an Achaemenid propylon, which allowed access to another building at Gurban Tepe. The partial excavation revealed a southern wall measuring 40 m in length, pointing at a considerable complex within the walls. As there is no local precedent for such buildings, Achaemenid control over the region meant a significant improvement in terms of political governance and the establishment of a local infrastructure. The building plan of the propylon is identical with that of the Tripylon, the Central Building, at Persepolis. Considering that the Tripylon was built by Xerxes I and completed by Artaxerxes I, the excavators suggested a date in the fifth century for the structure at Karajamirli (Figure 7.1). Ideal Tepe and Gurban Tepe align with a third Achaemenid foundation, Sari Tepe, about 70 km southwest of Gumbati, where part of an Achaemenid building was discovered in the 1950s, although much has been destroyed by the nearby river. This means that the satrapal residence at Karajamirli and the residences in Gumbati and Sari Tepe were established after Darius's campaigns in the Black Sea region.

As for Thrace, scholarship has tended to identify the region, together with Macedon, as a lesser satrapy under the Main Satrapy of Lydia. The inhabitants of this satrapy were the Skudra (Thracians), the *Saka paradraya*, or Scythians-beyond-the-Sea, identified as the Getae, and the *Yauna takabara*, the Ionians with the shield-like hat, that is, the Macedonians. Philippopolis (mod. Plovdiv) has been tentatively suggested as a satrapal centre. Herodotus mentions the Asian Thracians, but not the European Thracians, in the list of tribute-giving peoples. The Thracians and Macedonians, as well as the Colchians and their neighbours, were obliged to provide military service. European Thrace is mentioned in the lists of lands of Darius and Xerxes, and either

Figure 7.1   Photograph of the archaeological site of the Achaemenid palace near Karajamirli.
Source: With kind permission of Florian Knauss.

European or Asian Thracians are identified among the gift-bearers on the Apadana reliefs. Both regions west and east of the Black Sea came under Persian control at the same time. Also, in both cases, the Persians were dealing with areas wealthy in natural resources, although politically these regions were at an early stage of development. It could be argued that, unlike the conquered kingdoms of the Persian empire, which had possessed a fully functioning political organisation and administrative set-up when they were reverted into satrapies, or the city-kingdoms, which were self-governing and held a semi-autonomous status, regions which had less experience of political self-governance were integrated into existing satrapies.

Following the Persian retreat from Europe after 479/8, an independent kingdom, the Odrysian kingdom, emerged in Thrace over the following decades. It is rewarding to study the range of artefacts from Thrace and to recognise that the Thracian court was modelled on that of the Achaemenid kings. Jugs, vessels, *phialai* and even *rhyta* were modelled on Achaemenid art, yet these objects were produced in local workshops by Greek or local craftsmen. Achaemenid Persia set the standard for the way Thracian kingship and court life were expressed, and this meant the adaptation of Achaemenid court art. As diplomatic links may well have continued after 479/8, Thracian association with the Achaemenid court will have been welcomed. At the same time, the Thracian kings and the nobility ensured that they impressed their own identity on their art. Like the Persian kings, the Odrysian kings used a system of gift-giving and similarly created a court hierarchy through favour and privilege.

Box Text 7.1

Achaemenising Art

The observation we can make for Thrace and the Odrysian kingdom leads us to the exciting topic of Achaemenising art. As distinct from Achaemenid art, that is, the art of the Persian royal court, as can be identified in monumental architecture, in columned halls, in the imperial artistic depiction of the Persian dress, in jewellery, weaponry and metalware used in feasting and banqueting, Achaemenising art describes art objects that were crafted at local level, and, while emulating Achaemenid court style, adapted its forms and decorative motifs according to regional taste. This occurs in the satrapal regions of the empire as well as on its periphery and beyond.

The finds are particularly rich for western Asia Minor, where often Greek craftsmen can be identified as the makers of seals or as stonemasons creating funerary art. Satrapal centres such as Sardis and Dascyleium, with their governing Persian elite, doubtlessly facilitated the transfer of luxury goods, and with it the artistic expression and artistic motifs of the Persian court to the local elite. This mechanism is particularly intriguing when looking beyond the empire. One such extraordinary example is a marble slab found near Mouseion Hill in Athens, which, in two tiers, depicts Achaemenid motifs, although the craftsmanship is entirely Greek (Figure 7.2). The top shows a bearded male wearing Persian dress and holding two mythical beasts by the horns. It seems to be an adaptation of the royal hero motif well attested on the door jambs of the Hundred Column Hall in Persepolis and the Persepolis seals. The lower tier depicts a lion attacking a stag, a scene which emulates the lion-and-bull motif of Persepolis reliefs.

At the northeastern frontier region of the empire, the spectacular find of the burials in Pazyryk in the Altai Mountains has uncovered unique examples of Achaemenising art. The discoveries include a carpet which shows riders wearing tunic and trousers alternatively riding on horseback or walking alongside their bridled horses (Figure 7.3). They have been compared to the horsemen on the Persepolis reliefs.

A further piece of textile, a saddlecloth, shows rows of striding lions in the manner known from the Persepolis reliefs; although the motif is Achaemenid, the fabric was woven by local craftsmen. Equally intriguing is the motif on the remnants of a textile showing pairs of women, the taller of each pair wearing a crown, but all of them clad in the long Persian robe, centred around an incense burner (Figure 7.4).

Figure 7.2 Marble slab from Athens. The two-tiered slab depicts a royal hero scene in the upper tier in which a male figure wearing Persian dress fights two mythical winged and horned lions, while the lower tier depicts a lion killing a deer. *Source*: Athens 1487, after Boardman 2000, fig. 5.64.

Figure 7.3 Pile carpet, wool, from Pazyryk (St. Petersburg Inv. no. 1687/93). This is the oldest preserved carpet in the world, dating to the fifth or the fourth century. It depicts 28 horsemen alternating between riding and walking beside their horses. David Stronach suggested that the number may not be accidental but may represent the provinces of the Persian empire. *Source*: With kind permission of The State Hermitage Museum, St. Petersburg. Photograph © The State Hermitage Museum. Photo by Alexander Koksharov.

(a)

(b)

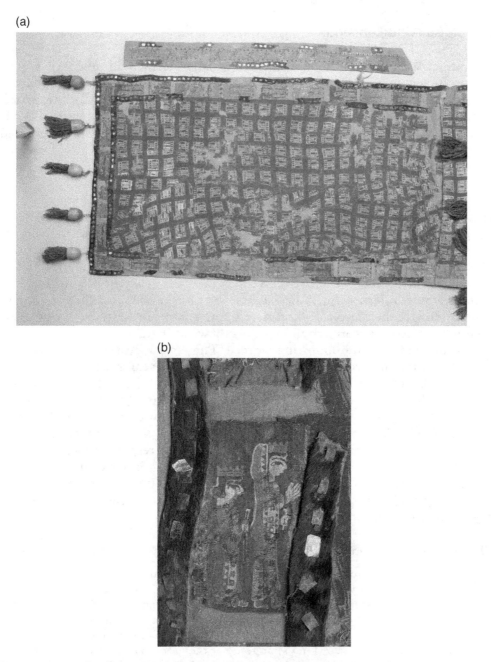

Figure 7.4   (a) Iranian saddlecloth, Pazyryk culture (Inv. no. 1687/100). *Source*: Photograph with kind permission of The State Hermitage Museum, St. Petersburg. Photograph © The State Hermitage Museum. Photo by Leonard Kheifets. (b) Detail of the Pazyryk saddlecloth depicting two women in Persian dress. The taller female wears a crown and a veil, which is hanging down her back; the smaller figure only wears a turreted crown and has a bobbed hairstyle, typical of Persian women. *Source*: Photograph with kind permission of The State Hermitage Museum, St. Petersburg. Photograph © The State Hermitage Museum. Photo by Leonard Kheifets.

7.2   Administering the Empire

7.2.1   *Royal Correspondence*

Communication between the king and his satraps and high administrative officials was conducted through letters; in the satrapies, royal decrees were put in force through these governors. The correspondence was conducted using Aramaic, the lingua franca, the shared written language of the multi-ethnic empire. At local level, the Aramaic text was translated into the language used in the individual satrapy, thus allowing for communication with the local elite and local bureaucrats in their language. This practice required scribes and interpreters to be fluent in at least two languages and/or scripts, a fact which may well be attested in the Persepolis texts, which record rations for Babylonian boys writing on parchment, which means they wrote in Aramaic, rather than Babylonian cuneiform on clay. Whether or not the Persian king himself was literate is an open question, and from all we can gather, the king dictated to a scribe or scribes and had letters and documents read to him aloud. It is highly likely that copies of the royal correspondence and royal decrees were kept in the palace archives, as the case of Cyrus II's decree regarding the Temple of Jerusalem shows. The Book of Ezra recounts that opponents to the rebuilding of the temple of Jerusalem wrote a letter in Aramaic to express their concern that the Jews were rebuilding the city walls (Ezra 4: 7), whereupon Artaxerxes responded with the following words: 'The letter you sent us has been read and translated in my presence. I issued an order and a search was made and it was found that this city has a long history of revolt against kings ruling over the whole of Transeuphratene, and taxes, tribute and duty were paid to them. Now issue an order to these men to stop work so that this city will not be rebuilt until I order so' (Ezra 4: 18–21). A letter of Darius I written to his governor Gadatas of Magnesia seemingly reveals the king's close attention paid to the respect of local deities. The letter, carved on a marble stele, is written in Greek, but it has been suggested that its original text must have been composed in Aramaic. Its authenticity, however, is strongly disputed among scholars, in part due to its being preserved only in a later copy dating to the second century CE.

> The King of Kings, Darius, son of Hystaspes, to Gadatas, his slave, thus speaks:
>
> 'I find that you are not completely obedient concerning my orders. Because you are cultivating my land, transplanting fruit trees from the province Across-the-Euphrates to the western Asiatic regions, I praise your purpose, and in consequence there will be laid up in store for you great favour in the royal house. But because my religious dispositions are nullified by you, I shall give you, unless you make a change, proof of a wronged (king's) anger. For the gardeners sacred to Apollo have been made to pay tribute to you; and land which is profane they have dug up at your command. You are ignorant of my ancestors' attitude to the god, who told the Persians all of the truth and [...]' (Meiggs and Lewis 1988: 20–22, no. 12; transl. Fornara 1983: 37, no. 35)

Sources in Translation 7.1

The Correspondences of Arsames and Akhmavazda

A. The Correspondence of Arsames

Each satrapy conducted its own administration guided by the central authority
of the king. In many cases, existing administrative systems were continued under
Persian rule, as is well attested for Babylonia, Egypt and Lydia; in other cases,
Achaemenid administrative practices will have been newly introduced. Within
this system, multiple languages and scripts were used, but Aramaic was the uni-
form written language used in the correspondence across the empire. One set of
such letters, being part of the correspondence of Arsames, the satrap of Egypt,
were found together in a leather pouch. Their provenance is unknown, but they
must have been found in Egypt, as Arsames was abroad and used the letters to
communicate with his officials back in Egypt. All but one of the 13 letters are
instructions given to his officials. The subject matter of these letters concerns
royal estates in Egypt and their administration. Though the letters bear no date,
they almost certainly belong to a period between 515/4 and 408/7 and some to a
period from 408/7 to 400. Arsames spent the time away from Egypt in Susa and
perhaps some time in Babylon.

Text 1

From Arsames to Ar[tavan]t.

I send yo[u abundant] (greetings of) welfare and strength.
[And now, the grant] was given [b]y the king and by me to Ahhapi my servant who
    was an offic[ial] in my domains which are in Up[per and Lower (Egypt).
Now, Ps]amshek, the son of Ahhapi, who now has been made an officer in his
    stead in my domains which are in Upper [and Lower] (Egypt), asked me
    to carry on] that grant whi[ch was gi]ven by the king and by me to Ahhapi.
Let Psamshek his son be permitted to carry out that grant there in Eg[y]pt.
(*Outside*) [Fr]om Arsames [the] prince to [Artavant who is in Egypt].
(*Summary*) concerning the grant of Ahhapi the official who (…). (Driver no. 2,
    transl. after Porten and Yardeni 1986: 104, A64)

Text 2

From Arsames to Artavant:

I send you abundant (greetings of) welfare and strength.
And [now], one named [Psa]mshek son of Ahhap[i], my servant, complained
    here. He says thus, 'When I was coming [t]o [my] lord … [sl]aves of Ahhapi
    my father whom I… […] after me to my lord – [1] named Psamshek-hasi [son
    of PN], 1 [PN son of …]twy, [1] Ahhapi son of P[…], 1 [PN] son of Psamshek,
    [1] Pashubasti son of Hor, [1 PN son of PN], 1 [PN] son of Wahpremahi,
    [1 PN son of PN], all (told) 8 persons – took my property and fled from me.

Now if it please my lord, let (word) be sent to Artavant [*that those slaves whom*] I shall present before him: the chastisement which I shall issue-an-order for them to be done to them.'

Now, Arsames says [thus]: 'That [P]samshe[khasi] and his colleagues, the slaves of Ahhapi, whom P[sa]mshek will present before you t[here] – you issue an order: the chastise[ment] which Psamshek will i[ssue]-an-order to be done to them – that shall be done to them. (Driver no. 3, transl. Porten and Yardeni 1986: 102, A6.3)

B. The Correspondence of Akhmavazda of Bactra

This correspondence is part of the private Khalili collection, comprising 30 documents written in Aramaic on leather and 18 inscribed wooden sticks. These documents were acquired on the antiquities market from several dealers and locations over a long period of time, but are thought to belong to one cache of documents. Their original findspot cannot be determined, but is thought to have been either Bactria, Central Asia or Mesopotamia. They are all associated with a high Bactrian official, most likely the satrap of Bactria himself; the period covered ranged from the reign of Artaxerxes III to the seventh year of the reign of Alexander III. Many of the letters are addressed to the governor of the city of Khulmi, called Bagavant. They were probably drafts to be copied at a later stage. This means that they must have belonged to the archive of the Bactrian satrap, and were kept as a record.

Text 1: A1

From Akhvamazda to Bagavant and the magistrates. And now: Vahuvakhshu son of Chithrabarzana said thus: 'I complained earlier to my lord Akhvamazda concerning Bagavant and the magistrates, how they removed (things) from the camel-keepers, my apprentice-servants; they despoiled and detained them, and extracted (from them) a tax which they (= the camel-keepers) are not obliged (to pay), not letting them guard the camels of the king. As a result of this, there will be(?) a flow(?) and a renewed flow(?) among the camels of the king. Therefore I inform (my lord). Thereafter Bagavant was interrogated by my lord. In the meantime, before the decision was issued to him, the same Bagavant went to Khulmi. I again complained to my lord. Afterwards (a message) was sent to Bagavant (and) an order was given to him to release those men, the detained camel-keepers, and to proclaim a prohibition concerning the camel-keepers, [and that which he] removed to give back. The same Bagavant refused to release those men. I again complained to my lord. Afterwards, (certain) men were appointed by the court of my lord, who released those men, the camel-keepers, from prison, and (who) issued a prohibition to Bagavant. Afterwards, finally, after the (issue of the) prohibition, because those men complained, Bagavant, Ahuradata, his foreman, and the magistrates removed from the camel-keepers one bull, two donkeys (and) 34 [sheep]. Furthermore, they imposed on them a surcharge(?) more than (is imposed on) another land. If my lord Akhvamazda deems this appropriate, may he consider (the issue) in my favour concerning the matter.'

Now, because you are removing (things from) those men and are imprisoning (them) against my decree, when you come (to me), you will be interrogated. But now, what you have removed, give back to them. Furthermore, do not extract (from them) a surcharge(?) more than what they owe you. Also, release those men, the camel-keepers, to do their own work. Do not impose on the land [a tax] which they do not have to pay. Hashavakhshu the scribe is aware of this command.

To [*blank space*] Bagavant and the magistrates who are in Khulmi.

... of Marsheshvan, Year 6 of Artaxerxes the king. Concerning a tax. Bring this letter. (Khalili A1, transl. Naveh and Shaked 2012: 69–70)

Text 2: A4

From Akhvamazda to Bagavant. And now: concerning that which you sent to me, saying: '(A message) was sent to me from you to give instruction to build the wall and the ditch around the town of Nikhshapaya. Subsequently I set a time and made the troops come close. Spaite, the magistrates and others (of) the garrison of the land came to me saying thus: "There is locust, heavy and numerous, and the crop is ripe (?) for reaping. If we built this wall, then the locust, the blight that is in the town, [will increase] and it will cause [a flow(?)] and a renewed flow(?) in the land." (But) I have no authority to let them go. And another (matter). That which you say, concerning that which you communicated to me (in your message), [...' And now ...] those troops that are appointed in your presence, set them free to go about their work. That locust let them [smash(?)], and let them reap the crop. And when the time comes, they will build that wall and ditch. Daizaka the scribe is in charge of this command.

Verso: To [*blank space*] Bagavant who is in Khulmi.

On (day) 3 of Sivan, [Year] 11 of Artaxerxes the king, concerning Nikhshapaya. Bring this letter. (Khalili A4, transl. Naveh and Shaked 2012: 96–97)

7.2.2 Taxes and Tribute

Through the satraps, the king collected tribute from the lands of the empire; this was called '*baji-*' in Old Persian, meaning '(the king's) share'. It is thought that this system was introduced, or least underwent a reform, under Darius I, since tribute had already been collected under his predecessors, Cyrus II and Cambyses II. Herodotus (III.89–97) accredited the amounts of paid tribute to Darius's reign, listing payments of silver for each of his 20 'satrapies', except for India, which paid in gold. Tribute payments were made annually and amounted to 14560 Euboean talents. We know very little about the criteria for determining the tax payments of each land of the empire. Most likely we need to differentiate between payments made to the king and those made to the satraps. Further taxes would have been paid to the cities and within private economies. For Babylonia there is evidence of land grants and payable duties. Such duties also had to be paid on the spot, as and when demanded by the king. Thus, for example, individuals were called upon to cater for the King's Table on state visits:

By day 15 of Arahshamnu, Year 2, (= 23 October 528) Cambyses, king of Baby-lon, king of lands, Zeriya, son of Nana-eresh, and Arad-Bel, son of Sharru-ukin, the Cattle Chiefs of the Goat and Sheep flocks of the Lady of Uruk (= the goddess Ishtar), will bring 100 each of ewes and nanny-goats giving suck, in all 200 head of sheep and goats, concerning which for day 28 of Arahshamnu there came an order of Parnaka, and have them ready for the king's meal in the palace which is in Abanu (or Amanu, south of Uruk). If they do not bring the 200 sheep and goats on day 28 of Arahshamnu and do not have them ready in the palace which is in Abanu, they will incur the punishment of the king. (*Witnesses, scribe, place, date*) (transl. after Kuhrt 2010: 711, no. 24 (i))

The correspondence of Akhmavazda already refers to a land tax payable to the satrap (see above, Text 2). A further reference, dated to the end of the fifth century, can be found in one of Arsames's letters addressed to Nakhtor, Kenzasirma and his colleagues:

Now, Arsa[mes] says thus: 'If it is so according to these words which Petosiri sent [to me that] that (one) named [Pamun], his father, when there was the unrest in Egypt, perished with [his household] personnel [and] the domain of that Pamun his father, of 30 a(rdab) seed capacity – (that) that was abandon[ed and] not made (over) [to my estate] and not given by me to another servant, then I do give the domain of that Pamun to Petosiri. You notify him. Let him hold-(it)-as-heir and pay to my estate the land tax just as formerly his father Pamun had been paying.' (Driver no. 8, transl. after Porten and Yardeni 1986: 118: ll.3–6)

7.2.3   The Administration of Persepolis

While Herodotus is emphatic that Parsa did not pay taxes, the texts from the Persepolis archive provide undeniable proof to the contrary. Under Darius I, the chief administrator was his uncle Parnaka, whom we already encountered as chief administrator under Cambyses II in the document above. As the head of the administration, he received the highest ration, receiving a daily amount of 90 quarts of wine or beer and two sheep. Like all members of the court and the administrators of the palace, Parnaka had his own seal, which bore his name in Aramaic. When this seal got lost, he annotated his letter order with the remark: '(…) the seal that formerly (was) mine has been replaced/lost. Now this seal (is) mine that has been impressed on this tablet'. (PF 2067, dated 5 June 500). This new seal bore the Aramaic inscription 'Seal (of) Parnaka son of Arsham' (Figure 7.5).

Parnaka issued letter orders to his subordinates, such as the chief of workers, the cattle chief or the wine steward. His orders were dictated in Persian, while his scribes noted them down in Elamite:

Tell Harrena the cattle chief, Parnaka spoke as follows: 'Shuddayauda the chief of workers in the shalir (place) spoke to me saying: "The cattle (for) which I am setting aside the king's 600 quarts (of) grain are not (at hand). And now you (are) to issue 30 male cattle to Shuddayauda. Within those cattle: (for) 20 (of) those cattle let him set aside the 600 (quarts of) grain; let him maintain 10 cattle in pasture (?)". Month 9, Year 18 (= of Darius I). Karkish wrote (the text). Maraza communicated its message (at) Persepolis.' (PF 1792)

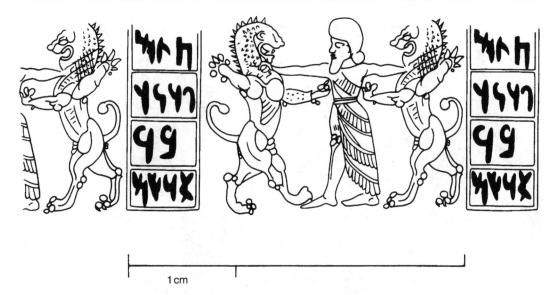

Figure 7.5   The seal of Parnaka (PFS16*) shows a royal hero scene with the hero fighting two lions. The Aramaic inscription reads: 'Seal (of) Parnaka son of Arsham'. Composite line drawing of impressions from the seal of Parnaka (PFS 16*). *Source*: Courtesy of M.B. Garrison, M.C. Root and the Persepolis Seal Project.

7.2.4   Royal Roads

One of the greatest accomplishments of the Persian government was the development of a complex road system (Map 7.2). Building on the model of the Assyrian road leading from Babylon north along the Euphrates River, and then turning west towards Sardis, the Achaemenid period saw the establishment of a network of Royal Roads leading not only south to north, but also west to east. The eastern route passed the former Median capital Ekbatana, and continued to Margiana and Bactra, and then on towards India.

A Babylonian text dated to the reign of Cyrus II reports the measurement of a stretch of road near Sippar:

> Measurement of the Royal Road (at the) head of the field in the Fifty (= a stretch of land) of (the place) Til-gubbi (in the hands of) the *erib-biti* (= the temple-enterers) of Shamash, undertaken by Bel-uballit, *shangu* of Sippar: Tebetu, day 7, Year 8 of Cyrus, king of Babylon, king of lands.
>   4400 (cubits) from the upper Fifty of Shamash-shum-lishir, son of Nabu-shum-iddin, descendant of Ile'i-Marduk, up to the boundary (of the territory) of Shamash, bordering (the land of the) Hummaeans.
>   88 measuring ropes; 26 date palm beams; which Nabu-appla-iddin received from Shamash-shum-iddin. (BM 79746; transl. Kuhrt 2010: 710, no. 22(i))

Herodotus, aware only of the Royal Road leading from Susa to Sardis, recorded that it took 90 days to travel that distance, covering c.18 miles per day, using the Persian distance measure *parasang* (5–6 km). Way stations along these Royal Roads secured

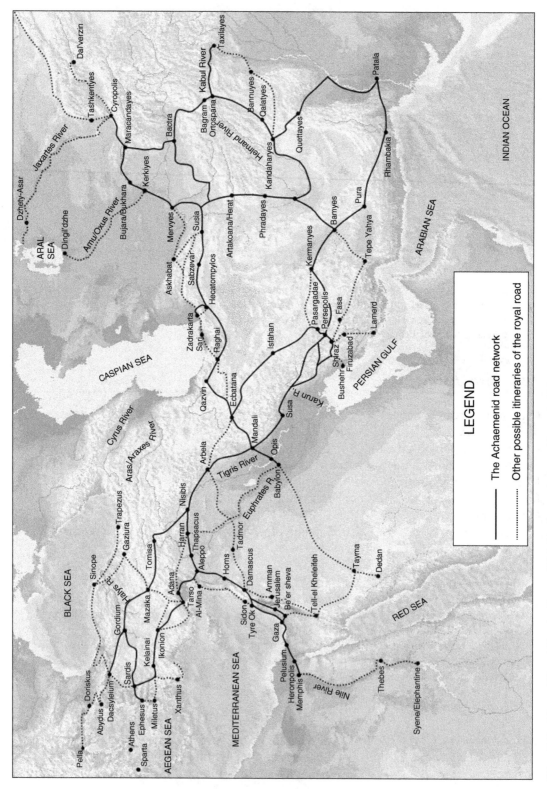

Map 7.2 Map of Royal Roads. *Source:* With kind permission of Joaquin Velazquez Muñoz.

Figure 7.6   A Royal Road station portico from Qaleh Kali. The Royal Road station shows the portico with three Achaemenid column bases. *Source*: Photograph with kind permission of Dan T. Potts.

the regular provision of the travellers and their horses, while guard stations controlled the safety of the roads (Figure 7.6). The Royal Road from Susa to Sardis boasted 111 stations to secure the maintenance of the 2470 km through the Zagros Mountains, across the Tigris and along the Euphrates to Cappadocia.

> Now the nature of this road is as follows. All along it are the royal stages and excellent inns, and the whole of it passes through country that is inhabited and safe. (…) Thus the total number of stages is 111, and that is the number of resting-places as you go up from Sardis to Susa. If I have rightly reckoned the *parasangs* of the Royal Road, and a *parasang* is 30 furlongs' length (= 5–6 km), which it is assuredly, then between Sardis and the royal palace called the city of Memnon (= Susa) there are 13 500 furlongs, the number of *parasangs* being 450. And if each day's journey is 150 furlongs, then the total of days spent is 90, neither more nor less. (Hdt.V.52–53)

The couriers were royal messengers sent on the king's order, who communicated information across the empire as fast as possible. A messenger changing his horse every 30 km at the road stations could manage the distance between Sardis and Susa in seven days, covering up to 300 km per day. 'Now nothing mortal travels faster than these couriers, by the Persians' skilful contrivance. It is said that the number of men and horses stationed along the road equals the number of days the whole journey takes – a man and a horse for each day's journey; and these are stopped neither by snow nor rain nor heat nor darkness from accomplishing their appointed course with all speed. (…). This equestrian post is called in Persian *angareion*.' (Hdt.VIII.98)

Xenophon already ascribed the system of Royal Roads to Cyrus II:

> We have observed still another device of Cyrus (II) to cope with the magnitude of his empire; by means of this institution he would speedily discover the condition of affairs, no matter how far distant they might be from him: he experimented to find out how great a distance a horse could cover in a day when ridden hard but not so hard as to break down, and then he erected post-stations at just such distances, equipped them with horses and men to take care of them; at each one of the stations he had the proper official appointed to receive the letters that were delivered and to forward them on, to take in the exhausted horses and riders and send on fresh ones. They say, moreover, that sometimes the express does not stop all night, but the night-messengers succeed the day-messengers in relays (…) it is at all events undeniable that this is the fastest overland travelling on earth; and it is a fine thing to have immediate intelligence of everything, in order to attend to it as quickly as possible. (Xen.*Cyr*.VIII.6.17–18)

We get a glimpse of the mechanisms as to how travel was permitted by the king and the daily withdrawal of foodstuffs for individuals and their horses were recorded at the way stations en route. An initial order was given either by the king himself or by the satrap; the traveller carried this sealed document with him to present to the royal storehouses en route, where any withdrawal was accounted for. One such initial order can be seen in a letter written by the Persian satrap Arsames to officials in Babylonia and Syria, advising them of the travel of his official Nahitur and ordering them to provide him with daily rations for the duration of his journey to Egypt.

> From Arsames to Marduk, officer in 'G.KD/R; Nabu-dalani, officer in Lahiru; Zatuva-hya, officer in Arzuhina; Upastabara, officer in Arbela, HL, and Matalubash; Bagafarna, officer in Salam; Fradafarna and HW[…], officers in Damascus.
>
> 'Now, he called Nakhtor, my steward, is going to Egypt. You are to give him rations charged to my estates in your province daily: white flour, 2 'handfuls'; rami flour, 3 'hand-fuls'; wine or beer, 2 'handfuls'; sheep(?) one. Also to his ten servants, each per day: flour, 1 'handful'; fodder for his horses.
>
> Giving rations to the two 'Cilicians' and one craftsman – all three are servants of mine who are going to Egypt with – each man per day: flour, 1 'handful'.
>
> Each officer in turn, according to the route from province to province until it reaches Egypt, is to give him these rations. If he should be more than one day in a place, then for these days do not give them any rations.
>
> Bagasrava knows this order: Rashta is the scribe.' (Driver no. 6; transl. Kuhrt 2010: 739–741, no. 4)

Box Text 7.2

Travel Rations from the Persepolis Archive

The Persepolis Fortification texts give a vivid impression of journeys undertaken by members of the royal family, members of the nobility, ambassadors from as far as India and the royal messengers. On an official journey, the traveller would be provided with a sealed document of the king, or sometimes of a high court official, which entitled the traveller to receive provisions of food and drink on a daily basis. Horses were also provided for receiving fodder and wine rations, the latter, perhaps, to be mixed with water to make it safe for drinking. People moved in groups or were accompanied by elite guides, as they are referred to in the tablets texts. Zishshawish, mentioned in Text 1, was Parnaka's second-in-command at Persepolis; Artaphernes, mentioned in Text 4, is the satrap of Sardis.

Text 1

Mushka received 1.5 quarts of flour, supplied by Bakadushda, as a fast messenger (Elam. pirradazzish). He went from the king to Zishshawish. He carried a sealed document from the king. Month 10 (of Darius I). (PF 1285)

Text 2

Abbatema received 110 quarts of flour. As his daily ration he receives 70 quarts. 20 men each receive 2 quarts. He carried a sealed document from the king. They went forth from India. They went to Susa. Month 2, Year 23 (of Darius I). Ishbaramishtima is his elite guide (Elam. barrishdama lakkukra). The seal of Ish-baramishtima was applied (to this tablet). (PF 1318)

Text 3

Turpish the caravan leader (Elam. karabattish) received 3.5 quarts of flour supplied by Karma and gave (them) to 1 gentleman and 2 servants. Month 9, Year 22 (of Darius I). (PF 1341)

Text 4

Dauma received 465 quarts of flour. 23 men each (received) 1.5 quarts. 12 boys each received 1 quart. He carried a sealed document of Artaphernes (Elam. Irdapirna). They went forth from Sardis (Elam. Ishparda) to Persepolis. Month 9, Year 27 (of Darius I). (At) Hidali. (PF 1404).

Text 5

400 quarts of grain were received and delivered as fodder for one(?) express horse. Year 20 (of Darius I). (PF 1700)

Special Topic 7.1

'Ordinary' People

A number of sources allow us to gain insight into the lives of 'ordinary' people, from the ration texts for workers at Persepolis to legal documents from Susa, Babylon and Egypt. We may glean from these sources that people pursued their lives in each satrapy under the social, legal and cultural conditions they had known prior to becoming part of the Persian empire. For Persis only, the Persepolis archives allow a remark on the workers in the province. These were remunerated according to their level of specialisation, and thus we find graded ration payments for male and female workers, and for boys and girls, whose payment most likely depended on their age. An average ration consisted of a monthly payment of 30 quarts of grain and 20 quarts of wine or beer. Highly specialised labour was paid up to 50 quarts of grain, an amount which was exclusively received by female chiefs of workers, called *arrashsharap* (sg. *arrashshara*), who were known by their personal name in some of the texts. The head of the workforce was called *kurda-battish*, and this office at the time of Darius I was held by a man named Irshena.

Work Forces

Text 1

> 8960 quarts (of) grain supplied by Irshena, treasury workers subsisting on rations, whose apportionments are set by Baratkama, received (at) Rakama, in the 28th year, fifth month. 1 scribe receives 40 quarts, 1 *etira* receives 40 quarts, 1 treasurer receives 30.5 quarts, x attendants each receive 40 quarts, 2 *ramikurrash* each receive 30 quarts, 1 *hazarna* handler receives 20 quarts, x *mulatap* each receive 30 quarts (…). x female *arrashshap* each receive 50 quarts, 75 female attendants each receive 40 quarts, 113 female *ramikurrash* each receive 30 quarts, 13 female *ammalup* each receive 20 quarts, 12 female 'ration makers' each receive 20 quarts (…) Total 311(?) workers received (it) as rations. (PF 866)

One of the most striking features of these ration texts is the special ration given to women who had just given birth to a child. For one month, the women received an additional ration consisting of wine and grain, and, oddly, women who gave birth to a son received twice the amount given to those who had a daughter.

> Lanunu, a woman (who) bore a male baby, received 10 quarts of wine, supplied by Irkezza.
> Parrkkuzzish, a woman (who) bore a female baby, received 5 quarts of wine.
> They were given to a total of 2 post partum women.
> Manzaturrush and his companions received it and gave it to them. Year 23, month 4 (of Darius I). (At) Tikrakkash. (PF NN-358)

Marriage

An undated marriage document from Achaemenid Susa written in Babylonian records the dowry and the terms for a possible divorce:

> Pisisamaska voluntarily [promised to give] to Harri-menna as dowry with Nahdi-Esu, his sister: One and two thirds minas of refined silver, two thirds of a mina (worth) of silver in jewellery for a woman; one roll of homemade(?) cloth; one *s.*-garment; three assorted garments, one of which has a multicoloured trim; one HUM-HUM-garment; [.....]; one [.....]-garment; [.....]; two couches. (…) Should Harri-menna release Nahdi-Esu his wife, and have another wife live (in the house) in preference to her, he will give her five minas of silver in addition to her dowry. And should Nahdi-Esu release Harri-menna her husband, she will forfeit(?) her

entire dowry in favour of Harri-menna, and thereby she will relinquish her means of support(?). (TBER 93–94:ll.14–23. ll.28–35; transl. Roth 1989: 108–112)

Similarly a marriage contract from Elephantine, dated to the reign of Artaxerxes I, stipulates the conditions for the marriage between Eshor and Miptahiah.

On the 24th [of] Tishri, [that is day] 6 of the month of Epeiph, [Y]ear [16 of Artaxerx]es [the] king, said Eshor son of Dje[ho], a builder of the king, to Mah[seiah, an A]ramaean of Syene, of the detachment of Vahyazdata, saying: 'I [c]ame to your house (and asked you) to give me your daughter Mipta(h)iah for wifehood. She is my wife and I am her husband from this day and forever. I gave you (as) *mohar* (= gift) for your daughter Miptahiah: [silver], 5 shekels by the stone(-weight)s of [the] king. It came into you and your heart was satisfied herein. [Your daughter] Miptahiah brought in to me in her hand: silver money, 1 karsh by the stone(-weight) s of the king, silver 2 q(uarters) to the ten. She brought into me in her hand: 1 new garment of wool, striped, with dye doubly-well; it was (in) length 8 cubits by 5 (in width), worth (in) silver 2 karsh 8 shekels by the stone(-weight)s of the king; 1 new (shawl), it was in length 8 cubits by 5 (in width), worth (in silver) 8 shekels by the stone(-weight)s of the king; another garment of wool, finely woven; it was (in) length 6 cubits by 4 (in width), worth (in) silver 7 shekels; 1 mirror of bronze, worth (in) silver 1 shekel, 2 q(uarters); 1 bowl of bronze, worth (in) silver 1 shekel 2 q(uarters); 2 cups of bronze, worth (in) silver 2 shekels; 1 jug of bronze, worth (in) silver 2 q(uarters). All the silver and the value of the goods (in) silver 6 karsh 5 shekels 20 hallurs by the stone(-weight)s of the king, silver 2 q(uarters) to the ten. It came into me and my heart was satisfied herein. 1 bed in which (there are) 4 oil vessels of stone; 1 tray of *slq*; 2 ladles; 1 new box of palm leaf; 5 handfuls of castor oil; 1 pair of sandals.

Tomorrow or (the) next day, should Eshor die not having a child, male or female, from Mipta[h]iah his wife, it is Miptahiah (who) has a right to the house of Eshor, and [hi]s goods and his property and all that he has on the face of the earth, all of it.

Tomorrow or (the next) day, should Miptahiah die not having a child, male or female, from Eshor her husband, it is Eshor (who) shall inherit from her her goods and her property.

Tomorrow o[r] (the) next day, should Miptahiah stand up in an assembly and say: "I hate Eshor my husband", silver of hatred is on her head. She shall place upon the balance scale and weigh out to Eshor silver, 6[+1] shekels 2 q(uarters), and all that she brought in in her hand she shall take out, from straw to string, and go away wherever she desires, without suit or without process.

Tomorrow or (the) next day, should Eshor stand up in an assembly and say: "I hate my [wif]e Miptahiah", her *mohar* [will be] lost and all that she brought in in her hand, she shall take out, from straw to string, on one day in one stroke, and go away wherever she desires, without suit or without process.

And [who]ever shall stand up against Miptahiah, to expel her from the house of Eshor and his goods and his property, shall give her silver, 20 karsh, and do to her the law of this document.

And I shall not be able to say: "I have another wife besides Mipta(h)iah and other children besides the children whom Miptahiah shall bear to me." If I say: "I have other ch[ildren] and a wife besides Miptahiah and her children", I shall give to Miptahiah silver, 20 karsh by the stone(-weight)s of the king. And I shall not be able to release my goods and my property from Miptahiah. And should I remove them from her [*erasure*], I shall give to Miptahiah [silv]er, 20 karsh by the stone(-weight)s of the king.'

Wrote: Nathan son of Ananiah [this document at the instruction of Eshor]. And the witnesses herein: *(names of four witnesses follow)*. (Cowley no. 15, transl. after Porten 2011: 178–184)

A Conveyance

Finally, we have an example of a conveyance of Mahseiah, the father of Miptahiah.

On the 21st of Kislev, that is day [20+]1(= 21) of Mesore, Year 6 of Artaxerxes the king (= 1 December 459) the king, said Mahseiah son of Jedaniah, a Jew hereditary property-holder in Elephantine, the fortress of the detachment of Haumadata, to lady Miptahiah, his daughter, saying: 'I gave to you in my lifetime and at my death a house, land, of mine. Its measurements was: (…).

That house, land – I gave it to you in my lifetime and at my death; you have right to it from this day and forever, and (so do) your children after you. To whomever you love you may give (it). I have no other son or daughter, brother or sister, or woman or other man (who) has right to that land but you and your children forever.

Whoever shall institute against you suit or process (against) you, or son or daughter of yours, or man of yours, in the name of that land which I gave you, or shall complain against you (to a) prefect or (a) judge shall give you or your children silver, 10 (that is ten) karsh by the stone(-weight)s of the king, silver 2 q(uarters) to the ten, without suit or without process, and the house is your house likewise and your children's after you.

And they shall be able to take out against you a new or old document in my name about that land to give (it) to another man. That document which they shall take out against you will be false. I did not write it and it shall not be taken in suit while this document is in your hand. And moreover, I, Mahseiah, tomorrow or the next day, shall not reclaim (it) from you to give to others.

That land of yours build up and/or give (it) to whomever you love. If tomorrow or the next day I bring against you suit or process and say: "I did not give (it) to you", I shall give you silver, 10 karsh by the stone(-weight)s of the king, silver 2 q(uarters) to the ten, without suit and without process, and the house is your house likewise. And should I go into a suit, I shall not prevail while this document is in your hand.

Moreover, there is a document of withdrawal which Dargmana, son of Khvarshaina the Khwarezmian, wrote for me about that land, when he brought (suit) about it before the judges and an oath was imposed (upon me) for him and I swore to him that it was mine, and he wrote a document of withdrawal and gave (it) to me. That document – I gave it to you. You, hold-it-as-heir. If tomorrow or the next day Dargamana or (a) son of his bring (suit) about that house, that document take out and in accordance with it make suit with him.

Wrote Attarshuri son of Nabuzeribni this document in Syene the fortress at the instruction of Mahseiah.' (*This is followed by a list of witnesses*) (Cowley no. 8; transl. Porten 2011: 165–172)

FURTHER READING

On satraps see Jacobs, B., 2011, Achaemenid Satrapies, available at http://www.iranicaonline. org/articles/achaemenid-satrapies). For the Persepolis texts see Hallock, R.T., 1969, *Persepolis Fortification Tablets*, Chicago: University of Chicago Press (Oriental Institute Publications 92) and Cameron, G.G. (1948). *Persepolis Treasury Texts* (Oriental Institute Publication 65). Chicago: University of Chicago Press; the Persepolis seals have been studied by Garrison, M. and Root, M.C. (2001). *Seals on the Persepolis Fortification Tablets. I: Images of Heroic Encounter* (Oriental Institute Publications 117). Chicago: University of Chicago Press. Briant, P. and Chaveau, M. (eds.) (2009). *Organisation des pouvoirs et contact culturels dans les pays de l'empire achéménide*. Paris: De Boccard (Persika 14). Tuplin, C. (1987). The Administration of the Achaemenid Empire. In: *Coinage and Administration in the Athenian and Persian Empires*, BAR series 34 (ed. I. Carradice), 109–166. London: British Archaeological Report. For Bactria see Francfort, H.-P. (1988). Central Asia and Early Iran. In: *CAH IV²*, 165–193. Genito, B. (2001). Dāhān-i Ghulmān: una 'vicina' periferia dell' Impero Achemenide. In: *Antica Persia. I tesori del Museo Nazionale di Tehran e la ricerca italiana in Iran* (eds. A. Gramiccia and G. d'Inzillo Carranza), XXXI–XXXV. Rome: De Luca. cf. Antela-Bernardez, B. and Vidal, J. (2014). *Central Asia in Antiquity: Interdisciplinary Approaches*. Oxford: British Archaeological Report. For Asia Minor see Dusinberre, E.R.M. (2003). *Aspects of Empire in Achaemenid Sardis*. Cambridge: Cambridge University Press. Dusinberre, E.R.M. (2013). *Empire, Authority, and Autonomy in Achaemenid Anatolia*. Cambridge: Cambridge University Press. Knauss, F. (2011). Residenzen achaimenidischer Beamter und Vasallen. In: *Kelainai – Apameia Kibotos: Développement urbain dans le contexte anatolien* (eds. L. Summerer, A. Ivantchik and A. von Kienlin), 391–410. Paris: Ausonius Éditions. The Black Sea region is discussed in Brosius, M. (2010). *Pax Persica* and the peoples of the Black Sea region: extent and limits of Achaemenid Imperial ideology. In: *Achaemenid Impact in the Black Sea Region* (eds. E. Rehm and J. Nieling), 29–40. Aarhus: Aarhus University Press. Babaev, I., Mehnert, G., and Knauss, F.S. (eds.) (2009). Die achaimenidische Residenz auf dem Gurban Tepe. Ausgrabungen bei Karčamirli. 3. Vorbericht. *Archäologische Mitteilungen aus Iran und Turan* 41: 283–321. Knaus, F. (2006). Ancient Persia and the Caucasus. *Iraniqua Antiqua* 41: 79–118. Jacobs, B. (2000). Achaimenidenherrschaft in der Kaukasus-Region und in Cis-Kaukasien. *Archäologische Mitteilungen aus Iran und Turan* 32: 93–102.

For the Arsames correspondence see Porten, B. and Yardeni, A. (eds.) (1986). *Textbook of Aramaic Documents from Ancient Egypt: Letters*. Jerusalem: Hebrew University Department of the History of Jewish People; On the Aramaic texts from Bactra see Naveh, J. and Shaked, S. (eds.) (2012). *Aramaic Documents from Ancient Bactria*. London: The Khalili Family Trust. For the difficulties determining the authenticiy of the Gadatas letter see Tuplin, C.J. (2009). The Gadatas letter. In: *Greek History and Epigraphy* (eds. L.G. Mitchell and L. Rubinstein), 155–184. Swansea: Classical Press of Wales.

On the emulation of Achaemenid court life at local level see Miller, M. (2007). The poetics of emulation in the Achaemenid world: the figured bowls of the 'Lydian Treasure'. *Ancient West & East* 6: 43–72; Miller, M. (2003). ii. Greco-Persian cultural relations. *EncIr* 11: 301–319. http://www.iranicaonline.org/articles/greece-ii. Summerer, L. (2007). Picturing Persian victory: the painted battle scene on the Munich Wood. *Ancient Civilizations from Scythia to Siberia* 13: 3–30. Summerer, L. (2007). From Tartalı to Munich: the recovery of a painted wooden tomb chamber in Phrygia. In: *The Achaemenid Impact on Local Populations and Cultures in Anatolia (Sixth-Fourth Centuries B.C.)* (eds. İ. Delemen, O. Casabonne, Ş. Karagöz and O. Tekin), 131–158. Beyoğlu, Istanbul: Türk Eskiçag Bilimleri Enstitüsü Yayinlari. Rudenko, I.S. (1970).

Frozen Tombs of Siberia. The Pazyryk Burials of Iron Age Horsemen. Berkeley: University of California Press. Stronach, D. (1993). Patterns of prestige in the Pazyryk carpet. Notes on the representational role of textiles in the first millennium BC. *Oriental Carpet and Textile Studies* 4: 19–26.

The Royal Roads were discussed by Graf, D.F. (1994). The Persian Royal Road System. *AchHist* 8: 167–189.Velázquez Muñoz, J. (2013). Las estaciones reales durante el período aqueménida / The royal stations in the Achaemenid period. *Lucentum* 22: 185–203. Briant, P. (2012). From the Indus to the Mediterranean Sea: the administration, organisation and logistics of the great roads of the Achaemenid empire. In: *Highways, Byways and Road Systems in the Pre-Modern World* (eds. S.E. Alcock, J. Bodel and R.J.A. Talbert), 185–201. Chichester: Wiley. Potts, D.T., A. Askari Chaverdi, A. Dusting, et al., 2007, The Mamasani archaeological project, stage two: excavations at Qaleh Kali (Tappeh Servan/Jinjun [MS 46]), *Iran* 45: 287–300.

8

Taking up the Baton: Diplomacy and Foreign Policy from Xerxes I to Artaxerxes II

8.1 The Reign of Xerxes

The designated heir to the throne, Xerxes I (ruled 486–465), was a worthy successor to Darius. He continued his father's policies in the empire and abroad. Upon ascending to the throne, his first concern was the quashing of the rebellion in Egypt. He continued his father's building programme in Persepolis, adding construction work to the Apadana, and began the building of his private palace south to that of Darius. He also constructed a new access to the palace complex, building an inverted double staircase and a monumental entrance gate. In style and sentiment his inscriptions follow those of his father. Yet by far the greatest impression he left on history was his execution of Darius's plan of a renewed attack on Greece. This time conducted on a much larger scale, and led by king Xerxes himself, the Persian War, or the Median War, as is was referred to by the Greeks, became a war of world historical importance.

8.1.1 Xerxes's Succession

Xerxes recalled his succession to the throne in a further inscription carved at Persepolis: 'King Xerxes proclaims: "Darius had other sons also, (but) thus was the desire of Auramazda: Darius, my father, made me the greatest (OP *maθista-*) after himself. When my father Darius went to his (allotted) place, by the favour of Auramazda I became king in my father's place."' (XPf §4; transl. after Kuhrt 2010: 244). There was a reason for emphasising his right to succeed to the throne. Darius already had a son named Artobarzanes by his first wife, the daughter of Gobryas. But Artobarzanes had been born before Darius became king, making Xerxes the first royal offspring born to Atossa, and thus born 'to the purple'. There were other full brothers: Masistes, Hystaspes and Achaemenes. A sister, Artazostre, was married to Gobryas's son Mardonius. Xerxes's marriage to Otanes's daughter Amestris produced three sons, Darius, the designated heir to the throne, Hystaspes and Artoxerxes, as well as Amytis and Rhodogune.

A History of Ancient Persia: The Achaemenid Empire, First Edition. Maria Brosius.
© 2021 John Wiley & Sons, Inc. Published 2021 by John Wiley & Sons, Inc.

Sources in Translation 8.1

Xerxes and Persepolis

Under Xerxes's reign, the construction of the palace complex of Persepolis continued to evolve. A monumental double staircase was added to the western Fortification Wall, leading to a grand entrance gate known as the Gate of All Lands (Figure 8.1). This gate features two pairs of human-headed winged bulls, a direct borrowing from Assyrian art, in which these *lamassus* served to protect the palace from any evil. Stone benches inside the entrance, still visible today, allowed visitors to the palace to recover from their journey, enjoy the cool space and gather themselves before being led to the king. It also gave them time to admire the trilingual inscription carved in Elamite, Babylonian and Old Persian and displayed in four copies on the inner walls of the gate:

Figure 8.1   The Gate of All Nations. *Source*: Author photograph.

Xerxes's Inscription from Persepolis (XPa)

§2 I am Xerxes, the Great King, king of kings, king of lands containing many men, king of this earth far and wide, son of Darius, an Achaemenid.

§3 Xerxes the king proclaims: 'By the favour of Auramazda I built this Gate of All Nations. Much other good (construction) was built within this (city of) Parsa, which I built and which my father built. Whatever good construction is seen, we built all that by the grace of Auramazda.'

A trilingual inscription on glazed bricks from the Apadana gives testimony of Xerxes's work here: 'Xerxes the Great King proclaims: "By the favour of Auramazda much that is good did Darius the king, my father. And also by the favour of Auramazda, I added to that work and built more. Me may Auramazda protect together with the gods, and my kingdom."' (XPg)

Another daughter, called Ratashah, was an infant at the time of Xerxes's accession in 486, attested in a Babylonian ration text for her wet-nurse, Artim (see Brosius 2000: 83, no. 163).

8.1.2 Quashing Rebellions in Egypt and Babylonia

Xerxes's immediate task was the suppression of the revolt in Egypt, which had erupted towards the end of Darius's reign in 486. Whether Xerxes adopted a harsher policy towards Egypt as a result, as Herodotus claims, remains a matter of dispute, as no Egyptian evidence corroborates this view. He installed his brother Achaemenes as satrap in Memphis, an office he held until his death in 459. In 484, two rebels rose in Babylon proclaiming themselves kings of Babylon. The first, Bel-shimanni, was soon eliminated by a second pretender to the throne, Shamash-eriba. Administrative records referring to their kingship cover a period of merely three months before Xerxes was able to restore control. However, it seems that as a consequence of these two rebellions, Xerxes took severe measures to curb the political influence of notable Babylonian families. This is evidenced in the sudden end of a number of archives in Babylon, Borsippa and Sippar dated to that same year, 484.

8.2 The War in Greece

In line with his father's policy, Xerxes began preparations for a renewed campaign against Greece, specifically against Athens. A canal was cut across the Chersonnese near Mt. Athos to allow the safe passage of the navy. It was the result of the experience of the strong north winds there that had destroyed a number of Persian ships during the campaign of 490. At Abydus a bridge was constructed to terminate at Sestus, thus allowing the army's crossing at the narrowest point of the Hellespont. In 482/1 Persian ambassadors were sent to the Greek cities asking for the confirmation of neutrality and acceptance of the Persian king by demanding Earth and Water. Thessaly, Thebes and

Boeotia, Argos, the region north of the Malian Gulf and Locris complied. No ambassadors were sent to Athens and Sparta; Persian diplomacy did not extend to those states that demonstrated opposition to her power.

8.2.1 The State of Play in Greece

In Greece, the battle of Marathon had not resulted in a political unity among the Greek city states, evidenced in a war between Athens and Aegina on account of Athens's refusal to return Aeginetan hostages. Sparta, too, was involved since king Leonidas (ruled 489–480) had judged that his Spartan co-king Leutychides (ruled 491–476) bore some responsibility for the hostages and he was taken to Athens to plead for their freedom. In reaction to Athens's refusal, Aegina kidnapped a number of noble Athenians during a religious festival at Sunium. This state of hostilities existed through most of the 480s, with fighting focused on naval battles. When a silver mine was discovered in Laurium in 483/2, Themistocles persuaded the Athenians to use this newly found resource to expand the city's navy, arguing that the Athenians could only win their fight against Aegina if they outnumbered their fleet. This constitutes a vital piece of information about Athens's attitude towards Persia during the 480s, as it demonstrates that her immediate focus was on internal conflicts, rather than on Persia, and that the primary reason for the expansion of the Athenian fleet was to employ it in the war against Aegina. This war probably ended around 481, at about the same time Athens must have become aware of Xerxes's preparations to return to Greece.

8.2.2 The Persian Army on the March

Xerxes gathered the Persian army at Sardis. Contingents were drawn from across the empire, each using their own equipment and armour. The size of the army is a much disputed subject. Herodotus's figure of five million people is far too exaggerated to be considered historical. More realistic estimates propose between 60 000 and 70 000 Persian troops. After crossing the first bridge, the land army and the Persian fleet met at Doriscus, which was secured with a fortification and a garrison. Herodotus's figure of 1207 Persian triremes seems rather high, and recent estimates allow for a navy half that size. Xerxes proceeded through Macedon and Thrace, where local forces joined his army, to Acanthus. Here the fleet used the canal and then proceeded towards Therma, where it was reunited with the army. In the meantime, the Greek fleet approached Artemisium on the northern shore of Euboea while the land forces advanced to Thermopylae on the southern coast of the Malian Gulf. But even before any battle was fought, the Persian fleet suffered naval losses due to heavy seas. Herodotus gives a figure of 400 ships wrecked in the storm, though we might need to be cautious in accepting such a high number. The remaining Persian fleet moved south to Aphetae, and two days later both fleets engaged in a three-day battle at Artemisium, which ended in a stalemate.

8.2.3 Thermopylae and Artemisium

The land battle at Thermopylae, a mountain pass which led into Boeotia and the plain of Attica, was commanded by king Leonidas. His Spartan force, 300 men strong and supported by Theban and Thespian soldiers, was in charge of the position; the

Xerxes disarmed the Samians. With Xerxes's fleet diminished and weakened, the Greeks had no great difficulty breaking through the Persian ramparts and defeating the Persians.

8.2.8   The Story of Xerxes and the Wife of Masistes

Herodotus ends his account of the Persian Wars with a tale about Xerxes that has all the makings of a palace intrigue. It completes his picture of Xerxes as a king unfit to rule, and as a man who placed emotion before rational thought. Thus the story shows Xerxes after his defeat in Greece, seeking refuge in extramarital affairs, becoming involved in a 'harem' intrigue and his behaviour being the cause of a revolt. Against Herodotus's presentation of Xerxes stands the fact that his rule continued until his death in 465, and that there are no indications that the Greek campaign had any effect on the stability of the empire.

After his return to Sardis, Xerxes is said to have fallen in love with the (unnamed) wife of his brother Masistes. In an attempt to get her attention, he married his son Darius to Masistes's daughter Artaynte. Returning from Sardis to Susa, Xerxes had a change of heart and no longer desired Masistes's wife but turned his amorous desire towards his daughter-in-law Artaynte. As a token of his love, she demanded a royal robe woven by the queen. When Amestris learned of this betrayal, she demanded nothing less than to punish the wife of Masistes. He, however, after learning what had occurred, made for his satrapy Bactria, from where he intended to rebel against the king. But Masistes and his sons were captured on the way and killed.

After three books of descriptions of military campaigns and battles, this episode appears as an anticlimax and out of context. Why narrate a story at this point that has barely any relation to the previous events? The formal position of the story is only one issue; the other is its actual contents, which sound rather inconclusive. In regard to the first aspect, it has been argued that by placing the story at the end of the *Histories* Herodotus completes his *Ringkomposition*, a ring composition which at its beginning narrates the story of another palace intrigue caused by the improper behaviour of a king. In this case, it is king Candaules of Lydia, who met his end when he betrayed his wife's dignity to the courtier Gyges. The queen, learning of their plot, persuaded Gyges to kill the king and take the kingship himself. Thus the story of Xerxes is deliberately positioned to close Herodotus's narrative. It implies, in accordance with the first story, the downfall of Xerxes, a literary means to achieve a dramatic effect.

8.2.9   ... And a Story Retold

What is intriguing about this particular story is that it seems to have been adapted for the story of Esther, the Jewess who is said to have become the wife of Xerxes and who saved the Jews from royal punishment. The story is recounted in *The Book of Esther* and was probably written in the third century BCE. Considered a fictional text, its author nevertheless drew on a historical reality in the description of the Persian court at Susa. It begins with a royal banquet given by the king and his queen Vashti's refusal to appear before his male guests. As a result, the queen was deposed, and Esther, as the king's new wife, received her crown from the king. Together with her uncle Mordechai, she uncovered a plot by the courtier Haman to eliminate all the Jews. Yet the collective punishment of a people is ahistorical, and such a policy against the Jews contradicts the Persian policy towards other peoples and religions, as we can observe throughout Achaemenid rule. The episode solely served to allow the storyline to work. Though it is a fictional account written for a Jewish audience with the aim to explain the Purim festival, and also a story with a moral purpose framed within a romantic storyline with all the 'real' elements of a court setting, it clearly presents itself as a real historical event. The Persian court provides a backdrop for that story, and in consequence, it is woven around a skeleton of historical facts to give it its own historicity.

The narrative elements of this story, namely the dismissal of the 'old' queen, Vashti, in favour of a 'new' queen, Esther, the plot by two courtiers to kill the king, which, however, is discovered by Mordechai and prevented through his intervention, Mordechai's seeming disobedience to the king, which leads to the king's order to punish the Jews, the familial link that exists between Esther and Mordechai, the gift of a royal robe and the reinstatement of Mordechai, bear striking similarities to Herodotus's story of Xerxes and Artaynte. Here the narrative elements are the chided queen Amestris and the 'new queen' Artaynte, who takes, or at least claims, her place, the familial relationship between Artaynte and Masistes, the gift of a robe demanded by, or given to, another family, the revolt staged by Masistes in Bactria and a plot to kill the king. Although Herodotus must have known about Xerxes's assassination in 465, he does not record it, and we must turn to Ctesias's *Persica* to complete Xerxes's story. Ctesias records that Xerxes was killed in a palace coup by two courtiers, Artabanus and Mithridates. Thus it is possible that the historical event of Xerxes's murder was used as a starting point for the story of Esther.

Some scholars suggested that Herodotus's story amalgamates strands of different stories into one. In historical reality, Xerxes's alleged affair and Masistes's rebellion may have been two distinctive events occurring at different periods in Xerxes's reign. It is possible that Masistes's rebellion occurred towards the end of Xerxes's reign, or perhaps at the onset of Artaxerxes's reign, as Ctesias reports. It may well have occurred in reaction to the murder of Xerxes and his heir Darius, with Masistes trying to seize the kingship from Artaxerxes. This is the point at which the transfer of the royal robe, symbolising the transferral of royal power, comes into play. In both Herodotus's narrative and the *Book of Esther*, the gift of the royal robe serves to enhance the status of another family. In Herodotus's version, it suffices to arouse the anger of the queen, yet at a political level, Xerxes's transferring the royal robe to a member of Masistes's family could signify that the latter laid claim to the kingship. In the *Book of Esther*, the robe, given as a gift to Mordechai, emphasises his standing with the king.

Yet, the most compelling argument to regard Herodotus's story as a template for the story of Esther is the similarity between Mordechai and Masistes. Both share a familial relationship to the king's mistress or the new queen, both are charged with disloyalty towards the king and subsequently are responsible for the punishment of a people, the rebelling Bactrians in the one, the Jews in the other version. Both men are, at some point, directly or indirectly, in possession of a royal robe. Above all, Mordechai's nomination as 'Second-after-the-King' matches precisely the meaning of the name Masistes (OP *maθista*) as 'the Second (or "Greatest") after the King'.

this image, Herodotus adheres to a literary structure of his narrative, namely to alternating his descriptions of the Persian kings from morally good king to morally bad king. Cyrus II and Darius I belong to the former category, Cambyses II and Xerxes I to the latter. This must be borne in mind when reading and evaluating his account of Xerxes. The means by which he does so include the depiction of irrational behaviour, such as the whipping of the Hellespont after a storm destroyed part of the bridge. One of his sacrileges was the destruction of the temple of Athena in Athens, an indication that Xerxes failed to respect foreign gods. He also mutilated the body of Leonidas, an act which echoes Cambyses's violation of the body of Amasis.

In fact, Xerxes I seemed to possess the same symptoms of 'madness' and *hybris* as Cambyses II: both are accused of disrespecting foreign religions, both commit sacrileges, both undertake military expeditions which cause their own ruin. For both kings, Herodotus uses the symbolism of crossing natural boundaries and thus showing contempt for the divine: Xerxes's crossing the Hellespont, Cambyses's invasion of Nubia and thus – in the Greek mind – transgressing the known world, 'overstepping' natural borders and therefore mocking the gods.

Against the accusation of sacrilege committed with the destruction of the temple of Athena stands Mardonius's peace offer to the Athenians, which included the rebuilding of the temple. The destruction of religious and civic buildings in the sacking of a city can also not exclusively be assigned to a Persian king, since we remember that the city of Sardis, including the temple of Cybele, was destroyed in a fire during the Ionian Revolt. Yet, in order to convey the image of a mad Persian king, interjecting anecdotes of Xerxes's alleged disrespect for foreign religions is essential for Herodotus's narrative tone. That we must employ caution before accepting his view of Xerxes has been demonstrated in the false accusation of Xerxes's sacrilege in Babylon where he allegedly removed the statue of the city-god Marduk. 'Outside the temple (= of Marduk/Bel in Babylon) is a golden altar, as well as another great altar, on which fully grown victims are sacrificed. On the golden altar only sucklings may be sacrificed, but on the larger altar the Chaldaeans (= Babylonians) yearly offer frankincense weighing a thousand talents when they celebrate the feast of this god. In the time of Cyrus, there was still in the precinct a statue of a man (Gr. *andrias*), 12 cubits high (= 6m), and made of solid gold. I did not see it myself, but I repeat what the Chaldaeans told me. Darius son of Hystaspes intended to remove this statue, but did not dare; but Xerxes son of Darius did take it and killed the priest who tried to prevent him' (Hdt.I.183.2–3). Yet closer scrutiny of this passage has changed the superficial assumption of sacrilege. First of all, statues of divinities were displayed in the inner part of the temple, not in the temple precinct. Secondly, the Greek text referring to the moved statue uses the word *andrias*, a term which is used to describe statues of mortals as well as divinities, whereas *agalma* explicitly only refers to a divine statue. Accordingly, it is by no means a foregone conclusion that the statue Xerxes removed from the precinct was that of a divinity, in this case, Marduk; it could well have been that of a former Babylonian king or a rebel king. Herodotus's claim that Darius I – who is not associated with committing any sacrileges – had already attempted to remove that statue may further support the argument that it represented a human figure. In any case, the reproach against Xerxes of committing a sacrilege must be dismissed.

8.2.10   The Beginning of the Myth

Immediately after the Persian War, it was Sparta, not Athens, that held the leadership of the Greeks, as their fighting at Salamis and Plataea defined what Jan Assman has called 'das kulturelle Gedächtnis', 'the cultural memory'. The term describes the collective knowledge of a group or an entire society through which it defines itself, its development and historical roots, and from which it draws self-confidence, consciousness about its character, identity and the stability of its time. This cultural memory feeds a society's outlook on its surroundings, its values and norms. It creates the identity of a group and ensures its constant reassertion. It does so through different means, mainly by constantly nurturing the event that created this identity. Writing its own history is one way of achieving it, visual presentation in art and architecture of the event another way, and finally, feast days which commemorate the event a further means. The Persian Wars were *the* event in Greek history that led to the establishment of such a collective memory. Initially, Marathon, the battle fought solely by the Athenians without Spartan support, took a back seat in comparison to Salamis and Plataea. Even Thermopylae, where mostly Spartan forces had fought, was acknowledged. The poet Simonides described the burial site of those who fell at Thermopylae as 'altar' (fr.531 PMG). But eventually, it was Salamis that came to embody Athens's fight against Persia. In Aeschylus's tragedy, the conflict between Greeks and Persians was reduced to a single battle – Salamis. It, too, was given a religious dimension when Themistocles declared after the Greek victory: 'Not we have accomplished this but the gods and the heroes' (Hdt.VIII.109.3). In laying the emphasis on Marathon and Salamis, Athens went to some lengths to claim that she was the sole victor over Persia. Around 460, the s*toa poikile*, a place for meeting and discussion built in Athens, was decorated with a painting of an Amazonomachia, a battle between the Amazons, as the embodiment of the people from the east, and Theseus, the most important hero of Athens. It was a figurative image which symbolised the battle of the Athenians against the Persians at Marathon. It became a prominent scene on Athenian pottery of the fifth century, and received official sanctioning with the dedication of Amazon statues in the Artemisium in Ephesus.

In addition to the Amazonomachia, the *stoa poikile* depicted other scenes of battle, including the capture of Troy and Marathon itself (Paus.I.15), all reminders of victories of Greeks over foreigners. The Athenian victory at Marathon was placed above all others: 'As forefighters of the Hellenes did the Athenians at Marathon defeat the might of the gold-wearing Medes' (Simonides, Epigram XXI, Page). The Athenian statesman Pericles put all the men who fell for the city on a level with the immortal gods (Plut.*Per*.VIII.9). A cult of Pan the goat-god was created on account of a vision which had appeared to the long-distance runner Philippides on his way to summon Spartan help at the time of Marathon (Hdt.VI.105).

Marathon came to epitomise the fight of the Greeks against the barbarians, the fight for freedom against despotism and the defence of the west against the wilfulness of the east. The reason is not difficult to understand: Marathon was a victory solely achieved by the Athenian hoplite citizens, which ensured the memory of a collective event by definition. Apart from the contemporary means of memory, such as the statue of Nike, Victory, dedicated by Kallimachus in Athens, epigrams inscribed on bases of marble found in Athens, the dedication of Persian spoils at the Treasury of Delphi, Miltiades's spoils offered to Zeus at Olympia, including a bronze helmet in Assyrian style with has been established, but afterwards it happened to others one by one' (Thuc.I.98.4). By c.470, Cyprus was back under Persian control, but Greek skirmishes in Asia Minor continued. At an unknown date between 469 and 462 the Greeks eliminated a large Persian fleet on the Eurymedon River: 'When the Persians began to assemble a large fleet, Cimon went with Athenian and allied ships, forced Phaselis to join the Delian League and continued east of the Eurymedon River in Pamphylia, where he destroyed the Persian ships in the mouth of the river and then landed and sacked their camp; then he marched further east to defeat Persian enforcements coming from Cyprus. This was a major campaign, in which 200 Persian ships were destroyed' (Thuc.I.110.1). Cimon also undertook a campaign against the Persians and Thracians in the Chersonnese, between the battle at the Eurymedon and the Thasian War.

While the 'Median War' had a considerable effect on the political and ideological attitudes in Athens, it was of little or no consequence to the stability of the Persian empire and to the kingship of Xerxes, who ruled until his death in 465. The defeats at Salamis and Plataea did not lead to any repercussions in the empire. No attempt at rebellion is reported that might have taken the opportunity of the Persian defeat to defect from the empire, nor was there anybody at court contesting Xerxes's authority after the war.

Sources in Translation 8.2

Xerxes's daiva-*Inscription (XPh)*

The tracks to identify Xerxes's religious intolerance having already been set by Herodotus, his accusation seemingly found first-hand confirmation in Xerxes's own inscription from Persepolis, which is known as the *daiva*-inscription (XPh), named after the *daivas*, or daemons, mentioned in the text. The inscription has given rise to the discussion about a possible change in Achaemenid religious policy. It has been suggested that it may reflect Xerxes's reaction to the revolts in Babylon as the land 'which was in commotion'. But while there is evidence of political measures Xerxes took to curb the power of the members of the Babylonian elite after 484, there is no evidence for any change in his religious policy towards Babylonia. In actual fact, the inscription is primarily concerned with a royal *caveat*, a caution, to uphold the law (OP *data*). This may be suggested on the grounds that Xerxes formulates the same generic sentiments we find expressed in Darius's Bisitun Inscription when he condemns the rebellious countries of Elam and Scythia, declaring: '[t]hose Elamites were disloyal and Auramazda was not worshipped by them. I worshipped Auramazda. By the favour of Auramazda, as (was) my desire, so I treated them' (DB col.V §72), and which are identically stated for the Scythians three paragraphs later. The attitude expressed in both texts is that a country's rebellion against the king is synonymous with a rebellion against Auramazda, synonymous with following the Lie, not the Order. Or, to put it in a different way, if a country does not follow Auramazda, it is not following the king. This is what Xerxes's inscription declared, and thus it merely used a more explicit wording than that used by Darius, but expressed the same sentiments.

§1. Auramazda is a great god, who created this earth, who created the sky, who created man, who created happiness for man, who made Xerxes king, one king of many, one lord of many.

§2. I am Xerxes, the Great King, king of kings, king of countries containing many men, king of this great earth far and wide, son of Darius the king, an Achaemenid, a Persian, son of a Persian, an Aryan, son of Aryan lineage.

§3. Xerxes the king says: 'By the favour of Auramazda these are the countries of which I am king outside Persia. I ruled over them, they brought me tribute, they did what I told them. My law (OP *data*) held them firm: Media, Elam, Arachosia, Armenia, Drangiana, Parthia, Aria, Bactria, Sogdiana, Chorasmia, Babylonia, Assyria, Sattagydia, Sardis, Egypt, Ionians – those who dwell by the sea, and those who dwell across the sea – men of Maka, Arabia, Gandara, Sind, Cappadocia, Dahae, Amyrgian Scythians, pointed-cap Scythians, Skudra, men of Akaufka, Libyans, Carians, Ethiopians.'

§4. Xerxes the king says: 'When I became king, there was one among these countries which are inscribed above, (one which) was in commotion. Afterwards Auramazda brought me aid. By the favour of Auramazda I struck that country and subdued it.

§5. Among these countries there was a place where previously demons (OP *daivas*) had been worshipped. Afterwards, by the favour of Auramazda, I destroyed that sanctuary of demons, and I made a proclamation: "The demons had been worshipped." Where previously the demons had been worshipped, there I worshipped Auramazda in accordance with Truth reverently.

§6. And there were other matters which had been done badly. These I made good. All that I did, I did by the favour of Auramazda. Auramazda brought me aid until I had completed the work.

§7. You, who will be there after me, if you think: "Happy may I be when living, and when dead may I be blessed", have respect for the law which Auramazda has established, and worship Auramazda in accordance with Truth reverently. The man who has respect for the law which Auramazda has established and worships Auramazda in accordance with Truth reverently becomes both happy while living and blessed when dead.'

§8. Xerxes the king says: 'May Auramazda protect me from harm, and my royal house, and this land. This I pray of Auramazda, this may Auramazda give me.'

8.3 Artaxerxes I

8.3.1 The Death of Xerxes I and the Succession of Artaxerxes I

The assassination of Xerxes and of the designated heir to the throne, Darius, in a palace coup in 465, caused a succession struggle which was won by a son only known by his throne name, Artaxerxes I, which means 'he who reigns through Arta'. Xerxes's

Special Topic 8.2

Persian Diplomacy in Asia Minor

Athens's control over her allies was soon threatened. Naxos attempted rebellion, as did Thasos in 465: 'Thasos revolted because of a dispute over trading posts and mines on the Thracian mainland, which were controlled by Thasos but coveted by Athens. The Thasians turned to Sparta for help, and Sparta wanted to distract Athens by invading Attica. However, they were held up by an earthquake and a revolt of the helots which followed it, and no invasion took place. In the third year of the dispute, Thasos was to demolish her city walls, surrender her warships and mainland possessions, presumably to Athens, and pay an indemnity and tribute.' (Thuc.I.100.2–101). The same fate awaited Aegina. The island was forced to join the Delian League in 458 and had to demolish her walls and surrender her warships.

In Asia Minor, too, Ionian cities began to resent Athenian dominance. A first resistance came from Erythrae, where upheaval began in 453/2 and from where about two years later Erythraean exiles fled to the Persian king. In reaction to her rebellion, Athens imposed regulations on the city, recorded in the decree of Erythrae of 451/0, including the establishment of a Council of 120, under the auspices of Athenian *episkopoi*, overseers, and a *phrouarchos*, a garrison commander. The council was forced to swear an oath of allegiance, promising not to revolt and not to take back those who had fled to the Medes, that is, the Persians. 'Nor shall I desert either on my own initiative nor shall I be persuaded by anyone else, not anyone. Nor shall I receive back any of the exiles either on my own initiative nor shall I be persuaded by anyone else. Of those who fled to the Medes without the assent of the Athenians and of the People, I shall not banish those who remained in Erythrae without the assent of the Athenians and the People.' (Meiggs and Lewis 1988: 89–94, no. 40: ll.24–29). The decree was a reaction to previous events during which a pro-Persian faction had revolted with Persian support, and sought refuge in Persian territory when Athens had regained control over Erythrae. The city paid for this attempt with an imposed democracy under the watchful eye of the Athenian officials there. Persia may only have offered passive support for the rebellion, but this incident exemplifies that the empire was willing to support Greek cities rebelling against Athenian imperial power.

About 10 years later, a similar observation can be made in regard to Samos, where, in 441, a conflict between Miletus and Samos forced Samian exiles to seek refuge with Pissouthnes the satrap of Sardis. He was the son of Hystaspes, who most likely is to be identified with the son of Darius I. With 700 troops, Pissouthnes restored order in Samos. When Samos revolted from Athens in c.440/39 she handed over Athenian officials operating on Samos to Pissouthnes. In the end, Samos was defeated by the Athenian navy, but both Erythrae and Samos provide evidence that Greek cities were willing to seek the protection of Persia.

Erythrae had been a member of the Delian League, but as the inscription of 453/2 makes amply clear, it was an unhappy ally. Forty years later, in 413/12, Erythrae was among the first cities to rebel against Athens. When she came under pressure from Sparta, the city accepted the offer of autonomy from the Persian satrap of Hellespontine Phrygia, Pharnabazus, and from Conon in 394. In this context, Erythrae honoured Conon as benefactor and *proxenos*. By c.390, however, Athens had regained control over the Aegean and Erythrae: 'It shall not be permitted to any of the generals to make a reconciliation with those on the Acropolis without the consent of the people of Athens; nor shall it be permitted to anyone to reinstate in Erythrae any of the exiles whom the Erythraeans drive out, without the consent of the people of Erythrae. Concerning not giving up Erythrae to the barbarians, reply to the Erythraeans that it has been resolved by the people of Athens (...)' (transl. Rhodes and Osborne 2003: no. 17).

Athens was setting the terms of political negotiations, and was emphatic about not allowing the 'barbarians', that is, the Persians, to take control of Erythrae. This section of the inscription has been interpreted to mean that this was an Athenian response to an earlier communication from Erythrae, which did not want to be 'given up to the barbarians'. Yet this interpretation is based on the mere assumption that such a request had in fact been made by some Erythraeans to Athens. Such a plea does not square with the evidence that Erythrae had wanted to leave the Delian League, and had rebelled twice against Athens. Under these circumstances, it is not likely that Erythrae would have welcomed Athenian control when it reappeared in 390. In contrast, there is no evidence to suggest that any pressure was exerted by Persia on the city, for which Erythrae would be seeking protection from Athens. Resentment towards Athenian or Spartan control was more explicitly expressed than for any involvement with the 'barbarian'. Perhaps the phrase, 'not giving up Erythrae to the barbarians' ought to be understood to mean that the Erythraeans had requested to be allowed to leave the League and join Persia, and that Athens had responded by saying that they were not going to hand Erythrae over to the 'barbarians'. Accordingly, the present text would provide a further argument to that effect. Looking ahead, this is what happened in the early fourth century: Athens ceded Erythrae to Persia in the King's Peace of 386.

An inscription dated sometime between 391 and 388 records a lawsuit, with the involvement of the Persian authority only at the point of solving an impasse. Within Greek–Persian diplomatic relations, this inscription probably shows Persian diplomacy at its best. It records a conflict over borderland between Miletus and Myus, but when Myus abandoned the suit, the matter was relegated to the Persian satrap of Ionia, Struses. The jurors were representatives from Erythrae, Clazomenae, Lebedos and Ephesos: 'When the Mysians had abandoned the suit, Struses, the satrap of Ionia, heard the Ionians' jurors and made the final decision that the land should belong to the Milesians' (transl. Rhodes and Osborne 2003, no. 16: ll.40–44). It is a rare example of diplomacy operating on a small scale and in a non-rebelling context: While the legal set-up followed the practice of Greek law courts, the Ionian jurors sought the final verdict on the case by appealing to the legal institution at next level higher up, the Persian satrap of Ionia. The inscription lends support to the argument that Persia's dealing with the Ionian cities, including Erythrae, seems to have been low-key. This also weakens the argument for Erythrae pleading with Athens not to hand her to the barbarian, for which we need reasons for resentment – political pressure, interference in local politics, fear – traits we find in Erythrae's relationship with Athens (and Sparta for that matter), but which we cannot discern from the literary and epigraphical records for Erythrae's relationship with Persia.

8.3.5   The Peace of Callias

With her limited military success in Cyprus and the growing resentment from Ionian cities, Athens was prepared to enter peace negotiations with Persia. The historic agreement meant that Athens ceased to interfere in Cyprus and Egypt, while the Persian king agreed that the Persian navy would stay clear of the Aegean coast. The question is why did either side agree to the peace? Greek sources claim that Persian morale had eroded due to Athenian actions in Cyprus. But it equally could be argued that the Persian king's priority was to keep control of Egypt, and that his forces were required there. In addition, the crucial concession that the king kept control over the lands in Ionia, matches precisely what he wanted before; tribute payments were not renounced by the king, not even for Ionia.

> [T]he Athenians and their allies concluded with the Persians a treaty of peace, the principal terms of which run as follows: All the Greek cities of Asia are to live under laws of their own making; the satraps of the Persians are not to come nearer to the sea than a three days' journey and no Persian warship is to sail inside of Phaselis or the Cyanean Rocks (= the place where the Bosporus and the Black Sea join); and if these terms are observed by the king and his generals, the Athenians are not to send troops into the territory over which the king is ruler. After the treaty had been solemnly concluded, the Athenians withdrew their armaments from Cyprus, having won a brilliant victory and concluded most noteworthy terms of peace. (Diod.Sic.XII.4.5–6)

Over the next decades, resentment against the Athenian empire grew across Greece, the Peloponnese and Asia Minor. At the outbreak of the Peloponnesian War in 431, Sparta sent envoys to Persia asking for aid, followed swiftly by an Athenian delegation. Both were refused. Meanwhile Pissouthnes had entered an alliance with exiles from Samos on account of their resistance towards an Athenian imposed democracy and took control of the Athenian garrison and magistrates there while the rebellion was successful. In 430, shortly after the outbreak of the Peloponnesian War, Colophon had been taken by Itamenes, a subordinate of Pissouthnes and the Persians. Fleeing to Notium, the Colophonians bought in Arcadian and Persian mercenaries, whom they had obtained from Pissouthnes, and kept them in a space walled off from the rest of the city. They were taken and killed by the Athenian admiral Paches. In 427, Ionian exiles and the people of Lesbos tried to win over the Spartan Alcidas in their attempt to bring Ionia to revolt against Athens and to get the support of Pissouthnes (Thuc.III.31). As has been pointed out by David Lewis, Pissouthnes's actions bordered on a breach of the Peace of Callias, but it could be argued that he was only meddling in Greek *stasis*, strife. Still, diplomatically he was walking a fine line.

8.3.6   Judaea Under Artaxerxes I

According to the *Book of Ezra*, troubles in Judaea had begun under Xerxes (Ezra IV.4–6), and flared up again when neighbouring inhabitants of Judaea objected to the rebuilding of the temple in Jerusalem. Opponents of the temple project, Rehum and Shimshai wrote a letter to the king accusing the Jews of rebuilding a rebellious city, with city-walls and repaired foundations. They feared that, were the city to be completed, the payment of revenues from this region would cease. In response, Artaxerxes brought the rebuilding of Jerusalem to a halt (Ezra IV.17–24). Artaxerxes I then appointed the priest and scholar Ezra to undertake a mission to Jerusalem to ensure that the Jewish laws were upheld. The text dates this mission to the seventh year of Artaxerxes, traditionally identified with Artaxerxes I, thus dating his arrival in Jerusalem to 459/8. Ezra travelled from Babylon to Judaea with a letter from the king (Ezra VIII.1–12; 12–26). A few years later, Nehemiah, the cup-bearer of Artaxerxes I, went on a royal mission to Jerusalem, where he then served as governor of Judaea, probably between 445 and 432.

8.3.7   Continuity in Persepolis

As successor to Xerxes, Artaxerxes I sought to continue his father's policy in the empire. This is best expressed in the continuation of Xerxes's building projects in Persepolis, completing the Hundred Column Hall and Xerxes's palace: 'I am Artaxerxes, Great King, king of kings, king of lands, king of this great earth far and wide, son of king Xerxes, son of Darius, the Achaemenid. Artaxerxes, the Great King proclaims: "With the protection of Auramazda this palace which my father, king Xerxes, made, I completed it"' (A¹Pa). And, like his predecessors, Artaxerxes had his tomb carved alongside those of his predecessors at Naqsh-e Rustam.

8.4   Succession Trouble in 424

The death of Artaxerxes I and his wife Damaspia probably occurred late in 424. But it was following the murder of the king's son and heir Xerxes II after only 45 days of rule that the empire was plunged into a series of rebellions. As these occurred shortly after the accession of Artaxerxes's son Umasu (Gr. Ochus), it seems that the problem centred on his contested succession. Babylonian tablets point to December 424 as the time of Artaxerxes's death and note the accession of Umasu, who took the throne name Darius II, by February 423. Prior to his kingship, Darius II had been satrap of Hycarnia. But, most importantly, he and his brother Arsites were not sons of the Persian queen Damaspia, but of the Babylonian Cosmartidene. This mixed descent allowed Greek sources to give him the epithet *nothos*, bastard. Darius had married his half-sister Parysatis, the daughter of a Babylonian lady called Andria. She most likely descended from a high-ranking Babylonian family; Parysatis herself could boast ownership of estates there, attested in several Babylonian documents. Greek sources locate others in Transeuphratene. Her marriage to Darius II produced four sons. The oldest, Arsaces, had been born when Darius was still satrap of Hyrcania, while Cyrus the Younger, Ostanes and Oxathres were born 'to the purple', that is, after Darius had been proclaimed king. One daughter, named Amestris, is also known. Darius's line was to continue the Achaemenid Dynasty, since, by default, one of his sons would succeed to the throne – a fact that may have caused resentment among the Persian nobility and may account for the troubled reign of Darius II. If nothing else, it shows how precarious the period of the transition of power was, how important the births of royal sons from a Persian noble woman and how a lack of eligible sons could throw the succession into turmoil. In the absence of a 'proper' Achaemenid heir, the remaining half-brothers all claimed the same right to the throne.

According to Ctesias, Sogdianus, a son of Artaxerxes with the Babylonian Alogune, declared himself king immediately after Artaxerxes's death. With a view to eliminating his half-brother and rival to the throne, Ochus, he summoned him to the court. Arriving with a large army and the support of the head of the cavalry as well as that of Arsites, the satrap of Egypt, and Artoxares, satrap of Armenia, Ochus was proclaimed king. Sogdianus was imprisoned and died shortly afterwards. Ctesias gives his reign as six and a half months. Yet neither this sequence of events nor the timeline is borne out in the Near Eastern sources. As stated above, Babylonian administrative documents date the death of Artaxerxes I and the accession of Darius II sometime between December 424 and February 423, the latest document for Artaxerxes I being dated to 24 December 424, and the first document for Darius II being dated to 10 January 423. That Darius's reign immediately followed that of Artaxerxes is also indicated by the fact that his accession year is equated with Artaxerxes's forty-first year. The only possibility is that Sogdianus staged a revolt, followed by that of Arsites, shortly after the beginning of Darius's reign. Babylonian documents attest that the king called out his feudal levies to Uruk in 422/1, a fact that may hint at these upheavals.

Sources in Translation 8.3

Levies in Babylonia

Archives from Babylonia attest to the tight link between the Persian elite and local entrepreneurs. The most notable amongst these is the archive of the Murashu family based in Nippur (454–404). Other archives belonged to Belshunu in Babylon (426–400), who is known in Greek sources as Belesys, and Tattannu in Borsippa (505–402), who has been identified with Tattenai mentioned in the Book of Ezra. The Murashu family conducted businesses with landowners and farmers, and also granted land to individuals who thus were tied to tax payments and military service. Several of the Babylonian documents from Nippur attest to the fact that Uruk served as a key military point at which archers, horsemen and chariot-riders were ordered to meet. The texts do not give a specific reason for the gathering, so it is not clear whether this occurred as a regular exercise or whether there was a particular military reason to muster an army there in 422/1. The *hatru* comprised holders of government land grants on which military service was owed. The reference to bow-land most likely means that these men were to serve as archers. If their service was not required, the men worked the land, but had to do their military service the moment they were called.

Text 1

80 gur dates, belonging to Rimut-Ninurta, descendant of Murashu, are owed by Hannani and Gubbaia, the sons of Ninurta-etir, Nadin and Arad-enlil, sons of Sa'ga' of the *hatru* of the Shushanu-mar-hisanni. In the month 7 of Year 3 of king Darius, they will deliver the 80 gur dates in the town of Hambari. The field planted with trees and fallow, which constitutes their bow-land in the town of Hambari, is surety for Rimut-Ninurta for the 80 gur dates. No other creditor has priority, so long as Rimut-Ninurta has not been paid his loan. They guarantee that the one nearest (to the place of payment) will pay for the others. The dates are equivalent to the silver which has been lent to them for clothing and military equipment for presenting themselves at Uruk. (*Witnesses, place, date*) (BE X no. 61, transl. Kuhrt 2010: 716, no. 31 (ii)).

Text 2

Gadalyma son of Rahim-ili, spoke of his own free will to Rimut-Ninurta son of Murashu, as follows:

'Because Rahim-ili adopted your brother Enlil-shum-iddina, you now possess the
  share of Barik-ili in the field planted and in stubble, held in tenure as horse-
  land by Rahim-ili. (Now),
1 horse together with its reins and harness
1 *suhattu* coat
1 iron corselet with 1 hood
1 neck-cover of the *suhattu*
1 hood of the *suhattu*
1 quiver of copper
120 arrows, some with heads, some without
1 sword(?) with its scabbard
2 iron lances
and 1 mina of silver for provisions,

give me (so that) I may go to Uruk in fulfilment of the royal order and (in return for this) I will fulfil the duty which rests on the horse-land as much as is your share.'

Upon (this) Rimut-Ninurta heard him, 1 horse and the battle equipment, all as it has been written down above, and 1 mina of silver for travel provisions he gave him; so that, in accordance with the royal command, he will go to Uruk to fulfil the duty of the horse-land mentioned.

The guarantee not to give this to someone else is borne by Gadalyma. Gadalyma will show it for registration by Zabin, the foreman of the scribes of the army. To Rimut-Ninurta, the son of Murashu, he will give (the deed of registration as proof).

(*Witnesses, scribe, place, date*) (Lutz 1928; transl. Kuhrt 2010: 722–723, no. 38)

8.4.1   Rebellions in the Empire

A further rebellion ensued at an uncertain date. It was led by Pissouthnes, satrap of Sardis, who had the support of an unspecified number of Greek mercenaries under the command of the Athenian Lycon. Perhaps this revolt, too, occurred early in Darius II's reign in reaction to his accession to the throne. However, some scholars have dated the rebellion to 416/5, which would make it less plausible that its reasons were connected with Darius's succession to the throne. It is also not clear how far Pissouthnes's aspirations went, but, as a grandson of Darius I, he might have considered himself more legitimate than his half-Babylonian uncles. Darius II ordered Tissaphernes to quash the rebellion and Pissouthnes was killed. Some years later, probably around 413, Pissouthnes's son Amorges staged a revolt in Caria with the support of Athenian ships. This rebellion, too, was put down, and Tissaphernes was awarded the satrapal office at Sardis.

There was more trouble to come. In c.415 a Phoenician named Abdemon seized the throne of Salamis on Cyprus, most likely with the allegiance of Darius II, and remained in office until 411, when Evagoras usurped his throne. A Median rebellion was put down in 407, as was the one staged by the Cadusians two years later. The Cadusians, a mountain people, were unwilling subjects of the Persian king. Their rebellion was quashed by a Persian army led by Darius II's son Cyrus the Younger; the Cadusians next were seen fighting on the king's side in 404/3 under the leadership of Artagerses against Cyrus the Younger, only to rebel again during Artaxerxes II's reign and that of his successor Artaxerxes III, who sent Ochus, the future king Darius III, against them.

8.4.2   The Royal Building Programme Continued

Despite the internal revolts, Darius II manifested himself as royal successor in a building inscription at Susa, and continued the building of another palace (OP *hadish*) there, which his father had begun: 'This palace of stone in its columns Darius the Great King built. May Auramazda together with the gods protect Darius the Great King' (D²Sa). And: 'Says Darius the king: This palace Artaxerxes previously built, who was my father; this palace I built afterwards (to completion) by the favour of Auramazda' (D²Sb: §1–2). In Egypt, a cartouche of Darius II carved on the Hibis temple el-Khargeh may point to his activities there.

8.4.3   Persia Re-enters Greek Politics

In regard to the empire's foreign policy, Darius II's most important achievement was the re-establishment of diplomatic relationships between Sparta and Persia, expressed in the bilateral treaty of 411. Persian involvement in Greek political affairs began in the summer of 412, when a first treaty was concluded between Sparta and Tissaphernes, satrap of Lydia since 415 and *karanos*, the military commander, of Asia Minor. This treaty, known in Greek sources as the treaty of Chalcideus after the Spartan general who participated in the negotiations, assured the king's claim that the land and cities of Asia Minor which the king or his predecessors held were his. The tribute payments to Athens were to cease; Sparta and the Persian king assured one another of their common enemies and their mutual assistance in war.

> The Spartans and their allies made a treaty of alliance with the King and Tissaphernes on the following terms: All the territory and all the cities held now by the King or held in the past by the King's ancestors shall be the King's. As for the money and everything else that has been coming in to the Athenians from their cities, the King and the Spartans and their allies shall co-operate in preventing the Athenians from receiving the money or anything else.
> The war on the Athenians shall be carried on jointly by the King and the Spartans and their allies. It shall not be permitted to bring the war with the Athenians to an end unless both parties are agreed, the King on his side, the Spartans and their allies on theirs. Any people who revolt from the King shall be regarded as enemies by the Spartans and their allies; and any people who revolt from the Spartans and their allies shall, in the same way, be regarded as enemies of the King. (Thuc.VIII.18)

Spartan dithering about this proposal led to an amendment in the winter of 412/11 under Therimenes, which in principle did not differ much from the first version. On the Persian side, the king's sons and Tissaphernes were now included in what the Spartans called a 'treaty of friendship'. The term *spondai*, which means the termination of hostilities, was inserted into the text and indicated that the Spartans had realised they technically were still at war with Persia, since they had not been included in the peace treaty of Callias. The Spartan concessions to Persia must have violated any diplomatic convention. It is not clear which cities and lands were meant in the treaty, and strictly speaking they could have included territory on the Greek mainland that had accepted the king's superiority in wider Greece, including Macedon and Thrace.

When the exiled Athenian politician Alcibiades, who had placed himself in Spartan service and in 413 had enticed Chios, Erythrae and Miletus to rebel against Athens, came under suspicion from the Spartans, he fled the country and found refuge at the court of Tissaphernes in Sardis. Here he tried to persuade the satrap to place his trust in the Athenians, not the Spartans. Under the circumstances, a seemingly odd decision, but perhaps Alcibiades expected that this might stave off Athenian defeat, while also hoping that his success in such negotiations would cause Athens to revoke his exile and allow him to return. In order to enhance Athens's chances for that support, Alcibiades schemed to topple the Athenian government and change the constitution there. To that end, he met some powerful men in Samos while the politician Pisander was sent as envoy to Athens in late December 411 with the message that the only hope for the Athenians was to trust Alcibiades and procure Persian help. Near the end of the winter, a conference took place including Tissaphernes and an Athenian delegation. When, in a third session of this meeting, the suggestion was put forward that the king be allowed complete freedom of shipbuilding and naval movement along his own coast, the Athenian ambassadors broke off the negotiations and returned to Samos. In consequence, Tissaphernes turned back to the Spartans and the treaty was finally concluded in the summer of 411 between Tissaphernes, Hieramenes and the sons of Pharnaces and the Spartans and their allies.

8.4.4   The Bilateral Treaty of 411

In the 13th year of the reign of Darius, in the ephorate of Alexippidas of Sparta, a treaty was made in the plain of the Maeander by the Spartans and their allies with Tissaphernes, Hieramenes and the sons of Pharnaces, concerning the interest of the King and the interests of the Spartans and their allies.

The country of the King in Asia shall be the King's, and the King shall take what measures he pleases with regard to his own country. The Spartans and their allies shall not go against the King's country with any hostile intent; nor shall the King go against the country of the Spartans and their allies with any hostile interest. If any of the Spartans and their allies makes an attack on the King's country, the Spartans and their allies are to prevent it; and if anyone from the King's country makes an attack on the country of the Spartans or their allies, the King is to prevent it.

Tissaphernes shall provide pay, as under the existing agreement, for the ships now present, until the arrival of the King's ships, and the Spartans and their allies may, if they wish, make themselves responsible for the payment of their own ships. But if they prefer to receive their pay from Tissaphernes, Tissaphernes is to provide it, and at the end of the war the Spartans and their allies are to repay to him the money which they shall have received.

After the arrival of the King's ships, the fleet of the Spartans and their allies and the King's fleet shall act together in carrying on the war in the way it seems best to Tissaphernes and to the Spartans and their allies. If they wish to make peace with the Athenians, the two parties shall each have their say in the peace. (Thuc. VIII.58)

The meeting of the two parties at the Maeander River is probably reflected in a Lycian inscription from Xanthos erected in honour of the Lycian dynast Kheriga (Gr. Gergis, ruled c.410–400):

The Spartans(?) ... began(?) to ... Tissaphernes ... son of Hydarnes and the Persians in Kaunos and in alliance with Spartialia against Athens they (= the Persians) fought the army. I became judge for them. They issued a double guarantee(?). Both in Hytenna a stele shall be set down for (the goddess) Maliya, in place (or: on the spot) ... the fighters(?) ... And in Kaunos likewise a stela shall be put down for the local precinct and for Maliya and for (the goddess) Artemis and for the King of Kaunos. (TAM I, 44 b.64–c9; transl. Kuhrt 2010: 339, no. 29)

The crucial insertion in the final version of the Treaty of Lichas concerns the payment for ships. The Spartan navy now was entitled to draw finances from Tissaphernes's personal funds; the shared view was to continue the war with Athens unless both Sparta and Athens would be willing to make peace. We also should take note of the mentioning of the king's fleet, that is, the Phoenician fleet, which, for the first time since 480/79, was, in this case in theory, employed for potential use in the Aegean against a Greek state. However, this fleet never materialised. Its mentioning, it has been suggested, may have simply been a ploy to speed up the negotiation process.

Still Athens remained a successful naval power until at least 407, when the battle at Notium was fought. Her victory meant that the Athenians even allowed their prodigal son Alcibiades to return from exile. Athenian collaboration with Persia had started when Pharnabazus, satrap of Hellspontine Phrygia at Dascyleium, offered aid to the Athenians in 411 when they fought Mindarus at Abydus (Xen.*Hell*.I.1.6.14; I.2.16). In 408,

Pharnabazus made an agreement with Alcibiades to provide 20 talents for Athens and lead an embassy to the king (Xen.*Hell*.I.3.9). Greek sources place great emphasis on a rivalry between Pharnabazus, supporting the Athenians, and Tissaphernes, favouring the Spartans, but the question is what each satrap thought he would gain from his respective support. The king seemed to have left matters entirely in the hands of the western satraps, allowing the conclusion that whatever Tissaphernes and Pharnabazus decided was their own responsibility.

In this first phase, in which both Sparta and Athens were eager to gain favour with Persia, Darius II was more concerned with keeping his satraps under control than with which Greek state was to get his support. But to bring the rivalry between Pharnabazus and Tissaphernes to a halt, in 408/7 Darius II sent his son Cyrus the Younger to take overall military command as *karanos* and to lead the war together with the Spartiates (Xen.*Hell*.I.4.13). Consequently, Tissaphernes's sphere of influence was reduced to Caria. Spartan-Persian success continued in September 405 with a victory in the battle of Aigospotami, which finally led to the surrender of Athens in April/May 404.

Special Topic 8.3

Egypt and the Jewish Garrison at Elephantine

At the time of Darius's reign his uncle Arsames was satrap of Egypt. It is during his period of office that a set of 11 letters can be dated which Arsames wrote to Egyptian officials while staying in Babylon and Susa. This so-called Arsames correspondence provides a unique insight into the responsibilities and day-to-day workings of a satrapal administration (See Sources in Translation 7.1). It is also during Darius's rule, perhaps sometime before 418, that an Aramaic copy of the Bisitun Inscription was written on Elephantine. The island of Elephantine is located near the first cataract of the Nile, opposite the ancient city of Syene, which was the administrative centre of the region headed by a governor called *fratarak*. Syene enjoyed a cultural mix of people, as Persians, Medes, Babylonians and Assyrians as well as Phoenicians and Khorasmians lived in the city. The sanctuaries of their different religious cults are all attested in Syene. Elephantine was a strategic point on the border to Nubia and was guarded by a Jewish garrison, which served the Persian king between 495 and 400. The garrison commander was Vidranga; his son, Nafaina, also served in the administration. The Aramaic documents from Elephantine cover about one hundred years of the first Persian domination between 525 and 400. The earliest letters belong to members of the Makkibanit family, who wrote from Memphis to individuals in Luxor and Syene. Three private archives can be identified in the Elephantine documents: the communal archive of Jedoniah, which begins in 419 with an important text regulating the Passover decree and the decree of Unleavened Bread, and ends about 12 years later; the archive of the family of the woman Miptahiah, which covers 11 documents over a period of 60 years; and the family archive of a temple official called Ananiah.

In 410, the Jews of Elephantine lodged a complaint against the Egyptians and Vidranga, the governor of Syene, writing to the governor of Judaea, Bagohi (OP Bagavahya). The Jews confirmed that the administrator of the sanctuary of Khnum had made an agreement with Vidranga according to which they were to be given money and other goods; in consequence, the Egyptians did not allow the Jews to carry an oblation into the sanctuary, or to make a fire for their god, Yahweh. The Egyptians took vases and destroyed other objects of the sanctuary; thereupon the Jews of Elephantine demanded its restoration. A delegate was sent to the authorities at Jerusalem, to Yahohanan and his colleagues, the priests of Jerusalem, and to Ostana, brother of Hanani, and the notables of Judaea.

The 'Passover Decree' of 419/8

To my [brothers Je]daniah and his colleagues the J[ewish T[roop], your brother Hanan[i]ah.

The welfare of my brothers may gods [seek after at all times].

And now, this year, Year 4 of Darius the king Darius, from the king it has been sent to Arsa[mes...],

[...] ... Now, you, thus count four[teen days of Nisan and on the fourteenth at twilight the Passover ob]serve and from day 15 until day 21 of [Nisan the Festival of Unleavened Bread observe. Seven days unleavened bread eat.

Now] be pure and take heed. Work [do] n[ot do] [on day 15 and on day 21 of Nisan. Any fermented drink] do not drink. And anything of leaven do not [eat and do not let it be seen in your houses from day 14 of Nisan at] sunset until day 21 on Nisa[n at sunset. And any leaven which you have in your houses b]ring into your chambers and seal (them) up during [these] days. [...] ...

[To] (sealing) my brothers Jedeniah and his colleagues the Jewish Troop, your brother Hananiah s[on of PN]. (transl. Porten 2011: 126–127)

Three years later, they turned again towards Bagavahya, as well as to Dalaiah and Selemiah, sons of Sanballat, the governor of Samaria, complaining that their sanctuary had remained in ruins for three years. They asked Bagavahya to intervene in Egypt to request permission for them to continue with the rebuilding of the temple. Their letter, dated to 25 November 407, notes the absence of the Persian satrap Arsames from Egypt:

To [our] l[ord Bagavahya governor of Judah,] your servants Jedonia]h [the] pri[est and his colleagues the priests who are in Elephantine the fortress and the Jews, all (of them).

The welfare of our lord] may the God of Heav[en] seek after (abundantly) at all times, (and) favour may He g[ra]nt [you before Da]rius (II) the king [and the princes more than now {a thousand times}, and] long [life] may He give you, and happy and strong may you be at all times.

Now, your ser[va]nt Jedoniah [and his colleagues the priests and the Jews thus say:

'In the month of Tammuz, Year 14 of Darius the king (= 14 July – 13 August 410), when Arsames had departed and gone [to] the king, [then the priests of Khnum, the god who are at Elephantine] the fortress, silver and goods gave to Vidranga the governor who was here, sa[ying: "The Temple of YHW the god which is in Elephantine the fortress] let them remove from there." Afterwards that Vidranga, the wicked, a letter sent to Na[fai]na his son w[ho was troop commander in Syene the fortress, saying: "The Temple] of YHW the God which is Elephantine the fortress let them demolish."

Afterwards Nafaina led [the] Egypt[ians with the other troops. They came to the fortress of Elephantine with] their weapons, broke into that Temple, demolished it to the ground, and [the] pillars of s[tone which were three – they smashed them. Moreover, it happened (that the)] 5 great gateways, built of hewn stone, which were in that Temple, [they demolished. And their standing doors, and the pivots of] those [doors] (of) bronze, and the roof of that Temple, all (of it) wood o[f] cedar, [which] with the r[est of the fittings and other (things), which were there – all (of these) with the fire they burned. But the basins of gold and silver and the (other) t[h]ings wh[ich] were in that Temple – all (of these) they took (and)] made [their own].

And from the day(s) of the kings of Egypt our fathers had built that Temple in Elephantine [the] fo[rtress and when Cambyses entered Egypt] that [Temple] built he found. And the temples of the god[s] of the Egyptians [a]l[l (of [them), they overthrew], but any[thing in that Temple] one [did not damage. ...

Moreover, all] the(se) things (in) a letter in our name we sent to Delaiah and Shelemiah s[ons of Sanballat governor of Samaria.

Moreover, about this] all (of which) was done to us, all of it, Arsames did not know.

On the 20th of Marcheshvan, Year 14[+3 (= 17) of Darius the king.]' (transl. after Porten 2011: 147–149)

The permission was granted, and the Jews committed themselves to provide 1000 artabes of wheat to the house of Arsames. The text was written by a group of five male residents of Elephantine.

If our lord (= Arsames?) [...] and the Temple of YHW-the-God of ours be (re-)built in Elephantine the fortress as former[ly] it was [bu]ilt – and sheep, ox and goat (as) burnt offerings are [n]ot made here but (only) incense (and) meal-offering [they offer there] – and should our lord a statement mak[e about this afterwards] we shall give to the house of our lord si[lver ... and] barley, a thousa[nd] artabs. (transl. Porten 2011: 152–153)

8.5   Artaxerxes II

8.5.1   The War of the Brothers

Darius II died sometime between April 405 and April 404 in Babylon, having ruled for 25 years. The last Babylonian document dating to his reign was written on 17 September 405. His son Arsaces succeeded to the kingship, taking the throne name Artaxerxes II. The ceremony of his investiture is recorded by Plutarch and is a reminder of the kings' sense of continuity and their own place in the history of the empire, as the passage evokes the memory of the empire's founder, Cyrus II: '[The king (= Artaxerxes

II)] made an expedition to Pasargadae, that he might receive the royal initiation at the hands of the Persian priests. Here there is a sanctuary of a warlike goddess whom one might assume to be Athena. Into this sanctuary the candidate for initiation must enter, after laying aside his own proper robe, must put on that which Cyrus the Elder used to wear before he became king, then he must eat a cake of figs, chew some turpentine wood and drink a cup of sour milk. Whatever else is done besides this is unknown to outsiders' (Plut.*Art*.III.3).

But Artaxerxes II's reign was contested by Cyrus the Younger, who mustered an army, including 10 000 Spartan mercenaries, to fight his brother. Cyrus had been appointed satrap of Lydia by Darius II and had been made *karanos*, overall commander-in-chief in Asia Minor, in c.408/7. Before Darius's death, he had been summoned to the king's court alongside Tissaphernes, no doubt to clarify their respective positions of authority in Asia Minor. When Artaxerxes II succeeded to the throne, Cyrus had tried to assassinate him during his coronation (Plut.*Art*.III.3.5), but his attempt had failed because Tissaphernes had warned the king. Thereupon Cyrus had returned to Sardis, probably in the summer of 403, where he had tried to persuade the Ionian cities to rebel against the king. He asserted that Tissaphernes had designs on the cities of Asia Minor and that these, above all Miletus, ought to go over to him to fight Tissaphernes. Claiming that he had the king's best interest at heart, Cyrus was given his brother's permission to fight Tissaphernes. In addition, he received support from Sparta, who sent 700 hoplites under Cheirisophus, and a fleet. Cyrus also recruited 14 000 Greek mercenaries, commanded by different generals. Gathering his army at Sardis, Cyrus explained that they would fight against Pisidia, a region north of Lycia and bordering on Caria in the west. His army advanced via Colossae, the satrapal seat Celaenae, Peltae, Caystru Pedium, Thymbrium and Tarsus to the Euphrates at the height of Thapsacus. In Cilicia, he had received support of the *syennesis*, the title of the ruler of Cilicia, and his wife Epyaxa against his brother, a step which probably cost Cilicia its semi-independent status. Under Artaxerxes II, the traditional office of *syennesis* was abandoned and control over Cilicia was handed over to a satrap.

After arriving in Thapsacus, Cyrus revealed his true objectives for the march. Tissaphernes, meanwhile, had realised that Cyrus's army was far too large just to fight the Pisidians and warned Artaxerxes II of his brother's expedition. In contrast, the Greek historian Ephorus claimed that it was Pharnabazus who alerted the king to the dealings of Cyrus. In any case, Artaxerxes II was made aware of Cyrus's plans in sufficient time to gather an army against his brother.

Greek sources insist that Parysatis had fuelled the rift between the two brothers, favouring her younger son Cyrus, offering him every support in his rebellion. 'And the villages in which the troops (= of Cyrus) encamped belonged to Parysatis, for they had been given her for girdle-money. From there, Cyrus marched five stages, 30 *parasangs* to the sources of the Dardas River, the width of which is a *plethrum* (= c.30.50 m). There was the palace of Belesys, the late ruler of Syria (= Transeuphratene), and a very large and beautiful park containing all the products of the season. But Cyrus cut down the park and burned the palace' (Xen.*an*.I.4.10). This Belesys appears in contemporary Babylonian sources as Belshunu. Belshunu, son of Bel-usurshu, is attested as governor (Bab. *pihātu*) of Babylon between 421 and 414, and between 407 and 401 as governor of Transeuphratene. His particular appointment as Babylonian satrap must be noted, as it is a change from the traditional appointment of a member of the Persian royal family. It may not be a coincidence that this change occurred at the same point in time that we hear of high-ranking Babylonian women entering the Persian court as women of the palace, who could be married to the king's sons. Why Parysatis should have favoured Cyrus over Artaxerxes is difficult to ascertain. The argument brought forward that Arsaces/Artaxerxes had been born before Darius became king, while, in contrast, Cyrus was born 'to the purple', and was therefore the legitimate successor, does not convince, since in either case Parysatis's status as king's mother was assured.

The armies of Artaxerxes II and Cyrus the Younger clashed at Cunaxa, about 80 km north of Babylon, on 3 September 401. The site has been identified with modern Nasiffiyāt. The size of Artaxerxes's army is difficult to discern, as Greek sources notoriously exaggerate the numbers. Given at 1 200 000 troops, this figure appears to have been arrived at simply by multiplying the figures of Cyrus's army by 100. On the basis of the presence of four generals, each of whom commanded 10 000 men, the army probably consisted of 40 000 soldiers. According to Persian tradition, both Artaxerxes and Cyrus took centre position in their respective army. Although Cyrus had ordered Clearchus to manoeuvre to the left in order to come closer to the centre, Clearchus disobeyed. Instead of attacking Artaxerxes, he moved forward to pursue the Persian left flank for about 7 km. This resulted in a gap in Cyrus's army line, allowing the Persian cavalry to attack. Cyrus made a last attempt at attacking Artaxerxes directly, charging with his cavalry through the royal guards around the king, killing the guard commander and wounding Artaxerxes with his javelin. But he immediately was struck down by a Persian javelin that pierced his temple. His death decided the battle. If Greek sources are to be believed, in due course those responsible for his death were killed on the order of Parysatis. Artaxerxes restored Tissaphernes to the office of *karanos* in Asia Minor. He honoured his loyalty with royal gifts and appointed him King's Friend. He was also given a royal daughter in marriage, the highest token of esteem that could be bestowed upon a Persian noble.

8.5.2 Persian Affairs in Asia Minor

In the winter of 400–399, Tissaphernes marched on the cities of Asia Minor, a punitive action in retaliation for their support of the rebellion of Cyrus the Younger; his first target was Cyme. The cities, however, had asked the Spartans for aid; they sent Thibron at the head of a force of 1000 Spartiates plus more from their allies, amounting to a total of 5000 men. Again playing out the animosity between Tissaphernes and Pharnabazus, Thibron achieved a truce with Pharnabazus for six months. In 397, Tissaphernes was prepared to come to an agreement with the Spartan commander Dercyllidas; one obvious reason was that Tissaphernes did not want to risk the ravaging of his territory, Caria. Negotiations between the two leaders included the demand for the withdrawal of Spartan troops and the *harmosts*, Spartan military governors, who had been installed there since the Spartan admiral Lysander, and the autonomy of the Greek cities. Both men decided to consult the king and the Spartan government, respectively. At the same time, Pharnabazus wanted a maritime battle with Athenian support against Sparta.

Understandably, after Sparta's support for Cyrus the Younger at Cunaxa, Artaxerxes II had little time for the Spartans and instead was open for negotiations with Athens.

the king, saw Athens, Corinth and Argos follow suit. The conditions for the peace were refused by the Athenians. Thebes, too, found it difficult to accept the independence of Boeotia, while Argos was afraid to lose control over Corinth, and Athens feared the loss of Lemnos, Imbros and Scyros. The concessions Sparta had made with the Treaty of 411 had a bad effect on these aspirations, in particular in regard to the Aegean islands. Control over the Hellespont also could not have been a small matter, since the grain supply from the Black Sea was a vital lifeline for Athens. In this context, the Athenians must have regarded the Spartan-Egyptian alliance as rather threatening, as it gave them access to a superb fleet and an unlimited grain supply.

Tiribazus, the Persian negotiator in this attempt, was met with disapproval by the king and was replaced by the strongly pro-Athenian Strouthas. As long as Egypt was rebelling from the empire, Sparta was not an option as an ally. The Spartans, seeing their chances dwindle at the replacement, rather undiplomatically opted for more aggression. Thibron laid waste to the king's territory in the Maeander plain, only to be killed by Struthas. In the same year, a pro-Spartan group took control in Rhodes, a crucial island on the grain route from Egypt, and on Cyprus, Evagoras's aspirations to become king of Salamis set him against the ruling king Abdemon. The other Phoenician cities called on the king for help, who sent the new Carian ruler Hecatomnus (ruled 395–377) to Cyprus. The Athenians were prepared to aid Evagoras's ambitions and promised to send 10 triremes in 390/89 which, however, never arrived, but were intercepted by the Spartan fleet. A second attempt under Chabrias, with 10 triremes and 800 *peltasts*, light-armed infantry, was made. The Athenian action was rather curious since it is difficult to explain why they supported Evagoras's ambitions while at the same time hoping for Persian support. Perhaps they wanted to find a way to be included in the affairs of the eastern Aegean in order to counterbalance Spartan involvement there. Tiribazus still had not given up hope of ingratiating himself with the king and continued his talks with Sparta. He offered money and ships to Antalcidas in 393/2 in return for Persian claims on the cities and lands of Asia Minor. By 388, Artaxerxes II, obviously drawing on the consequences of Athenian interference in Rhodes, considered Sparta's offer. An audience with the king in 387 resulted in the King's Peace, concluded in 386.

Sources in Translation 8.4

The King's Peace

King Artaxerxes thinks it just that the cities in Asia should belong to him, as well as Clazomenae and Cyprus among the islands, and the other Greek cities, both small and great, should be left independent (Gr. *autonomous*), except Lemnos, Imbros and Scyros, and these should belong, as of old, to the Athenians. But whichever of the two parties does not accept this peace, upon them I will make war, in company with those who desire this arrangement, both by land and by sea, with ships and with money. (Diod.Sic.XIV.110)

Xenophon commented on the peace as follows: 'Athens may not have been pleased with this result, seeing her chances of regaining her empire evaporate before her eyes, but with a joint adventure between the Sicilian fleet of

Dionysius I of Syracuse and the Persian fleet at the Hellespont, the prospect of an unavoidable famine due to grain shortage let them give up any resistance. Tiribazus announced the peace in the spring of 386 in Sardis' (Xen.*Hell.*V.1.31).

In 375, the King's Peace was re-affirmed: '[H]e (= Artaxerxes II) sent ambassadors to Greece to urge the cities to enter into a general peace by agreement. (...) all agreed to make peace on the condition that all the cities should be free and independent' (Xen.*Hell.*XV.38.2).

Agents were sent to ensure that the cities were freed of foreign garrisons. Only Thebes objected to the Peace, because the other Greek states refused to recognise her superiority over the Boeotians. A second renewal of the Peace occurred in 371 at the request of Artaxerxes: 'Artaxerxes, the Persian king, seeing that the Greek world was again in turmoil, sent ambassadors, calling upon the Greeks to settle their internecine wars and establish a Common Peace in accordance with the covenants they had formerly made' (Diod.Sic.XV.50.4; Philochorus FGrH 328 F151). All cities, with the exception of Thebes, agreed. Four weeks later, Thebes defeated Sparta in the battle of Leuctra, which led Artaxerxes II to change his views. Although Antalcidas travelled for a third time to the king for a peace conference in 367, his mission failed (Xen.*Hell.*VII.1.33–40). Instead, Persia now looked at Thebes as a potential partner. In 362/1, Spartan power was lost for good when she was excluded from the Common Peace of that year. According to an inscription, the Greeks settled their differences in a Common Peace in order that, free from war against each other, they would make their cities prosperous, would show no hostility towards the Persia king and would be at peace with him if he showed no aggression and provoked no trouble.

[...] share in the Common Peace.

Show to the man who has come from the satraps that the Greeks have resolved their disputes towards a common peace, so that, being freed from the war against themselves, they may each make their own cities as great as possible and happy, and remain useful to their friends and strong. They are not aware that the king has any war against them. If, therefore, he keeps quiet and does not embroil the Greeks, and does not attempt to break up the peace that has come into being for us by any craft or contrivance, we too shall keep quiet in matters with regard to the king; but if he makes war on any who have sworn the oath or provides money for the breaking-up of this peace, either himself in opposition to the Greeks who have made this peace or anyone else of those from his territory, we shall all resist in common, worthily of the peace that has now come into being and of what we have done before now. (transl. after Rhodes and Osborne 2003: 214–216, no. 42)

8.5.3   Evagoras of Salamis

On Cyprus, Evagoras had risen to power in Salamis in 411 with the support of the Solians from Cilicia. He had attacked the palace and exiled Abdemon of Tyre, who had ruled in Salamis since 415. Evagoras strengthened his position through fortifications and quickly from there; perhaps his decision was based on the swelling of the Nile, which had to be taken into account in terms of supply and safety for the Persian ships. Pharnabazus only retreated to Phoenicia to prepare for a renewed attack. After succession struggles in Egypt following the death of Akoris in 379/8, Nectanebo I (ruled 379/8–361/0) started the XXXth Dynasty at Sebennytus. Artaxerxes II sent Pharnabazus against Egypt again in 373, based in the city of Akoris in Palestine, while Nectanebo I, supported by the Athenian Chabrias and Greek mercenaries, prepared for war. Pharnabazus demanded the recall of Chabrias by the Athenians, as their involvement was a clear breach of the King's Peace. The Athenians obliged and immediately withdrew their forces from Egypt. Pharnabazus, aided by the Athenian general Iphicrates, fought the Egyptians at Memphis but was again defeated, and the Persian fleet returned to the Phoenician base. Efforts to subdue Egypt were continued under Artaxerxes III, who succeeded to power in 359, but before he could focus on Egypt, he had to deal with the revolt of Phoenician cities headed by Tennes king of Sidon. Tennes had received a considerable mercenary force from Egypt, but during the fight, initially going well for the rebelling city, the Sidonian king switched his allegiance and betrayed his city to the Persian king (Diod.Sic. XVI.41–45). Tennes's possible intention with this change of heart may have been to avert punishment from Artaxerxes III, but his effort failed. He was killed and part of the population of Sidon executed: '[Year] 14, Umasu (= 345), who is called Artaxerxes: (in the month) Tishri (= September/October) the prisoners which the king took [from] Sidon to Babylon and Susa [were brought.] That month, day 13 some o[f them] entered Babylon. Day 16, the remaining(?) women prisoners from Sidon, which the king sent to Babylon, that day they entered the palace of the king' (*ABC* 9, transl. Kuhrt 2010: 412, no. 76).

Egypt had had an obvious interest in prolonging any revolt in the eastern Mediterranean because it diverted the king's attention from Egypt and thus delayed military action against it. But once Phoenicia was back under Persian control, the way was paved for a Persian attack on Egypt, and now it was commanded by Artaxerxes III himself. After more than 60 years of independence, Egypt was defeated in 342 and once again was a Persian satrapy. An autobiographical inscription of Somtutefnakht shows that individual prominent Egyptians were as ready to collaborate with the Persian king as they had been before the revolt.

> My heart sought justice in your temple (= that of Harsaphes, god of Heracleopolis) night and day. You rewarded me for it a million times. You gave me access to the palace./ The heart of the Good God (= the Pharaoh Nectanebo II) was pleased with my speech./ You distinguished me before millions./ When you turned your back on Egypt,/ you put love of me in the heart of Asia's ruler./ His courtiers praised god for me./ He gave me the office of chief priest of Sakhmet./ In place of my mother's brother,/ the chief priest of Sakhmet of Upper and Lower Egypt, Nekhthenb (Stele of Somtutefnakht ll.6–10. transl. after Lichtheim 1980: 41).

8.6 The Winds of Change

8.6.1 City-Rulers and Local Dynasts of the Western Empire

The rule of city-kings had been a long-established form of government in Asia Minor. They governed in the Ionian cities of the coast and further inland. As early as Herodotus, we hear of the rulers of Cilicia based in the city of Tarsus. They bore the title

Map 8.2 Map of Lycia, Caria and Pisidia. *Source:* With kind permission of Elsbeth R.M. Dusinberre.

syennesis, erroneously thought by the Greeks to be a personal name. Equally, city-kings governed in the cities of Cyprus and Phoenicia. They held a double status as they were autonomous within their respective city and its environs, while at the same time they were the subject of the Persian king and accountable to the satrap of their respective Great Satrapy to which they were subordinate. In the fourth century, the number of local dynasties increased in western Asia Minor, enjoying both a level of independence and the protection of the Persian king, whose sovereignty they acknowledged. In Caria, the rise of the Hecatomnids is relatively well documented; at a level below them, but also in competition with the Hecatomnids, were the rulers of Lycia centred on Xanthos, and the ruler Perikle of Limyra, whose brief reign nevertheless displays a wealth of impressions as to how rulers like him regarded themselves within the Persian empire, showing, on the one hand, an affinity with a Greek way of life, and on the other, a strong emulation of Achaemenid court life. The emergence of local dynasts in southern Asia Minor signals a political development within Achaemenid rule which might place the revolts of the satraps during the 360s in context. Much more difficult to answer is the question of whether these developments reflect a loss of imperial control, or merely express a striving for more local political autonomy while remaining under the authoritative umbrella of the empire (Map 8.2).

8.6.2 The Hecatomnids

The dynasty of the Hecatomnids arose in 377 with its base in Mylasa. Hecatomnus had been appointed satrap of Caria in 392/1 and governed there until 377. Hecatomnus's son and successor Mausolus (ruled 377–353) moved his capital to the coastal

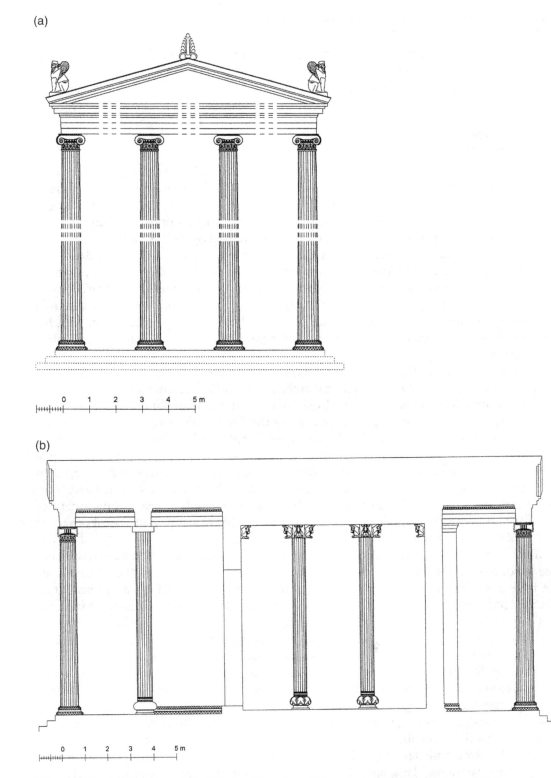

Figure 8.5 (a) Drawing of the Eshmun Temple at Sidon. Just as with the temple at Labraunda, the Eshmun Temple featured Persian-style sphinxes as corner ornaments. *Source:* With kind permission of Rolf A. Stucky, Basle. (b) Drawing of the columns of the Eshmun Temple featuring double-headed animal capitals which were modelled on those of Achaemenid palaces. *Source:* With kind permission of Rolf A. Stucky, Basle.

In consequence, the architecture at Labraunda is not indicative of a 'proto-hellenistic' kingdom, as has been argued, but of the self-representation of a local ruler who follows in its concept imperial Achaemenid ideology.

8.6.3 Perikle of Limyra

We may add to this observation the building activity of Perikle of Limyra, who established himself briefly as ruler in this city (ruled 380–362). Perikle was able to take control of the cities of Milyas, Rhodiapolis, Korydalla and Phaselis. He defeated the Lycian king Arttumpara, Arbinas's successor, and united Lycia under his kingship. His rule, however, was short-lived, and appears to have ended by 362. Scholars are divided as to whether Perikle's affinity lay with Greece, and thus he should be regarded as an opponent of the Achaemenid empire, or whether he was a loyal subject whose potential link with the satrapal rebellions of 370–362 brought on his downfall. Perikle's legacy, the Heroon of Limyra, in fact borrows artistic elements from both sides, and a middle position seems feasible, in which Perikle saw himself as an independent ruler with his own ideological values combining Greek, Persian and western Anatolian traditions (Şare 2013: 58).

A further example of Persian-influenced architecture can be found in Meydancıkkale, where a representational building in the architectural style of Achaemenid palaces has been excavated. Meydancıkkale probably is to be identified with Kirshu, the capital city of Luwian Pirundu mentioned in the annals of the Babylonian king Nergal-shar-usur/ Neriglissar (ruled 560–556) of 557/6, when he campaigned against this city. Finds of column bases allow the reconstruction of the main building as an Achaemenid-style hall, which, at a later point in the Achaemenid period, was enlarged. The building plan has been interpreted to reflect a simplified version of the audience hall in Persepolis. Most striking are the orthostatic reliefs, which show male gift-bearers, reminiscent of those we observe in Persepolis. The building most probably was that of a local governor in Meydancıkkale (Figure 8.6).

If we agree on the observation made by Held that the rulers of Halicarnassus and Sidon followed a grander imperial architectural design, and if we add the observations we have made for similar Persian-influenced mixed-buildings in Cilicia and Lycia, then the idea has several consequences for our investigation. First, it ascertains that Mausolus not only hinted at his link to the Persian king by using an imperial signifier, the sphinx, in his building project, but more importantly, that he adopted the royal concept of creating an all-inclusive architecture which would reflect the Ionian and Dorian Greek connection he had. But beyond that, the comparison of Mausolus's banqueting hall and the Eshmun Temple of Sidon means that Mausolus's position was not unique, but rather that a Phoenician city-king regarded himself at the same level of rulership as Mausolus considered himself: a local king who accepted imperial ideology, who used imperial signifiers to express his link with the king, presumably to declare his importance to his subjects, while at the same time demonstrating his allegiance to the king. At this point we need to ask whether we should designate all these rulers as 'satraps', irrespective of whether they were Achaemenids, Persians or local rulers, on the grounds that they were familiar with imperial architecture and imagery, which they adapted and may have used in different contexts, though with the same purpose: to express their own power.

8.6.5   Stele of the King of Byblos/Gubal

I am Yehawmilk king of Byblos, son of Yaharbal, grandson of Urimilk king of Byblos, whom the lady, Mistress of Byblos, made ruler over Byblos. I called upon my lady, Mistress of Byblos, and she heard my voice. And I made for my lady, Mistress of Byblos, this altar of bronze which is in this court, and this gateway of gold which is opposite of this gateway of mine, and the winged disc of gold which is (set) within the stone which is above this gateway of gold, and this portico and its pillars and the capitals which are upon them and its roof. I, Yehawmilk king of Byblos, made (them) for my lady, Mistress of Byblos, when I called upon my lady, Mistress of Byblos, and she heard my voice and did kindness to me. May the Mistress of Byblos bless Yehawmilk king of Byblos and give life to him and prolong his days and his years over Byblos; for he is lawful king! And may [the lady], Mistress of Byblos, give [to him] favour in the sight of the gods and favour in the sight of the people of this land! [Whoever you are], be you ruler or be you commoner, who may do further work on this altar, [or on] this gateway of gold, or on this portico, [you shall put] my name Yehawmilk [beside] your own on that work; and if you do not put my name beside your own but remove this work and [shift] this [(pillar)] along with its base from this place and

Figure 8.7   Stele of Yehawmilk (Louvre AO 22368). The stele shows the king of Byblos before the goddess of Byblos depicted in Egyptian dress. Yehawmilk wears a Persian-style dress and headdress. One hand is raised in prayer in the same manner we observe in the depiction of the Achaemenid kings in the tomb reliefs at Naqsh-e Rustam and Persepolis. In his other hand Yehawmilk holds a shallow bowl. *Source*: Photo © Musee du Louvre Dist. RMN-Grand Palais/ Christian Larrieu.

uncover its hiding place, may the lady, Mistress of Byblos, destroy both that man and his seed in the presence of all the gods of Byblos! (transl. Gibson 1982: 95)

What is striking is the image, which shows Yehawmilk presenting himself as a king and wearing Persian dress and a turreted crown reminiscent of those worn by the Persian king, and even Persian-style hair and beard (Figure 8.7). Above all, he is making a praying gesture, which we know from the praying gesture of Persian kings such as Cambyses and Darius.

Special Topic 8.4

The Rulers of Lycia

One of the ongoing scholarly debates concerns the question of a possible adoption or imitation of imperial policy, if not signs of identification on the part of local rulers with the Persian king. Here we may take a closer look at Lycia in southern Asia Minor. Lycia had come under Persian control in the 540s, when, in the course of Cyrus's conquest of Lydia, Harpagus defeated a Lycian army north of Xanthos. The inhabitants of the city, certain of their subjection to the Persian army, destroyed the buildings on the citadel and killed their women and children, a drastic measure against their own civilians. Geographically, Lycia entailed the region in the Xanthos valley, with its cities Tlos and Pinara, and Kragos whose location is still unknown. Under the Persians, Lycia flourished. Xanthos was rebuilt and its administration extended from Telmessos to Rhodiapolis. It is also thought that the Persians installed local rulers at Xanthos who remained in power until the early fourth century.

The archaeological and written evidence attests to Lycian rulers based at Xanthos. One example, the tomb of Arbinas, dated between 390 and 380, bears artistic motifs which strongly echo scenes from the Persian court, with servants carrying foodstuffs and wine jars for a banquet, banquet scenes and an audience scene. The inscription of Arbinas's funerary stele attests to his achievements and seems to echo sentiments we first encountered in Darius I's inscription at Naqsh-e Rustam.

[Arbin]as son of Gerg[is] (= Kheriga) [dedicated me, having accomplished deeds worthy of the] valour [of his forefathers]. [Within the tomb chamber lies] (this) cor[pse]. But the stele [that one] s[ees] here commemorates how he est[ablished his rule over the Lycians] by his resourcefulness, his s[upreme] might and po[wer]. In his youth, he conquered in one month three cities – Xanthos, Pinara and Tel[messos] with its fine harbour – striking terror into many Lycian and becoming their mas[ter]. A monument to these (achievements) he set up on the advice of the god Apoll[o]. Having sought counsel at Pytho, he dedicated me to Leto – his own image whose outward appearance (?) expres[ses the prowess?] of his achievements. Having slain many people, having brought honour to his father G[ergis], having conquered many cities, Arbinas made his own and his forefathers' name renowned [through the whole] land of Asia. He was conspicuous amongst all in

8.6.6   Rebellions in Western Asia Minor 366–359/8

The 360s witnessed four individual rebellions led by satraps of western Asia Minor. Contracted to a single event in 362/1 by Diodorus Siculus, our only source, these rebellions became known as the 'Great Satraps' Revolt' in modern scholarship. Diodorus presents them as one concerted action of unified satraps against the king, but in fact these were different revolts led by individual satraps, namely Datames of Cappadocia, Ariobarzanes of Hellespontine Phrygia, Orontes of Sardis, perhaps Mausolus of Caria, and in the reign of Artaxerxes III, Artabazus, also in Hellespontine Phrygia. To date these revolts precisely or to offer a safe chronology of events is not possible; it is clear, however, that at times they overlapped and saw at least two rebelling satraps join forces. Mutual mistrust of one another, however, ruled out any long-term coalition, ultimately contributing to the failures of the revolts. None of these attempts allows the conclusion that they posed a threat to Achaemenid kingship or the empire itself. Rather, they were attempts to extend the level of autonomy of the individual satraps. It is no accident that they happened when and where they did. As we have seen, the regions of the south coast of Asia Minor, including Cilicia, Lycia and Pisidia along the eastern Mediterranean coast and the Phoenician cities, as well as the cities on Cyprus, were ruled by local rulers and city-kings who minted coins and controlled armies while at the same time pledging their allegiance to the Persian king and paying tribute to him. The idea of semi-independent kingdoms, therefore, was right on their doorstep, and the satraps of western Asia may well have been inspired by them to attempt to strengthen their own position from satrap to local ruler.

Yet the rebellions of the satraps have given rise to a debate about the stability of the empire, namely, whether they were an indicator of the waning power of the Persian king, the loss central control, and, by extension, whether these rebellions served as evidence for the decline and the weakness of the king, if not the empire. Clearly, the political climate of late fifth-/early fourth-century Asia Minor was much changed from the earlier periods. The change of their status must be connected with the increased responsibilities the satraps of western Asia Minor bore in regard to their military and naval involvement in Ionia, Cyprus and, most of all, Egypt. Repeated campaigns against rebelling Egypt had placed considerable pressure on the naval forces of the coastal satrapies, while Persian involvement in Greek politics and, conversely, the interference of Athenian and Spartan forces in Asia Minor and Egypt, demanded their political and military engagement. In consequence, it seems logical to assume that the satraps of western Asia Minor were authorised to mint their own coins to pay soldiers and sailors.

8.6.7   Datames

Datames, the satrap of Cappadocia, began a rebellion, probably in 368/7. An entry in the Babylonian Astronomical Diary dated to May 367 recording a battle of the king's troops against a rebel has been interpreted to refer to Datames, but due to the lacunae in the text, the name of the rebel is not preserved.

> ... That month (= 20 May – 19 June 367), the lord(?) [of ...] The troops of the king did battle against the troops [of ...] the mountainous region of Mesopotamia. The tr[oops of ...] Mesopotamia were defeated.

That month the … […. pl.] of Esagil at the command of the king to the ho[use of the king?] were brought.

That month, day 19 (= 7 June 367) the steward [of …] in Susa to the office of satrap [was appointed?].

The 25th (13 June 367) Tattannu, the *rab umma* (= an officer who probably controlled the land of temple personnel) […]

That month, sickness … […]
                    (Sachs and Hunger 1988, no. -367 ll.2–10; transl. Kuhrt 2007a: 400, no. 68)

Datames had inherited the satrapy from his father, Kamisares, after his death in c.384. His mother, Scythissa, belonged to the Paphlagonian nobility and through her was related to the ruler of Sinope, Thuys. Serving in the royal guards of Artaxerxes II, he had fought against the Cadusians. In the same year, Datames had joined the Lydian satrap Autophradates against a group of rebels which included the Pisidians. He had subjected Paphlagonia on behalf of the king and delivered Thuys, his own relative, to the king, after his attempt at mediation had failed. Datames then had joined Pharnabazus and Tithraustes in their campaign against Egypt. When Pharnabazus was released from office, probably after 375, Datames was appointed commander for the next Egyptian campaign. Prior to that expedition, he subjected Aspis, the dynast of Cataonia, a region of Cappadocia between the Amanus and Antitaurus mountains, on the order of the king and then returned to Akke (Nep.*Dat.* 4–5.1). He probably began his revolt occupying part of Paphlagonia and attacking Sinope on the Black Sea coast. Datames concluded a secret alliance with Ariobarzanes, the satrap of Dascyleium, and sent his son Arsidaeus against Pisidia, but when he was killed in battle, Datames took command himself. But Datames was betrayed by his father-in-law, Mithrobarzanes, who went over to the Pisidians, and his own son Sysinas denounced him to Artaxerxes II. Autophradates of Lydia was commanded to deal with the rebel, concluding a treaty with him to avoid a military engagement (Nep.*Dat.* 7–8). In the following years, Datames repeatedly caused military skirmishes against the king, partly with the support of the Egyptian Tachos. In 362/1 he joined Artabazus in Cappadocia, but was killed in the same year by a stab wound delivered by Mithridates, the son of Ariobarzanes. As the case of Datames demonstrates, his was the rebellion of one satrap who even failed to secure the support of his own family.

8.6.8 Ariobarzanes

Almost parallel to Datames's rebellion occurred that of the Persian Ariobarzanes, the satrap of Dascyleium (Diod.Sic.XV.90.3), probably from 367 or 366 to 364 or 362. He had been installed as satrap of Hellspontine Phrygia as Pharnabazus's successor. It was to be a temporary arrangement until Artabazus, the son of Pharnabazus and Apame, herself a daughter of Artaxerxes II, reached a mature age to succeed his father in office. Ariobarzanes's revolt against the king probably was the result of his refusal to relinquish his satrapal power and restore it to Pharnabazus's successor. He received support from the Athenian Timotheus, who had replaced Iphicrates in Egypt, and in return gave him control over the Thracian sites of Sestus and Crithote. For this act, Ariobarzanes and his son received Athenian citizenship. Mausolus of Caria and Autophradates, the satrap of Lydia, were sent to deal with his rebellion at Adramyttium, perhaps located near modern

Edremit or at Assus. But when Athens and Sparta joined Ariobarzanes with forces commanded by Timotheus and the Spartan king Agesilaus, Mausolus and Autophradates abandoned the blockade. In the end, Ariobarzanes was betrayed by his own son Mithradates and was crucified. The satrapy of Lydia returned to the control of Artabazus.

8.6.9   Orontes

Towards the end of Artaxerxes II's reign and the beginning of that of Artaxerxes III, the rebellion of Orontes, satrap of Armenia, occurred. He was the son of Artasyras and married to a royal daughter. In 384, he had taken part in the campaign against Cyprus, where he tried to blacken Tiribazus's reputation, though with limited success, since Tiribazus was soon reinstated. In 361, he was satrap of Mysia, where a Greek inscription records his revolt from the king: 'Orontes, son of Artasyras, a Bactrian, revolted from Artaxerxes king of the Persians' (OGIS 264). Seemingly to increase his power in Mysia, Orontes collected money for mercenaries. Orontes led the revolt of the coastal satrapies between 368 and 358, then betrayed them, revolted against the king and took Pergamon. In the end, he came to an agreement with Artaxerxes III, was spared his life and was allowed to return to Pergamon.

8.6.10   The Death of Artaxerxes II

Apparently aged 94, Artaxerxes died after a 46-year-long reign. The last Babylonian tablet noting his reign is dated to 25 November 359. His successor, Artaxerxes III, was enthroned by early March 358. Despite the considerable political problems Artaxerxes II had faced during his reign, he was able to concern himself with internal affairs of the empire. He restored Darius's palace, which had been damaged in a fire: 'This palace Darius my great-great-grandfather built; later under Artaxerxes, my grandfather, it was burned; by the favour of Auramazda, Anaitis and Mithras, this palace I built. May Auramazda, Anaitis and Mithras protect me from all evil, and that which I have built may they not shatter or harm' (A^{2}Sa). He also constructed another palace in Susa, just across the Chaour River (Figure 8.8).

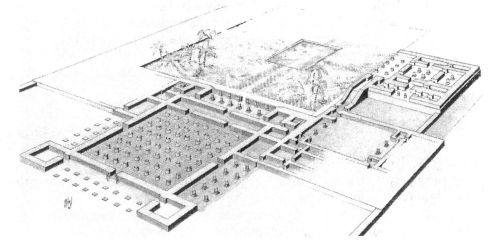

Figure 8.8   Plan of Artaxerxes's palace in Susa. *Source*: After Hesse 2013, fig. 429.

Special Topic 8.5

*Greek Historiography and the Depiction of Persia
as an Empire in Decline*

In the fourth century, negative views about Persia were propagated in Greece in a range of literary media. Book Eight of Xenophon's *Cyropaedia* was written as a diatribe against the Persian empire, leaving no doubt as to the empire's decline, which began soon after the reign of Cyrus II. As it differs considerably from the preceding books, it has been argued that it must have been written by a different author, who nevertheless attached his text to Xenophon's *Cyropaedia*. In any case, for the author of this chapter, the decadence of the empire began with the death of Cyrus, when his sons fought over the succession and the people started to revolt. The Persians became untrustworthy, and did not honour their promises. Militarily, they were unable to defend their territory. Enemies, according to the author, could run up and down the country and they would not need to strike a blow. No Persian was willing to engage in hand-to-hand conflict (Xen. *Cyr.* VIII.22).

Similarly, the Greek philosopher Plato (lived 427–347) used Persia following the rule of Cyrus II as an example of a weak form of government. In his view, the Persians never found the balance between slavery and freedom. As for their rulers, Cyrus II's tough, unspoiled upbringing had enabled him to become the successful king he was, but his sons, educated by women and eunuchs, turned out weak and incompetent. A brief respite was given by the reign of the outsider Darius, but his son, too, was educated in the same decadent manner. For Plato, the symptoms and the consequences of this moral decadence are most visible in the military aspect: they fight with no patriotism and no intention to endanger their lives in battle.

A third writer was the Athenian orator Isocrates (lived 436–338), who, in his *Panegyricus* and his *Speech to Philip*, declared that the Persians were without virtue, their population a mob without discipline and with no stamina for war. Their wealth got in the way of being decent human beings, as was the fact that they pampered their bodies and prostrated themselves before the king, a gesture the Greeks only performed before divine statues. In their criticism, neither the author of the *Cyropaedia's* Book Eight, nor Plato, nor Isocrates is concerned with historical facts and objective analysis. Their purpose was to convey an ideology. The realities of the Persian empire of their time did not take intellectual priority.

Xen. an. III. 2.25–26

I really fear, however, that if we once learn to live in idleness and luxury, and to consort with the tall and beautiful women and maidens of these Medes and Persians, we may, like the lotus-eaters, forget our homeward way. Therefore, I think it is right and proper that our first endeavour should be to return to our kindred and friends in Greece, and to point out to the Greeks that it is by their own choice that they are poor; for they could bring here the people who are now living a hard life at home, and could see them in the enjoyment of riches.

Xen. Cyr. VIII. 8.1–28

That Cyrus's empire was the greatest and most glorious of all the kingdoms in (...) of that it may be its own witness. For it was bounded on the east by the Indian Ocean, on the north by the Black Sea, on the west by Cyprus and Egypt and on the south by Ethiopia. And although it was of such magnitude, it was governed by the single will of Cyrus; and he honoured his subjects and cared for them as if they were his own children; and they, on their part, reverenced Cyrus as a father. Still, as soon as Cyrus was dead, his children at once fell into dissension, states and nations began to revolt and everything began to deteriorate. And that what I say is the truth, I will prove, beginning with the Persians attitude towards religion. I know, for example, that in early times the kings and their officers, in their dealings with even the worst offenders, would abide by an oath that they might have given, and be true to any pledge they might have made. For had they not had such a character for honour, and had they not been true to their reputation, not a man would have trusted them, just as not a single person any longer trusts them, now that their lack of character is notorious; and the generals of the Greeks who joined the expedition of Cyrus the Younger would not have had such confidence in them even on that occasion. But, as it was, trusting in the previous reputation of the Persian kings, they placed themselves in the king's power, were led into his presence and had their heads cut off. And many also of the barbarians who joined that expedition went to their doom, some deluded by one promise, others by another. But at the present time they are still worse, as the following will show: if, for example, anyone in the olden times risked his life for the king, or if anyone reduced a state or a nation to submission to him, or effected anything else of good or glory for him, such a one received honour and preferment; now, on the other hand, if anyone seems to bring some advantage to the king by evil-doing, whether as Mithradates did, by betraying his own father Ariobarzanes, or as a certain Rheomithres did, in violating his most sacred oaths and leaving his wife and children and the children of his friends behind as hostages in the power of the king of Egypt – such are the ones who now have the highest honours heaped upon them. Witnessing such a state of morality, all the inhabitants of Asia have been turned to wickedness and wrongdoing. For, whatever the character of the rulers is, such also that of the people under them for the most part becomes. In this respect they are now even more unprincipled than before. In money matters, too, they are more dishonest in this particular: they arrest not merely those who have committed many offences, but even those who have done no wrong, and against all justice compel them to pay fines; and so those who are supposed to be rich are kept in a state of terror no less than those who have committed many crimes, and they are no more willing than malefactors are to come into close relations with their superiors in power; in fact, they do not even venture to enlist in the royal army. Accordingly, owing to their impiety towards the gods and their iniquity towards man, anyone who is engaged in war with them can, if he desire, range up and down their country without having to strike a blow. Their principles in so far, therefore, are in every respect worse now than they were in antiquity. (...)

Again, this also was a native custom of theirs, neither to eat nor drink while on a march, nor yet to be seen doing any of the necessary consequences of eating or drinking. Even yet that same abstinence prevails, but they make their journeys so short that no one would be surprised at their ability to resist those calls of nature. Again, in times past they used to go out hunting so often that the hunts afforded sufficient exercise for both men and horses. But since Artaxerxes and his court became the victims of wine, they have neither gone out themselves in the old way nor taken the others out hunting; on the contrary, if anyone often went hunting with his friends out of sheer love for physical exertion, the courtiers would not hide their jealousy and would hate him as presuming to be a better man than they. Again, it is still the custom for the boys to be educated at court; but instruction and practice in horsemanship have died out, because there are no occasions on which they may give an exhibition and win distinction for skill. And while anciently the boys used there to hear cases at law justly decided and so to learn justice, as they believed – that also has been entirely reversed; for now they see all too clearly that whichever party gives the larger bribe wins the case. (...) Furthermore, they are much more effeminate now than they were in Cyrus's day. For at that time they still adhered to the old discipline and the old abstinence that they received from the Persians, but adopted the Median garb and Median luxury; now, on the contrary, they are allowing the rigour of the Persians to die out, while they keep up the effeminacy of the Medes. I should like to explain their effeminacy more in detail. In the first place, they are not satisfied with only having their couches upholstered with down, but they actually set the posts of their beds upon carpets, so that the floor may offer no resistance, but that the carpets may yield. Again, whatever sorts of bread and pastry for the table had been discovered before, none of all those have fallen into disuse, but they keep on always inventing something new besides; and it is the same way with meats; for in both branches of cookery they actually have artists to invent new dishes. Again, in winter they are not satisfied with having clothing on their heads and bodies and legs, but they must have also sleeves thickly lined to the very tips of their fingers, and gloves besides. In summer, on the other hand, they are not satisfied with the shade afforded by the trees and rocks, but amid these they have people stand by them to provide artificial shade. They take great pride also in having as many cups as possible; but they are not ashamed if it transpire that they came by them by dishonest means, for dishonesty and sordid love of gain have greatly increased among them. Furthermore, it was of old a national custom not to be seen going anywhere on foot; and that was for no other purpose than to make themselves as knightly as possible. But now they have more coverings upon their horses than upon their beds, for they do not care so much for knighthood as for a soft seat. And so is it not to be expected that in military prowess they should be wholly inferior to what they used to be? In times past it was their national custom that those who held lands should furnish cavalrymen from their possessions and that these, in case of war, should also take the field, while those who performed outpost duty in defence of the country received pay for their services. But now the rulers make knights out of their porters, bakers, cooks, cup-bearers, bathroom attendants, butlers, waiters, chamberlains who assist them in retiring at night and in rising in the morning, and beauty-doctors who pencil their eyes and rouge their cheeks for them and otherwise beautify them; these are the sort that they make into knights to serve for pay for them. From such recruits, therefore, a host is obtained, but they are of no use in war; and that is clear from actual occurrences: for enemies may range up and down their land with less hindrance than friends. For Cyrus had abolished skirmishing at a distance, had armed both horses and men with breastplates, had put a javelin into each man's hand and had introduced the method of fighting hand to hand. But now they neither skirmish at a distance any longer, nor yet do they fight in a hand-to-hand engagement. The infantry still have their wicker shields and bills and sabres, just as those had who set the battle in array in the times of Cyrus; but not even they are willing to come into a hand-to-hand conflict. Neither do they employ the scythed chariot any longer for the purpose for which Cyrus had it made. For he advanced the charioteers to honour and made them objects of admiration and so had men who were ready to hurl themselves against even a heavy-armed line. The officers of the present day, however, do not so much as know the men in the chariots, and they think that untrained drivers will be just as serviceable to them as trained charioteers. Such untrained men do indeed charge, but before they penetrate the enemy's lines, some of them are unintentionally thrown out, some of them jump out on purpose, and so the teams without drivers often create more havoc on their own side than on the enemy's. However, inasmuch as even they understand what sort of material for war they have, they abandon the effort; and no one ever goes to war any more without the help of Greek mercenaries, be it when they are at war with one another or when the Greeks make war upon them; but even against Greeks they recognise that they can conduct their wars only with the assistance of Greeks.

Plato, Laws 694a–698a

Athenian: Let us attend then. When the Persians, under Cyrus, maintained the due balance between slavery and freedom, they became, first of all, free themselves, and, after that, masters of many others. For when the rulers gave a share of freedom to their subjects and advanced them to a position of equality, the soldiers were more friendly [694b] towards their officers and showed their devotion in times of danger; and if there was any wise man amongst them, able to give counsel, since the king was not jealous but allowed free speech and respected those who could help at all by their counsel – such a man had the opportunity of contributing to the common stock the fruit of his wisdom. Consequently, at that time all their affairs made progress, owing to their freedom, friendliness and mutual interchange of reason.

Clinias: Probably that is pretty much the way in which the matters you speak of took place. [694c] Athenian; How came it, then, that they were ruined in Cambyses's reign, and nearly restored again under Darius? Shall I use a kind of divination to picture this? (...)

[694d] Athenian: Probably he spent all his life from boyhood in soldiering, and entrusted his children to the women folk to rear up; and they brought them up from earliest childhood as though they had already attained to Heaven's favour and felicity, and were lacking in no celestial gift; and so by treating them as the special favourites of Heaven, and forbidding anyone to oppose them, in anything, and compelling everyone to praise their every word and deed, they reared them up into what they were. (...)

Athenian: And their father, while gaining flocks and sheep and plenty of herds, both of men and of many other chattels, [695a] yet knew not that the children to whom he should bequeath them were without training in their father's craft, which was a hard one, fit to turn out shepherds of great strength, able to camp out in the open and to keep watch and, if need be, to go campaigning. He overlooked the fact that his sons were trained by women and eunuchs and that the indulgence shown them as 'Heaven's darlings' had ruined their training, whereby they became [695b] such as they were likely to become when reared with a rearing that 'spared the rod'. So when, at the death of Cyrus, his sons took over the kingdom, over-pampered and undisciplined as they were, first, the one killed the other, through annoyance at his being put on an equality with himself, and presently, being mad with drink and debauchery, he lost his own throne at the hands of the Medes, under the man then called the Eunuch, who despised the stupidity of Cambyses. (...)

Athenian: Let us follow the story and see how things went. Darius was not a king's son, nor was he reared luxuriously. When he came and seized the kingdom, with his six companions, he divided it into seven parts, of which some small vestiges remain even to this day; [695d] and he thought good to manage it by enacting laws into which he introduced some measure of political equality, and also incorporated in the law regulations about the tribute-money which Cyrus had promised the Persians, whereby he secured friendliness and fellowship amongst all classes of the Persians, and won over the populace by money and gifts; and because of this, the devotion of his armies won for him as much more land as Cyrus had originally bequeathed. After Darius came Xerxes, and he again was brought up with the luxurious rearing of a royal house: 'O Darius' – for it is thus one may rightly address the father – 'how is it that you have ignored the blunder of Cyrus, [695e] and have reared up Xerxes in just the same habits of life in which Cyrus reared Cambyses?' And Xerxes, being the product of the same training, ended by repeating almost exactly the misfortunes of Cambyses. Since then there has hardly ever been a single Persian king who was really, as well as nominally, 'Great'. And, as our argument asserts, the cause of this does not lie in luck, [696a] but in the evil life which is usually lived by the sons of excessively rich monarchs; for such an upbringing can never produce either boy or man or greybeard of surpassing goodness. (...)

Athenian: It was our investigation of the polity of the Persians that caused us to discuss these matters at greater length. We find that they grew still worse, the reason being, as we say, that by robbing the commons unduly of their liberty and introducing despotism in excess, they destroyed [697d] in the state the bonds of friendliness and fellowship. And when these are destroyed, the policy of the rulers no longer consults for the good of the subjects and the commons, but solely for the maintenance of their own power; if they think that it will profit them in the least degree, they are ready at any time to overturn states and to overturn and burn up friendly nations; and thus they both hate and are hated with a fierce and ruthless hatred. And when they come to need the commons, to fight in their support, they find in them no patriotism [697e] or readiness to endanger their lives in battle; so that, although they possess countless myriads of men, they are all useless for war, and they hire soldiers from abroad as though they were short of men, and imagine that their safety will be secured by hirelings and aliens. And besides all this, [698a] they inevitably display their ignorance, inasmuch as by their acts they declare that the things reputed to be honourable and noble in a State are never anything but dross compared to silver and gold.

Isocrates, Panegyricus 150–152

And none of these things has happened by accident, but all of them have been due to natural causes; for it is not possible for people who are reared and governed as are the Persians, either to have a part in any other form of virtue or to set up on the field of battle trophies of victory over their foes. For how could either an able general or a good soldier be produced amid such ways of life as theirs? Most of their population is a mob without discipline or experience of dangers, which has lost all stamina for war and has been trained more effectively for servitude than are the slaves in our country. [151] Those, on the other hand, who stand highest in repute among them have never governed their lives by dictates of equality or of common interest or of loyalty to the state; on the contrary, their whole existence consists of insolence towards some, and servility towards others – a manner of life than which nothing could be more demoralising to human nature. Because they are rich, they pamper their bodies; but because they are subject to one man's power, they keep their souls in a state of abject and cringing fear, parading themselves at the door of the royal palace, prostrating themselves and in every way schooling themselves to humility of spirit, falling on their knees before a mortal man, addressing him as a divinity and thinking more lightly of the gods than of men. (…) So it is that those of the Persians who come down to the sea, whom they term satraps, do not dishonour the training which they receive at home, but cling steadfastly to the same habits: they are faithless to their friends and cowardly to their foes; their lives are divided between servility on the one hand and arrogance on the other; they treat their allies with contempt and pay court to their enemies.

FURTHER READING

For Xerxes and Babylon see Waerzeggers, C. (2010). Babylonians in Susa. Travels of Babylonian businessmen to Susa reconsidered. In: *Der Achaimenidenhof / The Achaemenid Court* (eds.

B. Jacobs and R. Rollinger), 777–813. Wiesbaden: Harrassowitz. Baker, H. (2008). Babylon in 484 BC: the excavated archival tablets as a source for urban history. *Zeitschrift für Assyriologie* 98: 100–116. Waerzeggers, C. (2003/4). The Babylonian revolts against Xerxes and the "end of archives". *Archiv für Orientforschung* 50: 150–178. Briant, P. (1992). La date des révoltes babyloniennes contre Xerxès. *Studia Iranica* 21: 7–20. Kuhrt, A. and Sherwin-White, S. (1987). *Xerxes' destruction of Babylonian Temples. AchHist* 2: 69–78.

Monographs on the Persian Wars are abound Burn, A.R. (1984). *Persia and the Greeks. Second Edition with a Postscript by David M. Lewis*. London: Duckworth still provides a balanced narrative of events. The problems in Herodotus's story of Xerxes and the wife of Masistes were discussed by Sancisi-Weerdenburg, H. (1983). Exit Atossa: images of women in Greek historiography on Persia. In: *Images of Women in Antiquity* (eds. A. Cameron and A. Kuhrt), 20–33. London: Croom Helm for the story of Esther see Brosius, M. (2015), From fact to fiction: Persian history and the book of Esther. In: *Assessing Biblical and Classical Sources for the Reconstruction of Persian Influence, History and Culture* (ed. A. Fitzpatrick), 193–202. Wiesbaden: Harrassowitz. The central publication on cultural memory is Assman, J. (1992). *Das kulturelle Gedächtnis: Schrift, Erinnerung und politische Identität in frühen Hochkulturen*. Munich: Beck.

The Greek–barbarian antithesis has received intensive scholarly discussion; two of the key contributions are Edith Hall's monograph from 1989. *Inventing the Barbarian. Greek Self-Definition through Tragedy*. Oxford: Oxford University Press and Hall, E. (1993). Asia unmanned: images of victory in classical Athens. In: *War and Society in the Greek World* (eds. J. Rich and G. Shipley), 108–133. London: Routledge. The debate has been strengthened by the following contributions: Zenzen, N., Hölscher, T., and Trampendach, K. (eds.) (2013). *Aneignung und Absterrung: wechselnde Perspektiven auf die Antithese von 'Ost' und 'West' in der griechischen Antike*. Heidelberg: Verlag Antike. Carey, C., Edwards, M. (eds.) (2013). Marathon – 2,500 Years: Proceedings of the Marathon Conference 2010. London: Institute of Classical Studies, University of London (Bulletin of the Institute of Classical Studies Supplement 124); Madreiter, I. (2012). *Stereotypisierung – Idealisierung – Indifferenz. Formen der Auseinandersetzung mit dem Achaimeniden-Reich in der griechischen Persika-Literatur*, Classica et Orientalia 4. Wiesbaden: Harrassowitz. Rhodes, P. (2007). The impact of the Persian wars on classical Greece. In: *Cultural Responses to the Persian Wars. Antiquity to the Third Millennium* (ed. E. Bridges, E. Hall, P.J. Rhodes), 31–45. Oxford: Oxford University Press; Cerf, W.J. (2001). Thermopylai: myth and reality in 480 BC. In: *Gab es das griechische Wunder?* (eds. D. Papenfuss and V.M. Strocka), 355–364. Mainz: Von Zabern Hoelteskamp, K.-J. (2001). Marathon – vom Monument zum Mythos. In: *Gab es das griechische Wunder?* (eds. D. Papenfuss and V.M. Strocka), 329–353. Mainz: Von Zabern. Hornblower, S. (2001). Greeks and Persians: west against east. In: *War, Peace and World Orders in European History* (eds. A.V. Hartmann and B.V. Heuser), 48–61. London: Routledge. Hoelscher, T. (ed.) (2000). *Gegenwelten zu den Kulturen Griechenlands und Roms in der Antike*. Munich: De Gryter. Harrison, T. (ed.) (2000). *Greeks and Barbarians*. Edinburgh: Edinburgh University Press.

For Greece and Persia in the fourth century see Lewis, D.M. (1977). *Sparta and Persia*. Leiden: Brill. Hornblower, S. (1994). Persia. In: *CAH VI²* (eds. D.M. Lewis, J. Boardman, S. Hornblower and M. Ostwald), 45–96. Cambridge: Cambridge University Press. Tuplin, C. (ed.) (2004). *Xenophon and his World*, Historia Einzelschriften 172. Wiesbaden: Steiner. The satrapal rebellions have been analysed by Weiskopf, M. (1989). *The So-called 'Great Satraps' Revolt', 366–360 BC*, Historia Einzelschriften 63. Stuttgart: Steiner. For Datames's identification in the Babylonian Astronomical Diaries see Van der Spek, R. (1998). The chronology of the wars of Artaxerxes II in the Babylonian Astronomical Diaries. *AchHist* 11: 239–256. On Persian diplomacy see Brosius, M. (2012). Persian diplomacy between 'Pax Persica' and 'zero tolerance'. In: *Maintaining Peace and Stability in the Greek World* (ed. J. Wilker), 1–13. Heidelberg: Verlag Antike. For the documents from the Jewish garrison at Elephantine see Porten, B. (2011). *The Elephantine Papyri in English: Three Millennia of Cross-Cultural Continuity and Change*, 2nd. rev.e. Leiden: Brill. A comprehensive study of Lycia is provided by Bryce, T. (1986). *The Lycians*. Copenhagen: Museum Tusculanum Press. For the Aramaic version of the Leto trilingual stele Lemaire, A. (2017). The Aramaic inscription of the Xanthos trilingual stele (4.30). In: *Context of Scripture Online* (ed. W. Hallo). Leiden: Brill https://doi.org/10.1163/2211.436X_cos_aCOSB_4_30>. The dynasts of Asia Minor are discussed by Borchardt, J. (2000). Dynastie und Beamte in Lykien während der persischen und attischen Herrschaft. In: *Variatio Delectat: Iran und der Westen. Gedenkschrift Peter Calmeyer* (eds. R. Dittmann, B. Hrouda, U. Löw, et al.), 73–140. Münster: Ugarit. (AOAT 272)Held, W. (2011). Mischordnungen in Labraunda als Repräsentationsform persischer Satrapen. In: *Keleinai-Apameia Kobotos. Developpement urbain dans le contexte anatolien* (eds. L. Summerer, A. Ivantchik and A. von Kienlin), 383–390. Munich: Ugarit. Held, W. and Kaptan, D. (2015). The residence of a Persian satrap in Meydancıkkale, Cilicia. In: *Mesopotamia in the Ancient World*, Melammu Symposia 7 (eds. R. Rollinger and E. van Dongen), 175–191. Münster: Ugarit.On the Hecatomnids see Hornblower, S. (1982). *Mausolus*. Oxford: Oxford University Press. For Perikle of Limyra see Şare, T. (2013). The sculpture of the Heroon of Perikle at Limyra: the making of a Lycian king. *Anatolian Studies* 63: 55–74. For the eastern Mediterranean see Lemaire, A. (2013). *Levantine Epigraphy and History in the Achaemenid Period (539–332 BCE)*. Oxford: Oxford University Press for the British Academy. Cross, F.M. (1978). A recently published Phoenician inscription of the Persian period from Byblos. *Israel Exploration Journal* 28 (4): 40–44.

On the subject of 'Persian decadence' see Sancisi-Weerdenburg, H. (1987). Decadence in the empire or decadence in the sources? From source to synthesis. *AchHist* 1: 33–46 and Briant, P. (2000). History and ideology: the Greeks and 'Persian decadence'. In: *Greeks and Barbarians* (ed. T. Harrison), 193–210. Edinburgh: Edinburgh University Press.

9

A Whole New Ballgame: The Reign of Artaxerxes III and Artaxerxes IV

9.1 The Succession of Artaxerxes III

In 359/8, Ochus succeeded to the Achaemenid throne as Artaxerxes III. Greek sources recount the death of the designated heir, Darius, allegedly put to death for his intended palace revolt, which was triggered, if we are to believe Plutarch, by the king's refusal to give his favourite concubine, Aspasia, to Darius. To ascend to the throne, Ochus had to rid himself of Darius's full brother Ariaspes as well as his half-brother Arsames. According to Curtius Rufus, Ochus was married to a daughter of Oxathres, and a late source claims he was married to his niece. For Plutarch, Artaxerxes III 'outstripped all in cruelty and bloodlust' (Plut.*Art*.XXX.5). Yet politically and militarily, Artaxerxes III proved himself immensely astute. Immediately after his accession, he disbanded the Greek mercenary armies of the coastal satraps (Schol.Dem.IV.19), thus curbing their military strength. These mercenaries hired themselves out to the Athenian Chares, who in turn put himself into the service of the rebelling Artabazus. Artaxerxes III swiftly put an end to this action, threatening Athens with his support of Athens's rebelling allies. Athens withdrew immediately. He quashed the rebellion of Artabazus with the support of 5000 Theban mercenaries originally hired by Artabazus himself. The son of Pharnaspes and Apame, Artabazus became satrap of Hellespontine Phrygia in 362. Six years later he rebelled, but in 352 fled to the Macedonian court of Philip II. He was pardoned by the Persian king in 345 and allowed to return to Persia. No reason is given as to what triggered his revolt in the first place. Theban–Persian diplomatic relations must have been good, because in 351 Thebes was given 300 talents of silver from the king in support of her Sacred War against Phocis (Diod. Sic.XVI.40.1–2). Yet Artaxerxes III's main focus was on quashing the revolt of Egypt, ongoing since 404, as well as those of the Cypriote cities (c.346–344) and of Tennes of Sidon (345/4).

A History of Ancient Persia: The Achaemenid Empire, First Edition. Maria Brosius.
© 2021 John Wiley & Sons, Inc. Published 2021 by John Wiley & Sons, Inc.

9.2   Egypt

For Artaxerxes III, the reconquest of Egypt was a priority, but an attack in 351 failed. Phoenicia rose in revolt headed by Tennes of Sidon and supported by Pharaoh Nectanebo II and most of the cities of Cyprus, with nine kings declaring their independence. Idreius, the Carian dynast, was sent with a Babylonian force to deal with Cyprus. Mazaeus, satrap of Cilicia, and Belshunu II, satrap of Syria, led the first operations against Phoenician cities. Tennes of Sidon meanwhile was supplied with mercenary forces from Egypt. When other Phoenician cities surrendered, opening their gates to the king's forces, the Sidonians resisted. In the end, Sidon fell by treachery and Tennes was executed. Mentor and his Egyptian mercenaries switched sides and now served the king. He became one of the commanders against Egypt alongside Rhoesaces, satrap of Lydia and Ionia.

The defeat of Sidon is indicated in a Babylonian chronicle dated to the fourteenth year of Artaxerxes (= 345) in which female prisoners from Sidon were taken into the king's palace. Immediately after bringing the Phoenician cities back under Persian control, the king prepared for a further attack on Egypt, which was carried out at the end of 343. Thebes sent 1000 hoplites under Lacrates, 3000 Argives and 6000 Asiatic Greeks, a total of 10 000 troops, to support Artaxerxes III. They were confronted with a 20 000-strong force from Nectanebo II, plus further troops from Libya and Egypt. In the summer of 342, the king entered Memphis and defeated Nectanebo II in battle. Almost 60 years since the beginning of the revolt, Egypt was back in Persian hands and placed under the control of the satrap Pherendates (Diod.Sic.XVI.51.3) (Figure 9.1). Artaxerxes's punishment was harsh: 'Artaxerxes, after taking over all Egypt and demolishing the walls of the most important cities, by plundering the shrines gathered a vast quantity of silver and gold, and he carried off the inscribed records from the ancient temples which later on Bagoas returned to the Egyptian priests on the payment of huge sums by way of ransom' (Diod.Sic.XVI.51.2). A Demotic papyrus records an Egyptian reaction to the renewed subjugation under the Persian king: 'Our ponds and islands are filled with weeping: that is, the houses of the Egyptians will be bereft of people to dwell in them; that is, one will say of this time: the Medes will bring them to ruination; they will take away their houses and dwell therein' (BN Pap.215 obv.IV 22–3; transl. after Kuhrt 2010: 416, no. 79 (i)).

9.3   Athenian–Persian Relations 349–342

The Athenian attitude towards Persia was still ambiguous in the mid-340s. While Athens claimed that her friendship with Persia was dependent on the king's attitude towards Hellenic cities (Anaximenes FGrH 72 F28), she supported the Persian cause during the revolt of Cyprus in 346–344, when the Athenian Phocion and Idreius of Caria were entrusted by the king to suppress the revolt (Diod.Sic.XVI.42.6–9; Strabo XIV.656). In 343/2, Thebes returned the favour to Artaxerxes, sending 1000 hoplites under the command of Lacrates to the king. The Argives also sent 3000 hoplites under the command of Nicostratus; and the Greeks at the coast of Asia Minor joined the venture with 6000 soldiers (Diod.Sic.XVI.44.4). All these forces were used in Artaxerxes's third attempt to reconquer Egypt.

Figure 9.1   Seal of Artaxerxes III (St. Petersburg 19499). It shows the Persian king killing the defeated rebel leader and pretender to the Egyptian throne. *Source:* With kind permission of The State Hermitage Museum, St. Petersburg. Photo © The State Hermitage Museum, Konstantin Sinyavsky.

Yet a new player had appeared on the Greek political stage in 360, when Philip II succeeded to the throne of Macedon. Philip's ambition was to become hegemon of Greece, and he achieved this goal in a series of military aggressions, beginning with the occupation of Amphipolis in 357 and ending with the defeat of the Greek forces in the Battle of Chaeronaea in 338. The Greek city-states were slow to react to Philip's aggressions in the 350s, and were equally slow to form alliances against him. Eventually, Thebes's request for aid from Artaxerxes III brought Persia back into the Greek vision as a potential ally and supporter, whose unlimited resources could be used against Philip II. After 343, in light of the growing threat coming from Philip and Macedon, Athens followed suit. An alliance with Persia was concluded in 342. This political move had only become possible after Persia's successes in Phoenicia and Egypt, as her military and financial resources could now be redirected elsewhere. The fact that Greece sought this alliance must also indicate that, against all propagandistic 'noise', Persia's military and financial power was regarded to be as strong as ever. But the Athenian–Persian alliance alarmed Philip, as it posed a serious threat to his ambitions in Greece.

In the summer of 340, Philip attacked Perinthus (Diod.Sic.XVI.74), possibly with a view to occupying the Bosporus to gain control over Athens's food supply from the Black Sea. In response to the request of the Athenian embassy for Persian aid, Artaxerxes III ordered the Persian satraps of Asia Minor to send mercenary troops and supplies; the Macedonians were forced to withdraw from Perinthus but moved in

Sources in Translation 9.1

The Military Campaigns of Artaxerxes III

He (= Artaxerxes III) began to make war also on the Phoenicians for the following reasons. In Phoenicia there is an important city called Tripolis, whose name is appropriate to its nature, for there are in it three cities, at a distance of a stade from one another, and the names by which these are called are the city of the Aradians, of the Sidonians, and of the Tyrians. This city enjoys the highest repute amongst the cities of Phoenicia, for there, as it happens, the Phoenicians held their common council and deliberated on matters of supreme importance. Now since the king's satraps and generals dwelt in the city of the Sidonians and behaved in an outrageous and high-handed fashion towards the Sidonians in ordering things to be done, the victims of this treatment, aggrieved by their insolence, decided to revolt against the Persians. Having persuaded the rest of the Phoenicians to make a bid for their independence, they sent ambassadors to the Egyptian king Nectanebo, who was an enemy of the Persians, and after persuading him to accept them as allies, they began to make preparations for the war. Inasmuch as Sidon was distinguished for its wealth and its private citizens had amassed great riches from its shipping, many triremes were quickly outfitted and a multitude of mercenaries gathered, and, besides, arms, missiles, food and all other materials useful in war were provided with dispatch. The first hostile act was the cutting down and destroying of the royal park in which the Persian kings were wont to take their recreation; the second was the burning of the fodder for the horses, which had been stored up by the satraps for the war; last of all they arrested such Persians as had committed the acts of insolence and wreaked vengeance upon them. Such was the beginning of the war with the Phoenicians, and Artaxerxes, being apprised of the rash acts of the insurgents, issued threatening warnings to all the Phoenicians and in particular to the people of Sidon. In Babylon, the king, after assembling his infantry and cavalry forces, immediately assumed command of them and advanced against the Phoenicians. While he was still on the way, Belesys (= Belshunu II), the satrap of Syria, and Mazaeus, the governor of Cilicia, having joined forces, opened the war against the Phoenicians. Tennes, the king of Sidon, acquired from the Egyptians 4000 Greek mercenary soldiers, whose general was Mentor the Rhodian. With these and the citizen soldiery, he engaged the aforementioned satraps, defeated them and drove the enemy out of Phoenicia' (Diod.Sic.XVI.41–42).

The End of the Revolt in Egypt

Then when he had rewarded the Greeks who had accompanied him on the campaign with lavish gifts, each according to his deserts, he dismissed them into their native lands; and, having installed Pherendates as satrap of Egypt, he returned with his army to Babylon, bearing many possessions and spoils and having won great renown by his successes. (Diod.Sic.XVI.51.3) response to attack Byzantium. In the autumn of the same year, Philip seized 230 grain ships at the Bosporus (Philochorus FGrH 238 F54.162; Dem.XVIII.73, 139). Byzantium received support from Athens, as well as from Chios, Rhodes, Cos and Persia. In October 340, Athens declared war on Philip, certain of receiving Persian money to finance the war. History had shown that whatever side Persia and Persian money was on would win the war. Philip had to abandon his attack on Byzantium. It is after this withdrawal that Philip declared war on Athens in return, accusing her of breaching the peace and even instigating Persia to declare war on Macedon (Dem.XII.6).

By 340, the political balance in Greece had shifted strongly against Philip. The Athenian-Persian coalition meant the end of Macedonian ambitions of supremacy over Greece. Demosthenes brought the matter to a point: '... quite recently the satraps of Asia Minor sent a force of mercenaries and compelled Philip to raise the siege of Perinthus, but today their hostility is confirmed, the danger, if he reduces Byzantium, is at their very doors, and not only will they eagerly join the war against him, but they will prompt the king of Persia to become our paymaster; and he is richer than all the rest together, and his power to interfere with Greece is such that in our former wars with Sparta whichever side he joined, he ensured their victory and so, if he sides with us now, he will easily crush the power of Philip' ([Dem.]XI.5–6). Accordingly, Philip needed to keep Persia out of Greek affairs in order to subject Athens and end Greek resistance to Macedonian power. To do so, he planned to attack those Persian forces which had – and would – support Athens against him, that is, the satrapies of Asia Minor. As some scholars suggested, the attack on the satrapies of Asia Minor most likely had been the primary target of Philip's Persian War. Unable to declare his motives for the Persian War openly, since it would have revealed his ambitions in Greece, Philip 'created' an enmity with Persia. The revenge motive, to avenge the Greeks for Xerxes's attack, and the revival of the slogan of 'freedom of the Greek cities of Asia' cloaked his real intentions perfectly.

Philip first subjected the Greeks: their defeat at the battle at Chaeronaea of 338, the culmination of the aggressions between Greek states and Macedon, led to the subjected Greek member states' agreement to the 'Common Peace' and they were forced to immediately declare war on Persia under Philip's leadership. Now he took the second step, an attack on the satrapies of Asia Minor. In 337, Philip called for a war of revenge and the liberation of the Greeks of Asia. He sent a force under Attalus and Parmenion into Asia Minor. Further actions were curtailed when Philip was assassinated in 336, and the Greeks took advantage of his death to renew their resistance to Macedonian control. Diodorus recalls that at news of Philip's death many Greeks wanted to free themselves from Macedonian supremacy (Diod.Sic.XVII.3.1–5). Thebes, which had been discontent having a Macedonian garrison stationed on the Cadmeia, the Theban citadel, wanted to revolt against the new king, Alexander III, and began by killing the two Macedonians who held the Cadmeia (Arr.*an*.I.7; Diod.Sic.XVII.8–14) in 335/4. Alexander's wrath at Theban obstinacy was overpowering: the city was razed to the ground, 6000 Thebans were remorselessly killed and 30000 were enslaved. These actions were justified by the claim that the Thebans had allied with the Persians in the Persian Wars (Diod.Sic.XVII.14.1–2). After the destruction of Thebes, Alexander demanded the elimination of 10 other Greek politicians, those who opposed his own and his father's policy.

9.4   The Death of Artaxerxes III and the Reign of Artaxerxes IV

On 26 July 338, a few weeks before the battle between Philip and the Greek city-states took place at Chaeronaea, Artaxerxes III had died. A Babylonian document states: '(an eclipse of the moon passed by) on the 29th of the month Du'uzu in year 21 (of Artaxerxes III) (= 26 July 338). Month Ululu. Umakush (went to his) fate; his son Arshu sat on the throne' (BM 71537; Walker 1997: 22). Arshu, or Arses, took the throne name Artaxerxes IV.

Following the Greek sources, the final years of Achaemenid rule appear to be dominated by palace intrigues instigated by a courtier named Bagoas. While, on the one hand, he was described as a courageous and successful member of Artaxerxes III's army, a *chiliarch* even, he was also labelled a 'eunuch' and a 'king-maker' in the classical sources. Diodorus ascribes to him the murder of Artaxerxes III and the enthronement of the king's son Arses. Bagoas killed him two years later when Arses suspected him of wrongdoing, and replaced him with Arsanes, who took the throne name Darius III. He must have seen through Bagoas's machinations and had him killed soon after his accession.

> While Philip was still king, Ochus (= Artaxerxes III) ruled the Persians and oppressed his subjects cruelly and harshly. Since his savage position made him hated, the chiliarch Bagoas, a eunuch in physical fact but a militant rogue in disposition, killed him by poison administered by a certain physician and placed upon the throne the youngest of his sons, Arses. He similarly made away with the brothers of the new king, who were barely of age, in order that the young man might be isolated and tractable to his control. But the young king let it be known that he was offended at Bagoas's previous outrageous behaviour and was prepared to punish the author of these crimes. So Bagoas anticipated his intentions and killed Arses and his children also while he was still in the third year of his reign. The royal house was thus extinguished, and there was no one in the direct line of descent to claim the throne. Instead, Bagoas selected a certain Darius, a member of the court circle, and secured the throne for him. He was the son of Arsanes and grandson of that Ostanes who was a brother of Artaxerxes who had been king. As to Bagoas, an odd thing happened to him and one to point a moral. Pursuing his habitual savagery, he attempted to remove Darius by poison. The plan leaked out, however, and the king, calling upon Bagoas, as it were, to drink to him a toast and handing him his own cup, compelled him to take his own medicine. (Diod.Sic.XVII.5.3.)

Two issues stand out in Diodorus's account. Firstly, the power of the courtier Bagoas as 'king-maker', and secondly, the astuteness of Darius III. Bagoas had proved himself in 350/49 in the Persian campaign against Egypt. Diodorus further describes him as a man whom the king trusted most, who was exceptionally daring and impatient of propriety. Bagoas shared the king's trust with the Persian Aristazanes, an usher of the king. Assigned to him were 5000 elite soldiers and 80 triremes. He was ordered to take Pelusium and then encamped with Mentor of Rhodes at Bubastis. According to Diodorus, the 'result of this was that these two by their co-operation in the service of the king attained later on the greatest power of all the friends and relatives at Artaxerxes's court', and he continues, '[a]s for Bagoas, after he had administered all the king's affairs in the Upper Satrapies, he rose to such power because of his partnership with Mentor that he was master of the kingdom and Artaxerxes III did nothing without his advice. After Artaxerxes's death, he designated in every case the successor to the throne and enjoyed all the functions of kingship save the title' (Diod.Sic.XVI.50.8.).

The question that has rarely been asked is what Bagoas's motive would have been to kill not only Artaxerxes III but also the successors he himself had selected. By all accounts, he was held in high esteem by Artaxerxes III – that his moral compass would have told him to eliminate a harsh king is not convincing. What did he hope to achieve in placing Arses, and then Astanes, on the throne? As it is, the story of Bagoas's actions and the killing of the king and the two royal heirs is reminiscent of the story of the courtier Artabanus, who killed Xerxes and the heir to the throne, Darius, and also aimed to kill Artaxerxes I, who, however, saw through his scheme and killed him, just like Darius III eliminated Bagoas. Courtiers and eunuchs with 'great influence on the king' are a literary theme which we find in Greek fourth-century writers on Persia, and it seems appropriate to exercise caution in the later accounts of Diodorus, which seem to embellish history, where standard clichés are readily employed to emphasise the image of the Persian court and, by extension, the empire as being in a state of decline and decadence.

But there is an even more tangible reason to question his outline of events. The record of the Babylonian Astronomical Diary contradicts the Greek claim of the murder of Artaxerxes III, noting the succession of Arses as the logical consequence of Artaxerxes's natural death. As we have seen in the case of Xerxes's death, the authors of the Astronomical Diaries would not shy away from recording the truth. Instead, we find that the entry simply states the death of Umakush/Artaxerxes and the succession of his son Arshu. And again, the Babylonian Dynastic prophesy states explicitly for the death of Artaxerxes IV that his death was not accidental but caused by a *sha-rēshi*, a term which tends to be translated 'eunuch', though it could merely refer to a palace courtier: '[...] kings [...] which/of his father. [...]. For two(?) years [he will exercise the kingship]. That king a eunuch [will murder]. Any prince [...] will attack and [seize] the thro[ne]. For five years [he will exercise] kingsh[ip]' (transl. after Kuhrt 2010: 425, no. 4 (i)).

Artaxerxes IV's reign was accepted in local administration, as the dating formula of a sales document from Samaria shows: 'On the twentieth of Adar, the second year (of Arses/Artaxerxes IV), the accession year of [D]arius the king, in Samari[a the fortified city which is in Samaria the province]' (Samaria Papyrus no. 1; transl. Lemaire 2013: 78–79).

FURTHER READING

For the main narrative of the reigns of Artaxerxes III and Artaxerxes IV see Briant, P. (2006). *From Cyrus to Alexander*, 680–690. Winona Lake, IN.: Eisenbrauns. The entry in the Astronomical Diary regarding the death of Artaxerxes III is discussed by Walker, C. (1997). Achaemenid chronology and the Babylonian sources. In: *Mesopotamia and Iran in the Persian Period. Conquest and Imperialism 539–331 BC* (ed. J. Curtis), 17–25. London: British Museum Press. For an assessment of the relationship between Persia and Greece in the mid-fourth century see Brosius, M. (2003). Why Persia became the enemy of Macedon. *AchHist* 8: 227–238.

10

A Good King in the End: Darius III

10.1 The Succession of Darius III

When Artaxerxes IV died after a two-year reign, Artashata, the son of Oarsanes/ Arsanes and Sisygambis, and the grandson of Ostanes, succeeded to the throne in 336 aged around 45 and took the throne name Darius III. He is said to have been the satrap of Armenia (Just.10.3), which would fit geographically, considering that Artaxerxes III had commanded him to fight the Cadusians. Darius III was married to Stateira, by some authors thought to have been his sister (Plut.*Alex.*XXX.3; Curt.Ruf.IV.10.2), while others identify her as the sister of the Persian noble Pharnaces (Diod.Sic.XVII.35.2). Among their children were the brothers Ariobarzanes and Ochus and the sisters Stateira and Drypetis. Since the mother of Stateira is not known, we must allow for the possibility that she was Darius's half-sister rather than a full sister, in which case theirs was an accepted union amongst members of the royal family. Immediately after his accession, Darius quashed a renewed rebellion in Egypt, which may have broken out at the death of Artaxerxes III. It was led by the mysterious Khababash, who claimed the kingship of Upper and Lower Egypt, but ended in the winter of 336/5. In Babylon, an uprising under Nidintu-Bel, if it indeed happened, was probably quashed by 335, at which point Darius III was listed in a king-list from Uruk.

10.1.1 Battling Negative Propaganda

Greek and Latin authors writing about Darius III are torn between describing him, on the one hand, as a weak king, an illegitimate successor to the throne, a king who had entered an incestuous marriage, and on the other hand, as a courageous leader in war. Arrian called him 'as soft and unsound of mind in war as anybody ever was' (Arr.*an.* III.22.2–5), and Plutarch's *On the Virtue of Alexander* (326E) described him as 'a slave

A History of Ancient Persia: The Achaemenid Empire, First Edition. Maria Brosius.
© 2021 John Wiley & Sons, Inc. Published 2021 by John Wiley & Sons, Inc.

and courtier of the king, him did you (= Fortune) make the mighty lord of Persia'. Diodorus gave him some credit:

> Darius's selection for the throne was based on his known bravery, in which quality he far surpassed the other Persians. Once, when king Artaxerxes (III) was campaigning against the Cadusians, one of them with a wide reputation for strength and courage challenged a volunteer among the Persians to fight in single combat with him. No other dared accept, but Darius alone entered the contest and slew the challenger, being honoured in consequence by the king with rich gifts, while among the Persians he was conceded the first place in prowess. It was because of this prowess that he was thought worthy to take over the kingship. This happened about the same time as Philip died and Alexander became king. (Diod.Sic.XVII.6.1–2)

Modern scholarship reflects the bias of the sources. Tarn described him as a 'worthless' king (Tarn 2014), and Hornblower referred to Darius III as 'Alexander's cowardly opponent' (Hornblower 1994). For Bengtson, the Achaemenid empire had become 'a colossus on clay feet' (Bengtson 2009), and the Persian army consisted of nothing but 'hordes' of people according to Hammond (Hammond 1986). In fact, we are to see the failure of the army as the manifestation of Persian decadence and the failure of Darius III to confront a Greek force with superior weaponry and courageous soldiers. Particular attention is being paid to the use of (Greek) mercenary forces in the Persian army – clearly a sign of its weakness, as it had to use foreigners to fight for it. Thus, Arrian states that at the battle at the Granicus River, the satraps used 20 000 foreign mercenaries with an equal number of Persian cavalry (Arr.*an*.I.14.1).

A more balanced view is offered by few: Nylander (1993) argued that the king's fleeing the battlefield cannot be equated with cowardice but with the maxim that the king must live. As the worldly representative of Auramazda, he could not die in battle. If he did, so would the kingship and the power; accordingly, while present in battle, and indeed in its centre, he had to withdraw to save his life. The fact that he intended to assemble more forces from the east when he retreated after Gaugamela does not reflect the action of a king deserting his army or his empire. Equally, the fact that the Athenians as late as 331 still sent a delegation to him asking for support against Macedonian hegemony in Greece, demonstrates that the trust in the Persian king was still very much alive. Seibert (Seibert 1988: 437–456) called Darius's operations and defence strategies sensible, coherent and well organised. For one thing, in reaction to his defeat at Issus, Darius was able to analyse the battle and improve his tactics, lengthening the lances and swords of his men in light of past experience. He increased the cavalry and created a tank force of 200 scythed chariots.

The bias in the sources and modern literature reflects a problem which concerns Alexander III himself. On the one hand, one is eager to demonstrate that the Persian empire was at the brink of collapse, that the king, the court and the army all showed clear signs of weakness, unfitness to rule, disorder, intrigue and chaos. On the other hand, one had to have a worthy enemy in order to allow Alexander III to emerge as the heroic warrior, the conqueror of an empire that was worth conquering. After all, it was this conquest which gave him legendary status. Claiming victory over a weak empire did not quite have the same glorious effect as had fighting a formidable enemy. Therefore, Darius III had to be an illegitimate successor to the throne, enter an incestuous marriage and flee the battlefield when faced with Alexander, while at the same time having suppressed rebellions in the empire, fought bravely in the Cadusian War and been held in high regard by the Persians.

10.2   External Threat

Darius III may indeed have been a good Persian warrior, but for the first time in the 230-year history of the empire, a Persian king was faced with a foreign invasion, something which was hugely different from quashing rebellions, dealing with palace revolts or being involved in Greek politics. Although aware of the Macedonian threat in the early stages of the conflict, it must have been difficult for Darius III, and indeed the Persians, to realise Alexander's ultimate ambition. If we trust the Greek sources, after the battle of Issus, a letter written by the king and addressed to Alexander noticed the failed diplomacy after Alexander's accession, and the king's attempts to mediate a peace agreement.

10.2.1   The Macedonian Invasion

Macedonia's war against Persia remains clouded in uncertainties about its actual aim – did Philip II only want to campaign against the satraps of Asia Minor or was he set to conquer the whole empire? Even more puzzling is his revival of the memory of the Persian Wars and his declaration of Macedon as champion of the Greeks in revenge for Xerxes's invasion of Greece of 480/79. This slogan was first voiced by Philip II in 337, shortly after his victory over Athens at Chaeronaea. 'He spread the word that he wanted to make war against the Persians on behalf of the Greeks and to punish them for the profanation of the temples' (Diod.Sic.XVI.89.2). Alongside it went the platitude of the 'freedom of the Greeks of Asia', proclaimed as the reason for the campaign in Asia Minor of the Macedonian generals Attalus and Parmenion. Alexander adopted both slogans wholesale.

Whether the revenge motif pulled any weight with the Greeks themselves must be doubted. What could be its significance 150 years after the event, after decades of co-operation between the Greek states and Persia since then, the last being the Athenian–Persian alliance of 342? For Alexander, the revenge for Xerxes's invasion became tangible in many aspects of his campaign, from the route taken to Sestus to the symbolism at Troy to the 300 Persian panoplies which he dedicated to the temple of Athena after the battle at the Granicus River, and which were, in his words, 'taken from the barbarians of Asia by Alexander, son of Philip, and the Greeks, except for Sparta', and, finally, the burning of Persepolis in the summer of 330, which was started deliberately by setting fire to Xerxes's palace – the symbolic end to his revenge for Xerxes's invasion.

10.2.2   Granicus

Alexander's campaign began in the spring of 334. With a force estimated at c.50 000 men, including 5000 cavalry, Alexander led his army overland to Sestus, taking the same route Xerxes had taken 150 years before. Arrian notes his march, covering

500 km in 20 days, that is, moving the army at 25 km per day. He met the Persian army at the shore of the Propontis near Zeleia. This army had a different balance: a cavalry of 20 000 and an infantry that included 20 000 Greek mercenaries and troops levied at local level. While Memnon proposed a scorched earth policy to avoid battle, Arsites, the satrap of Hellespontine Phrygia, favoured a direct confrontation, a decision that was accepted by the other generals. The army positioned itself on the east bank of the Granicus River. Arrian's description of the cavalry being positioned at the edge of the river (where they could not be deployed effectively) and separate from the infantry, which was stationed behind them on the high ground, is regarded as unrealistic. However the Persian army was organised at the Granicus River, the challenge for the Macedonian army was to avoid suffering collapse at the steep river banks. Many attempts have been made to reconstruct the ensuing battle, but none of the ancient accounts allow a coherent scenario. In the ensuing fight, it seems that the Persians Rhoesaces and Spithridates made for Alexander directly, and this attack went as far as shattering Alexander's helmet when Cleitus the Black, commander of the *ile*, the elite cavalry, came to his rescue, and his life was saved. The battle was won because, in the end, the Macedonian cavalry gained ground as their lances proved more effective than the Persian javelins. The Persian cavalry was forced to retreat, and with the death of many Persian commanders, the battle order collapsed. Alexander's army then attacked the infantry, foremost the mercenaries, and all but 2000 of them lost their lives. They were taken prisoner and sent to Macedon in chains as forced labour. The battle was lost for the Persians. The satrap Arsites committed suicide in the face of the now inevitable Macedonian occupation of Asia Minor. Atizyes and Arsames withdrew to their respective satrapies, while Memnon returned to the coast.

Alexander secured Dascyleium and then proceeded to Sardis. In both satrapal centres, he installed Macedonian officials. After taking control of Ephesus, he met with resistance at Miletus, and the city was taken by force; its city-walls were demolished. Still, by late 333, Miletus was back under Persian control. A battle at sea against the superior Persian fleet was avoided. Thinking that he could control the Persian fleet by denying it access to the shore, and thus the ability to renew supplies, Alexander demobilised most of his own fleet. The short-sightedness of this action became apparent in early 333 when he had to employ a new fleet. His siege of Halicarnassus had to be abandoned when the Persian forces put up a strong defence. When his troops finally were able to break through the city walls, the Persian general Memnon set the city alight and the Macedonian army was forced to abandon the burning city. Halicarnassus resisted a Macedonian force until 332.

10.2.3   Issus

In early 333, Darius III levied an army at Babylon, consisting mainly of Greek mercenaries recruited from across the empire. The historian Callisthenes (lived 360–328) gives a figure of 30 000 men, but it is impossible to determine whether this is accurate, as most figures given for the Persian army are an exaggeration used to underline the greatness of Alexander's achievement. Darius III moved north with the army and his entourage, but the latter were re-routed to Damascus when Darius learned of Alexander's illness and decided to move faster. But Alexander III was already moving via Soli and Mallus to Issus. Darius III wanted his army to fight in the plain, but Alexander wanted to meet them near the coast. It became a waiting game, each king waiting for the other to move first. In the end, the Persian army descended onto the plains north of Issus, cutting communications between Alexander and his bases in Cilicia. The battle location, impossible to reconstruct given the description in the ancient sources and the fact that the landscape and coastal lines have changed over the past two millennia, will remain unknown, but it is thought that it happened in a narrowed part of the plain which provided only a 4-km-wide space, thus preventing the Persian infantry from lining itself up to its fullest extent. The cavalry was concentrated by the sea to the right, the centre was commanded by the mercenary forces and the Persian army was next to it. The remainder made up the depth of the formation. Alexander filtered his infantry and cavalry down to the plain. His cavalry attacked first, making for Darius in the centre of the Persian army. His charge opened a gap between him and his infantry. Darius's mercenaries were able to attack the Macedonians from the side. On the left, the Persian cavalry forced the Thessalians back across the river.

But, faced with the Macedonian lances, the Persian infantry folded, and Alexander advanced further towards Darius. The Persian javelins were no match for the Macedonian onslaught. In the end, Darius fled the battlefield in his chariot, then on horseback, to save his life. This action caused uncertainties among his soldiers, who began to withdraw, leaving the mercenaries to face the Macedonian cavalry. By now, the Macedonian infantry had recovered its phalanx position, and the combined force resulted in the collapse of the mercenaries' ability to fight. The Persian retreat was made worse by the deeply positioned infantry forces, which were now in each other's way, and the fleeing Persian cavalry caused further deaths by having to escape right through the infantry. More Persians met their deaths in this retreat than in the actual fighting. The figures, given at 100 000 Persian losses against 500 for the Macedonians, are, as always, to be regarded with caution, but there can be no doubt that the bulk of the Persian army had been annihilated in this battle.

Alexander now had unhindered access to the Syrian coast. In Damascus, he captured the king's entourage, including the royal family, his mother, wife and children, and took possession of the royal treasury. In the following year, he took the cities of Tyre and Gaza, albeit in the face of considerable resistance, which, in the case of Tyre, meant a seven-month siege, ending in the complete destruction of the city and the enslavement of its population, while in Gaza, the siege ended in the massacre of the soldiers who withstood the Macedonian attack, and the women and children became prisoners of war. In the winter of 332/1, the Persian satrap of Egypt, Mazaeus, surrendered Memphis to Alexander without resistance. In the spring of 331, Alexander moved towards Phoenicia and undertook a punitive campaign against Samaria. The people of Samaria had resented the Macedonian take-over and had killed Alexander's governor Andromachus. Alexander retaliated with brutal measures and executed the governor's murderers.

10.2.4   Gaugamela

Immediately before Gaugamela, Darius offered Alexander the territory up to the Euphrates River, a ransom payment of 30 000 talents in return for his captured family and one of his daughters in marriage. Alexander refused, and a further battle became inevitable. Darius's army consisted of Bactrian and Sogdian cavalry, as well as units from western India and the Sacae. They were led by Bessus, the satrap of Bactria and Darius's kin. Additional forces came from Areia, Arachosia and Parthyene. Darius had their weapons improved, better swords and longer lances – a valiant effort, but not with sufficient time to experiment and improve fighting tactics. In addition, he had 200 scythed chariots. Darius and his army moved towards Arbela and halted at Gaugamela. He positioned his army between the River Bumelus and the Jabal Maqlub hillside. An eclipse of the moon on 20 September was interpreted as an ominous sign by both sides.

Darius, again taking centre position in the army, surrounded by 50 scythed chariots, his kinsmen and the *melophoroi*, the 'apple-bearers', came under increasing pressure from the Macedonian army, and at some point he fled the battlefield. The Persian line had been breached and, with Darius's flight, the army was left in disarray. At this point, the ancient sources describe Alexander's single-minded intention to pursue Darius to the end, which he did over the whole day, covering a distance of 30 km to the River Lycus (mod. Great Zab). Darius fled to Arbela and then towards Media, together with a small circle of royal guards led by Bessus.

The Babylonian Astronomical Diaries report on the battle of Gaugamela as follows: 'That month (Ulul), on day 11 (= 18 September 331); panic broke out in the camp of the king. [...] lay/encamped(?) opposite the king. On day 24 (= 1 October 331), in the morning: the king of the world [...] the standard(?). They fought with each other, and a severe(?) defeat of the troops of [...] The troops of the king deserted him and to their cities [...]. They fled [to the l]and of Gutium [...]' (Sachs and Hunger 1988, no. -330, obv.14–18; transl. after Kuhrt 2010: 447, no. 27).

10.2.5 The Royal Cities

In the winter of 331/0, Alexander took Babylon, which surrendered without offering resistance. About three weeks after the battle of Gaugamela, Alexander staged an official entrance into Babylon: 'That month (= Tashritu), from day 1 (= 8 October 331) until [...] came to Babylon saying: "Esangil [...] and the Babylonians for the treasury of Esangil [...]. On day 11 (= 18 October 331) in Sippar an order from Al[exander ...] as follows: '[...] one shall not enter your houses.' On day 13 (= 20 October 331), [... sikil]la-gate, the outer gate of Esangil, and [...]. On day 14: these Ionians [...] short [...], fatty tissue [...] Alexander, king of the world, entered Babylon [...] horses and equipment of [...] and the Babylonians and the people [...] a letter on parchment to [...] thus: [...]"' (Sachs and Hunger 1988, no. -330 rev. 3'–15'; transl. after Kuhrt 2010: 447, no. 27).

After a 20-day march from Babylon, Alexander reached Susa, which was surrendered by the satrap Abulites. He confiscated royal property and 50 000 talents of silver from the royal treasury. Next, Alexander took Persis and the centre of the Persian empire, Persepolis. Although the city's commander, Tiridates, had offered the peaceful surrender to Alexander, he was set on destroying it. Diodorus provides a detailed description of the brutality and destruction which the Macedonian army inflicted upon Persepolis and its inhabitants. Alexander allowed his soldiers to plunder the city and slaughter, kill and deport its population, women taken as the soldiers' prisoners.

Sources in Translation 10.1

The Destruction of Persepolis

The destruction of the royal terrace, which was begun deliberately in Xerxes's palace, symbolised the fulfilment of the Greek revenge for Xerxes's invasion of Greece. The pretext of the war had become a reality, and with the burning of the centre of Persian power, the task was fulfilled. Technically, the burning of Persepolis thus brought Alexander's campaigns to an end.

> It was the wealthiest city under the sun, and the private houses had been filled with all kinds of luxury over many years. The Macedonians stormed it and slaughtered all the men whom they met, plundering the houses, many of which belonged to the ordinary inhabitants, and which were furnished and decorated with all kinds of ornaments. From there a lot of silver was carried off and no small amount of gold, and many elaborate dresses, in sea purple or with gold embroidery, became the reward of the victors. The enormous palaces, known throughout the entire world, were turned to ruins through *hybris* and utter destruction. (Diod.Sic.XVII.70.6)

> He (= Alexander) burned the palace of the Persian kings, though this act was against the advice of Parmenion, who urged him to spare it for various reasons, chiefly because it was hardly wise to destroy what was now his property and because the Asians would, in his opinion, be less willing to support him if he seemed bent merely upon passing through as their conqueror rather than upon ruling it securely as a king. Alexander's answer was that he wished to punish the Persians for their invasion of Greece; his present act was retribution for the destruction of Athens, the burning of the temples and all the other crimes they had committed against the Greeks. (Arr.*an*.III.18.11)

Persepolis marked a turning point in Alexander's conquest of Persia. During the months Alexander spent at Persepolis, his ambition to become 'king of Asia' opened up a new political and military perspective and must have seemed a real possibility. But the destruction of the city meant the loss of the central focus point of the Persian satrapies, because Persepolis had symbolised the empire in its entirety since its foundation by Darius I. Among the royal cities of the empire, Persepolis took first place. It was the utmost expression of royal kingship and of Persian rule. Heleen Sancisi-Weerdenburg has argued that with his destruction of Persepolis, Alexander severed the link between the king and the satraps. As representatives of the king, they were the immediate embodiment of royal power in the Persian satrapies; their palaces and *paradeisoi* reflected Achaemenid court life and royal architecture on a smaller scale. The satraps were members of the royal family or related to the royal household by marriage. The loss of the Persian centre of power meant the loss of a vital link between the king and his satraps, as well as the king and the peoples of the lands of the empire. Even though Alexander took over the satrapal system and appointed members of the Persian nobility as satraps or confirmed them in their office, their power was hugely infringed by Macedonian officials controlling the military forces and financial resources of the satrapy, clearly manifesting their role as conquerors. On Alexander's return from India in 325/4, most satrapies were in revolt against Macedonian domination. Their loss of status, as well as the lack of affinity with the king, led to the disloyalty of the satraps.

Special Topic 10.1

The Irony of it All

Philip's and Alexander's pretext for the war, the Greek revenge for Xerxes's invasion of 480/79, cynically denied the long-standing diplomatic relations between Macedon and Persia, and crucially the fact that Macedonian forces had fought in Xerxes's army against the Greeks in 480/79. We are reminded that, in 513, the Macedonian king Amyntas had offered Earth and Water to Darius I, thus recognising the supremacy of the Persian king. Amyntas also offered refuge to the pro-Persian Hippias after his expulsion from Athens. In 492, during the revolt of Ionia, Thasos and Macedon were secured for Persia. But the most paradoxical aspect of Macedonia's claim that it sought to be champion of Greece to avenge Athens is the fact that during Xerxes's invasion of Greece in 480/79, Macedonia's relationship to Persia meant that the Macedonian infantry fought on the Persian side, under the Persian command, against the Greeks (Hdt.VII.185). With this in mind, Macedonia's justification for the punishment of the Thebans exposes their own manipulation of the historical facts, denying their own role in their historical past, when they themselves fought on the Persian side against the Greeks.

Macedonian support for the Persian side is undeniable: After the occupation of Athens, Alexander I acted as mediator between Mardonius and the Athenians, proposing the Persian peace terms. Alexander strengthened his ties with Persia through a marriage alliance between his sister Gygaea and a Persian nobleman, Bubares, the son of Megabazus, the governor of Thrace; their son, Amyntas, later became the Persian governor of the city of Alabanda in Caria. After the Persian Wars, Macedon did not join the Delian League against Persia. The rebelling Artabazus had fled to the Macedonian court in 359. We know that at least one other Persian noble, Aminaspes, stayed at the court of Philip II (Curt.Ruf. VI.4.25). And a further expression of the peaceful relationship between Macedon and Persia was the offer made by Pixodarus, the satrap of Caria, to give his daughter in marriage to Philip's son Arrhidaeus.

Apart from the political closeness, it can be argued that other links existed between the Macedonian and the Persian court, such as the political marriage alliances forged to bind other powerful families to the royal house and to seal a treaty concluded with another ruler, the royal hunt and the institution of the circle of the King's Friends, the gift-giving to elevate individuals to the special status of a King's Friend. Thus, for example, Arrian (Arr.*an*.I.5.1) recalls that Langaros, the king of the Agrianes, was presented with gifts by Alexander because of his services to the king. These gifts were considered 'to be of the highest value [including the promise of Alexander's sister Cyna in marriage]'. In another instance, when Alexander had fallen ill before the battle at Issus, his doctor, Philip the Arcarnanian, gave Alexander fast-remedy drugs. In return,

Alexander honoured him with 'magnificent gifts and assigned him to the most loyal category of Friends' (Diod.Sic.XVII.31.6).

That the Greeks were opposed to Macedonian control was evident in their attitude towards Alexander. At news of Philip's death, many Greeks wanted to free themselves from Macedonian supremacy. Before the battle at Issus, Alexander learned that Chios, Lesbos and Mytilene had joined forces with Memnon, who planned to carry the war into Macedon with 300 ships and land forces, with many Greeks ready to revolt (Diod.Sic.XVII.31.3–4). In 332, king Agis III of Sparta (died 330) gathered the mercenaries who survived the battle of Issus, 8 000 in number, and wanted to change matters in Greece with the aid of Darius, who provided him with ships and money to gather forces on Crete. Still as late as 331/0, the Greeks hoped to get the support of Darius III for their fight against Alexander (Diod.Sic.XVII.621–3).

Alexander the Philocyros

And it is here that the revenge motif, the pretext for the war, stands in contrast to Alexander's ambition to be recognised as king of Asia. His desire to be recognised as a king, as expressed in his increasing 'Persianisation', that is, wearing Persian dress, the royal diadem or tiara and the girdle, adopting the procedure of *proskynesis* and including Persians in the group of Companions as well as in his army, could not be reconciled with his behaviour as conqueror, manifestly demonstrated in the destruction of Persepolis.

Perhaps most revealing in his aspiration to be recognised as king was his desire to follow in the footsteps of Cyrus II, the founder of the Persian empire, whom he regarded as the exceptional model of a conqueror-king. Whenever an opportunity arose, Alexander demonstrated his affinity with the founder of the empire, wanting to be regarded as a *philocyros* (Strabo XI.11.4). His 'respect' for Cyrus II was explicitly demonstrated in his concern for Cyrus's tomb at Pasargadae (Arr.*an.* VI.29.4–11). During his campaigns, Alexander made frequent gestures underlining his kinship with Cyrus II. Among these, his entry into Babylon, reminiscent of Cyrus's entry into the city in 539, must have carried a considerable propagandistic weight. Continuity of benign rule was further expressed in Alexander's granting freedom to the Ariaspians because their people had been made Benefactors of the King by Cyrus II. He also followed in Cyrus's footsteps on his march to India, a fact which apparently inspired him. Arrian even invites a comparison between the Indians encountered by Alexander and the Persians who first supported Cyrus's conquest of Media (Arr.*an.*V.4.5). Alexander's disastrous march through the Gedrosian desert was apparently inspired by Cyrus's – failed – attempt to cross the desert. All these gestures served to pursue a carefully orchestrated ideological agenda. They were meant to invite comparison with Cyrus, and to link Alexander with the Persian king hailed for his noble spirit and humane rulership, as they were depicted in Xenophon's *Cyropaedia*.

Some scholars argue that Alexander went even further and that he regarded himself as the last Achaemenid king, but the question is whether he ever could be. Alexander may have claimed a kingship as 'king of Asia', but no source reveals that he was ever regarded by the Persians as 'Great King, king of kings, king of lands', the traditional royal title. The title 'king of lands' was given to him in Babylon

(Sachs and Hunger 1988: no. -329, B obv.), but equally he was regarded as a foreigner, 'Alexander the king who is from the land of Hani (= Macedon)' (Sachs and Hunger 1988: -328 LE). No contemporary Persian sources survive that could shed light on the way the Persians perceived the Macedonian conqueror. But Alexander wanted to achieve political union between Persians and Macedonians, expressed in the foundation of cities populated with mixed populations: 'His highest concept of government, as far as the evidence at our disposal permits us to see, was the Macedonian-Persian Empire embracing geographically Greece proper, the Balkans to the Danube (as a deep frontier-zone) and the satrapies of the Persian Empire, from Egypt to the Jaxartes and the Indus' (Fraser 1996: 181). Yet, in the absence of any attempt at consolidating the empire, the creation of a Macedonian-Persian empire was hardly feasible. The mutual resentment between Macedonians and Persians likewise made this idea impossible. The 30 000 Persian youths who were taken from Persian noble families, trained in Macedonian warfare and clothed in Macedonian-style dress (Arr.*an*.VII.6.1; Diod.Sic.XVIII.108.1; Plut.*Alex*.71.1), gave Alexander a direct hold over the Persian nobility. Their male offspring were in fact hostages of Macedonia, forcing the Persian nobles to give in to Alexander and to abandon their hopes for resistance. This group was, in fact, meant to act as a counter-group to the Macedonians. The lack of co-operation on the part of the Persian nobles and the resentment of his Macedonian officers at his growing 'Persianisation' meant that Alexander's vision was bound to fail. Macedonian acceptance of Persian nobles was limited.

His failure to maintain a link with the satraps meant that, for the Persian nobility, Alexander was a non-Persian, a foreign usurper who wore the royal tiara and Persian dress, but who had little understanding of the ideology of Persian kingship.

10.2.6 The Death of Darius III

In the spring of 330, Darius III, who had wintered in Ecbatana in Media, moved northeast towards the Caspian Gates with a force of 3300 cavalry and a larger infantry force. Alexander, who had begun his move from Persepolis in early May, now pursued Darius with a reduced force consisting of his cavalry, most of the phalanx and the light infantry. Alexander reached Rhagae after a 10-day march, but learned that Darius had passed the Caspian Gates. Darius, meanwhile, was dependent on the support of Bessus, the Bactrian satrap, and Nabarzanes, the chiliarch. Alexander, in pursuit, covered about 200 km in four nights and three days, riding from Choarene to the borders of Parthyene. Shortly after dawn, he saw the first Persian unit marching behind the king. At the Macedonians' approach, Darius III was stabbed to death by Satibarzanes and Barsaentes, the satraps of Areia and Arachosia. His death can be seen in two ways: The immediate impression is that the courtiers wanted to rid themselves of their weak and defeated king. Alternatively, the courtiers might have killed Darius because death was preferable to becoming a prisoner of war of the foreign invader. When Alexander discovered the king's body, a complete change of heart occurred, and he turned from pursuer to defender. Alexander mourned the king and ordered his body to be returned to Persepolis, in line with the Persian custom that the king's body had to find his final resting place there. He then resolved to pursue Darius's murderers and avenge his death. After the destruction of Persepolis, this marked a second turning point in Alexander's attitude towards Persia. It was a first step towards his own 'Persianisation', in which he, the king of Asia, saw himself in a new realm far removed from Macedon.

10.3 In the Footsteps of the Persian Kings?

Darius's death did not lead to the collective surrender of the Persian satraps to Alexander. He was forced to conquer the lands of the empire one by one on his eastern conquest, only to discover on his return that many satrapies were in rebellion against him. His attempts to establish himself as 'king of Asia', or even as the last Achaemenid king, as has sometimes been argued, never took hold. These efforts began with Alexander's pursuit of the murderers of Darius and ended with the mass wedding at Susa in 324, in which he married two Achaemenid princesses – demonstratively a symbol of his legitimate succession to the Persian throne.

Alexander gathered his forces at Shar-e Qumis/Hecatompylos to begin the formal defeat of the remaining army. In the course of this pursuit, Nabarzanes surrendered to Alexander, and the satrap of Hyrcania, Phrataphernes, followed suit. Artabazus and his sons joined Alexander's court; the Greek mercenaries who had fought under Darius were incorporated into Alexander's army. At Susia (mod. Tus, near Mashad), Satibarzanes surrendered to Alexander and was confirmed in office. Resistance came only from a few fronts: The Mardi were fought in a five-day campaign, but Bessus, who had retreated to his satrapy of Bactria, assumed the upright tiara and declared himself the new Achaemenid king, as Artaxerxes (V). At this point, Alexander reacted by making himself 'more Persian': he adopted the Persian diadem, the striped tunic and girdle, and clothed senior Companions in the scarlet robes of Persian courtiers. Darius's brother, Oxathres, was made to join his entourage. These all served as clear signals that Alexander regarded himself as the legitimate successor of Darius.

Alexander marched towards Bactria, but after Alexander had left Areia, Satibarzanes rebelled against him and slew the Macedonian cavalry force that had been left to guard the garrison. Alexander returned with his forces in an attempt to quash Satibarzanes's rebellion, but Satibarzanes had already left to join forces with Bessus. The Persian Arsaces was appointed to take over the satrapy; Alexander now wanted to pursue the murderers of Darius III so that they would receive their just punishment. Barsaentes fled to India, and the Macedonian army occupied Phrada, the satrapal centre of Drangiana.

In Ariaspa, Alexander rested his army for about 60 days. Meanwhile, Satibarzanes and Bessus continued to stir unrest in the eastern satrapies; Satibarzanes also sent troops from Bactria to Media. His rebellion lasted for about two years; he was killed in the summer of 329 and replaced as satrap of Bactria by Stasanor, who, however, had difficulties establishing himself. In the late winter of 328, Alexander led his forces up the Helmand valley, through heavy snow and with insufficient provisions. The pass across the Hindukush was blocked, and he was stuck somewhere near Kabul for at least one month.

Bessus had been unable to get the Bactrian nobility behind him; he retreated beyond the Oxus River, and Alexander was able to take Bactria unopposed. Artabazus was put in charge of the province. Alexander's next goal was the capture of Bessus. His army crossed 75 km of desert, his troops suffering significant losses from thirst. After the Macedonians had crossed the river with makeshift rafts made of stuffed hides, Bessus was handed over to Alexander by Dataphernes and Spitamenes. He suffered a cruel death: he was disrobed, fettered and then scourged, and sent to Bactria, where he was to be mutilated, and then on to Ecbatana, where he was executed. On the outside, it may have looked like the harsh punishment for the murder of Darius, but Bessus was also made an example of for any pretender to the Achaemenid throne.

Moving on to Maracanda and to the Banks of the Iaxartes River, Alexander concluded a peace treaty with the Scythian tribes across the river, as he regarded this territory outside his empire. Here he founded a new city, Alexandria Eschate. Meanwhile, Spitamenes and Dataphernes continued to stir unrest in Sogdiana and Bactria. Macedonian soldiers stationed at garrisons there were massacred. Alexander reacted severely, conquering seven fortresses close to the Iaxartes, massacring rebels and enslaving survivors. To the north, the Scythians were eager to attack his new city. They received instant punishment from Alexander, who sent a barrage of artillery, followed by the cavalry, which was flanked by archers and light infantry. The Companions, marching in column, broke the main Scythian formation. There followed an extended pursuit, and eventually, caused by the Scythian king's illness, the Scythians offered peace.

At Nautaca, the local dynast, Sisimithres, was shocked into submission by siege engineering, while at Coenus, an invasion of Spitamenes and his Scythian allies was repulsed. At Parthyaea and Areia the satraps entered a ceasefire. After two years, the eastern satrapies were relatively quiet. Amyntas was placed as satrap of Bactria and Sogdiana and a large network of military colonies set up. A native cavalry was recruited, while 30 000 Iranian youths were recruited to be trained in the Macedonian army. At this point, Alexander married Roxane, daughter of the Bactrian Oxyartes. The implications were manifold: the fact that he married a foreigner no doubt caused more tensions among the Macedonians, as this act emphasised the increasing 'orientalising' of their king.

Macedonian resentment towards Alexander grew stronger when he attempted to introduce *proskynesis*, and this was heavily resisted by the Macedonians, to whom this amounted to committing a sacrilegeous act. On his return from India and the Hydaspes River, Alexander discovered that most of the satrapies were in rebellion against him. Greek soldiers in the satraps' service were demobilised on his orders, but refused to be conscripted by him. Instead, led by the Athenian Leosthenes, they returned to Greece. Those who remained lived like renegades in the countryside.

In January 324, Alexander was back in Pasargadae, where he discovered that Cyrus's tomb had been neglected and made a point of ordering its restoration. A month later, he staged mass weddings at Susa, in which 10 000 Macedonians were made to marry Persian women. These weddings have been regarded as a demonstration of the Macedonian–Persian union Alexander aimed for. But in actual fact, they were a demonstration of Macedonian domination and presumption of power (cf. Bosworth 1988: 157; Bosworth 1994: 840). The success of these marriages and their long-term effect was limited. Those of the Macedonian soldiers were dissolved almost immediately after Alexander's death in June 323, since the Macedonians were not allowed to take their wives and children home. Stateira/Barsine, a daughter of Darius III who had been married to Alexander, was killed by Roxane. The fate of Parysatis, a daughter of Artaxerxes III also married to him, is unknown, but if Alexander's wife Roxane was afraid that the offspring of the Persian princesses would rank higher than her own son in the succession stakes, she most likely eliminated her, too. Roxane even regarded Darius's daughter Drypetis as a threat, because she killed her a short time after the death of Hephaistion.

Darius's niece Amastris was married to Craterus (Memnon FGrH 434 F1 4.4; Arr.*an.* VII.4.5), but was abandoned by him after Alexander's death. She then married Dionysius of Heraclea Pontica, with whom she had three children, Clearchus, Oxathres and Amastris. Dionysius died in 306, and four years later, Amastris married Lysimachus, with whom she had a son, Alexandros (Poly.VI.12). As regent of her city-foundation, Amastris, she minted coins bearing the legend '(of) Queen Amastris'. Her daughter also was to carry the ancient Achaemenid name Amestris. Two daughters of Artabazus, Artacama and Artonis, were married to Ptolemy and Eumenes (Arr.*an.*VII.4.6), respectively, but Ptolemy soon abandoned Artacama in order to marry Antipater's daughter Eurydice (Berve 1926:52, no. 97). A daughter of Barsine was married to Nearchus.

It is Apame, the daughter of the rebellious Spitamenes, who rose to fame as the wife of Seleucus. As the mother of Antiochus I (Arr.*an.*VII.4.6; Strabo 16.2.4; App.*Syr.*57; cf. Plut.*Demetr.*31) she embodied the Persian side of the Seleucid Dynasty. After a bitter power struggle between Alexander's generals following his death in June 323, Seleucus eventually emerged as the ruler of most territories of the former Achaemenid empire, basing his empire on a newly founded city, Seleucia-on-the-Tigris. His son Antiochus I became co-regent in 294/3. Seleucus named three cities after his queen, Apamea-Euphrates, Apamea-Silhu and Apamea-Zeugma, founded between 301 and 281.

FURTHER READING

On Macedonia's aims in Persia see Seibert, J. (1998). 'Panhellenischer' Kreuzzug, Nationalkrieg, Rachefeldzug oder makedonischer Eroberungskrieg? Überlegungen zu den Ursachen des Krieges gegen Persien. In: *Alexander der Grosse. Eine Welteroberung und ihr Hintergrund,* Antiquitas Reihe I, Abhandlungen zur Alten Geschichte 46 (ed. W. Will), 5–58. Bonn: Habelt. The literature on Alexander is ever growing: Bosworth, A. (1988). *Conquest and Empire: The Reign of Alexander the Great.* Cambridge: *Cambridge University Press* provides a comprehensive and balanced narrative of events. Most recent critical studies on aspects of Alexander's reign have been presented in Roisman, J. (ed.) (2003). *Alexander the Great,* The Classical Tradition. Leiden: Brill.A notably level-headed assessment of Alexander is the article by Worthington, I. (2003). Alexander, Philip, and the Macedonian background. In: *A Companion to Ancient Macedonia* (eds. J. Roisman and I. Worthington) 2010, 69–98. Oxford: Wiley.Fraser, P. (1996). *Cities of Alexander the Great.* Oxford: Oxford University Press.

For Darius III see Nylander, C. (1993). Darius III – the coward king. Points and counterpoint. In: *Alexander the Great: Reality and Myth* (eds. J. Carlsen and B. Due), 145–160. Rome: L'Erma di Bretschneider (Analecta Romana Instituti Danici Suppl. 20). Seibert, J. (1988). Darius III. In: *Zu Alexander d.Gr. Festschrift G. Wirth* (eds. W. Will and J. Heinrichs), 437–456. Amsterdam: Adolf M. Hakkert. See also Jacobs, B. (1994). *Die Satrapienverwaltung im Perserreich zur Zeit Darius III.* Wiesbaden: Ludwig Reichert.and Briant, P. (2015). *Darius III in the Shadow of Alexander.* Paris: Harvard University Press for the depiction of Darius in the classical and early islamic literature.

11
Epilogue

As Alexander's conquest of the Achaemenid empire and the subsequent Seleucid rule in Iran took a dominant political role in the ancient Near East, the history of the first Persian empire slipped into the background. When less than 100 years later a new Persian power arose in Parthia, eventually conquering Mesopotamia in 141 and pushing the Seleucids back to the territories west of the Euphrates River, the Persian memory of the Achaemenids seemed to have all but disappeared. The emergence of the Sasanian Dynasty under its king Ardashir in 224 CE triggered the question to what extent the Sasanians were aware of their famous ancestors. There were several reasons for this. Their rise to power occurred in Parsa, the Achaemenid homeland, and the city from whence they arose against the last Parthian king, Artabanus IV, was Istakhr, situated in the immediate vicinity of Persepolis. The Sasanians used the site of Naqsh-e Rustam to add their own royal rock reliefs with scenes of investiture and knightly combat beneath the tombs of the Achaemenids. More forceful, however, were their claims, demanded from the Romans, who had replaced the Seleucids in the Near East, and recorded in the histories of Latin authors, that the territories that their ancestors had possessed be returned to them.

> Believing these regions to be his (= Ardashir's) by inheritance, he declared that all the countries in that area, including Ionia and Caria, had been ruled by Persian governors, beginning with Cyrus, who first made the Median empire Persian, and ending with Darius, the last of the Persian kings, whose kingdom was seized by Alexander the Great. He asserted that it was therefore proper for him to recover for the Persians the kingdom which they formerly possessed. (Herodian VI.2.1–2)

This idea was echoed by several writers in antiquity and thus found acceptance in modern scholarship. It was seemingly enforced by the Persian historian Tabari (lived 838–870 CE), who claimed that Ardashir 'wanted to return the kingdom to his owners and to place it under the command of one ruler and one king as was the case in the time of his ancestors and prior to the time of the feudal states' (Tabari I: 814). It led some scholars to argue that these passages were a clear indication that the Sasanians

A History of Ancient Persia: The Achaemenid Empire, First Edition. Maria Brosius.
© 2021 John Wiley & Sons, Inc. Published 2021 by John Wiley & Sons, Inc.

considered themselves heirs to the Achaemenids and that, accordingly, there must have existed a cultural memory across the centuries. This memory must have been transmitted orally, as no extant Persian sources indicate the existence of a written historical tradition. Yarshater (1971) proposed that the Romans took their information from the Greek authors on Achaemenid Persia and constructed the Sasanians' claim accordingly. Likewise, early islamic texts will have been informed by a Greco-Babylonian and Jewish-Babylonian tradition for their references to early Persian kings. Others argued for a more complex picture. Neither the memory of the Achaemenids nor the prevalence of Achaemenid art and culture could have disappeared wholesale with Alexander's conquest. For one thing, in Persis, a local dynasty arose in the second century known as *frataraka*, and their images on their coinage echo features of the Achaemenid kings, such as the soft cap, the *kyrbasia*. The *frataraka* continued to rule in Persis under the Parthians, not being regarded as a threat to Parthian power. For another, traces of Achaemenid heritage were thought to be evident in the Parthian kings' use of the title 'King of Kings'. But, as Rahim Shayegan (2011) has argued, the knowledge about this title may have been derived from Babylonian sources, and thus independently of a Persian tradition. As for the claim made by the Parthian king Artabanus II (ruled 10–38) on the territories 'held first by Cyrus and afterwards by Alexander' (Tac.*Ann*.VI.31), those 'cornerstones' of Persian rule, were, of course, also known figures in the classical tradition in which Cyrus featured as the best of the Persian kings, and Alexander became the model conqueror many Roman emperors aspired to. The problems thus identified have led to the current and ongoing debate about the prevalence of an oral Iranian tradition alongside other written traditions followed by different cultural communities within the Persian empires.

Thus, while evidence for a traceable idea of memory of the Achaemenids is lacking for the Persians themselves, we nevertheless find indications elsewhere. The earliest Parthian coins depict a seated archer wearing the riding costume, holding a bow in his hand. It is most likely the figure of Arsaces, the founder of the empire, whose name became the generic title for the kings, in the same way the name Caesar evolved from personal name to imperial title in the Roman period. The image of the archer clearly echoes that found on the coins of Datames, and thus could be regarded as a direct borrowing from Achaemenid coinage. Outside Persia proper, we encounter vestiges of the Achaemenids in visual and written evidence from the kings of Commagene, a small principality bordering on Cappadocia and Osrhoene. Here, king Antiochus I Theos of Commagene (ruled c.69–31) built several cultic centres, most notably on top of Nemrud Dağ, with its colossal statues of three Greek-Persian divinities, one of the goddess of Commagene and one of himself as the deified king. On the same site, he set up two rows of stelae with representations of his ancestors from both his paternal and his maternal side. Stelae of his paternal ancestors include Darius I, Xerxes I, Artaxerxes I and Darius II, while another refers to Aroandas/Orontes, the Persian satrap of Armenia and then Mysia, who had been married to Rhodogune, daughter of Artaxerxes II, and thus established his line to the Achaemenids. The inscriptions reads: '(...) Aroandas (= Orontes) son of Artasyr[as], [who] married Quee[n] [Rho]dogune daughter of the ki[ng of] [k]ings, the Gre[at Arta]xerxes [II] who is also Arsakes' (transl. Shayegan 2017,429).

What holds true of the Sasanians, however, may do so, too, for the kings of Commagene. Their knowledge about the Achaemenids may have derived from Greek sources rather than from a Persian written tradition. In fact, the name of the princess, Rhodogune, strongly suggests it, as it is a purely Greek name, not a Persian one. But perhaps where Antiochus I, or the Sasanians, for that matter, obtained this information is less important than the fact that he sought it out to remember his Persian ancestry. The key point Antiochus made with these stelae is that he was expressing his honour and respect for his Persian ancestors, and that they bore relevance to his kingship and authority. Their importance lies in the fact that the Achaemenids were part of Antiochus's heritage and as such belonged to his cultural memory.

FURTHER READING

The debate about the Persian cultural memory was discussed by Yarshater, E. (1971). Were the Sasanians heirs to the Achaemenids? In: *La Persia nel Medioevo*, 517–531. Rome: Accademia Nazionale dei Lincei, followed by a further key article by Wiesehöfer, J. (1986). Iranische Ansprüche an Rom auf ehemals achaimendisichen Territorien. *Archäologische Mitteilungen aus Iran* 19: 177–185. For Alexander and the Persians see Wiesehöfer, J. (1994). Zum Nachleben von Achaimeniden und Alexander in Iran. *AchHist* 8: 389–397. Shahbazi, S. (2003). Iranians and Alexander. *American Journal of Ancient History* 2: 5–38. Brosius, M. (2003). Alexander and the Persians. In: *Alexander the Great*, The Classical Tradition (ed. J. Roisman), 169–193. Leiden: Brill.

For the later Persian and Hellenistic empires and the question of continuity see Shayegan, M.R. (2011). *Arsacids and Sasanians. Political Ideology in Post-Hellenistic and Late Antique Persia.* Cambridge: Cambridge University Press. Canepa, M. (2015). Seleucid Sacred architecture, royal cult and transformation of Iranian culture in the Middle Iranian period. *Iranian Studies* 48: 71–97. Shenkar, M. (2007). Temple architecture in the Iranian world before the Macedonian conquest. *Iran and the Caucasus* 11: 169–194. Smith, R.R.R. (2012). *The Gods of Nemrud. The Royal Sanctuary of Antiochus and the King of Commagene.* Istanbul: Ertug & Kocabiyik. Jacobs, B. (2017). Tradition oder Fiktion? Die "persischen" Elemente in den Ausstattungsprogrammen Antiochos' I. von Kommagene. In: *Persianism in Antiquity*, Oriens et Occidens 25 (eds. R. Strootman and M.J. Versluys), 235–248. Stuttgart: Franz Steiner.

Bibliography

Álvarez-Mon, J. and Basello, G.P. (eds.) (2018). *The Elamite World*. London: Routledge.

Álvarez-Mon, J. and Garrison, M.B. (eds.) (2011). *Elam and Persia*. Winona Lake, IN: Eisenbrauns.

Antela-Bernardez, B. and Vidal, J. (2014). *Central Asia in Antiquity: Interdisciplinary Approaches*. Oxford: Archaopress.

Assman, J. (1992). *Das kulturelle Gedächtnis: Schrift, Erinnerung und politische Identität in frühen Hochkulturen*. Munich: Beck.

Babaev, I., Mehnert, G., and Knauss, F.S. (2009). Die achaimenidische Residenz auf dem Gurban Tepe. Ausgrabungen bei Karčamirli. 3. Vorbericht. *Archäologische Mitteilungen aus Iran und Turan* 41: 283–321.

Bäbler, B. (1998). *Fleissige Thrakerinnen und wehrhafte Skythen. Nichtgriechen im klassischen Athen und ihre archäologische Hinterlassenschaft*. Stuttgart: B.G. Teubner.

Baker, H. (2008). Babylon in 484 BC: the excavated archival tablets as a source for urban history. *Zeitschrift für Assyriologie und Vorderasiatische Archäologie* 98: 100–116.

Balcer, J.M. (1987). *Herodotus and Bisutun*. Stuttgart: Steiner (Historia Einzelschriften 49).

Benech, C., Boucharlat, R., and Gondet, S. (2012). Organisation et aménagement de l'espace à Pasargades: Reconnaissances archéologiques de surface 2003–2008. Arta 3: 1–37.

Bengtson, H. (2009). *Griechische Geschichte von den Anfängen bis in die römische Kaiserzeit*. Munich: Beck.

Berve, H. (1926). *Das Alexanderreich auf prosopographischer Grundlage*, vol. 1: Darstellung. Munich: Olms.

Bigwood, J.M. (2009). 'Incestuous' marriages in Achaemenid Iran: myth and realities. *Klio* 91: 311–341.

Boardman, J. (2000). *Persia and the West*. London: Thames & Hudson.

Borchardt, J. (2000). Dynastie und Beamte in Lykien während der persischen und attischen Herrschaft. In: *Variatio Delectat: Iran und der Westen. Gedenkschrift Peter Calmeyer* (eds. R. Dittmann, B. Hrouda, U. Löw, et al.), 73–140. Münster: Ugarit (AOAT 272).

Borger, R. (1956). *Die Inschriften Asarhaddons, Königs von Assyrien*. Graz: Biblio Verlag (Archiv für Orientforschung, Beiheft 9).

Bosworth, A.B. (1988). *Conquest and Empire: The Reign of Alexander the Great*. Cambridge: Cambridge University Press.

A History of Ancient Persia: The Achaemenid Empire, First Edition. Maria Brosius.
© 2021 John Wiley & Sons, Inc. Published 2021 by John Wiley & Sons, Inc.

Bosworth, A.B. (1994). Alexander the Great, Part I: The events of the reign. In: *CAH VI²* (eds. D.M. Lewis, J. Boardman, S. Hornblower and M. Ostwald), 791–845. Cambridge: Cambridge University Press.

Boucharlat, R. (1997). Susa under Achaemenid rule. In: *Mesopotamia and Iran in the Persian Period. Conquest and Imperialism 539–331 BC. Proceedings of a Seminar in Memory of Vladimir G. Lukonin* (ed. J. Curtis), 54–67. London: British Museum Press.

Boucharlat, R. (2001). The palace and the Royal Achaemenid City: two case studies – Pasargadae and Susa. In: *The Royal Palace Institution in the First Millennium BC* (Monographs of the Danish Institute at Athens vol.4), 113–123. Athens: Danish Institute at Athens.

Briant, P. (1992). La date des révoltes babylonniennes contre Xerxès. *Studia Iranica* 21: 7–20.

Briant, P. (2000). History and ideology: the Greeks and 'Persian decadence'. In: *Greeks and Barbarians* (ed. T. Harrison), 193–210. Edinburgh: Edinburgh University Press.

Briant, P. (2006). *From Cyrus to Alexander.* Winona Lake, IN: Eisenbrauns.

Briant, P. (2012). From the Indus to the Mediterranean Sea: the administration, organisation and logistics of the great roads of the Achaemenid empire. In: *Highways, Byways and Road Systems in the Pre-Modern World* (eds. S.E. Alcock, J. Bodel and R.J.A. Talbert), 185–201. Wiley.

Briant, P. (2015). *Darius III in the Shadow of Alexander.* Paris: Harvard University Press.

Briant, P. and Chaveau, M. (eds.) (2009). *Organisation des pouvoirs et contact culturels dans les pays de l'empire achéménide.* Paris: de Boccard (Persika 14).

Bridges, E., Hall, E., and Rhodes, P.J. (2007). *Cultural Responses to the Persian Wars. Antiquity to the Third Millennium.* Oxford: Oxford University Press.

Brinkman, J.A. (1965). Elamite military aid to Merodach-Baladan. *Journal of Near Eastern Studies* 24: 161–166.

Brosius, M. (1996). *Women in Ancient Persia (559–331 BC).* Oxford: Oxford University Press.

Brosius, M. (2000). *The Persian Empire from Cyrus II to Artaxerxes I.* London: London Association of Classical Teachers – Original Records Committee (LACTOR 16).

Brosius, M. (2003a). Alexander and the Persians. In: *Alexander the Great* (ed. J. Roisman), 169–193. Leiden: Brill (The Classical Tradition).

Brosius, M. (2003b). Why Persia became the enemy of Macedon. *AchHist* 8: 227–238.

Brosius, M. (2006). *The Persians. An Introduction.* London: Routledge.

Brosius, M. (2010a). Keeping up with the Persians: between cultural identity and Persianization in the Achaemenid period. In: *Cultural Identity and the Peoples of the Mediterranean* (ed. E. Gruen), 143–157. Los Angeles: Getty Publications.

Brosius, M. (2010b). *Pax Persica* and the peoples of the Black Sea region: extent and limits of Achaemenid imperial ideology. In: *Achaemenid Impact in the Black Sea Region* (eds. E. Rehm and J. Nieling), 29–40. Aarhus: Aarhus University Press.

Brosius, M. (2012). Persian diplomacy between 'Pax Persica' and 'zero tolerance'. In: *Maintaining Peace and Stability in the Greek World* (ed. J. Wilker), 1–13. Heidelberg: Verlag Antike.

Bryce, T. (1986). *The Lycians in Literary and Epigraphic Sources.* Copenhagen: Museum Tusculanum Press.

Burn, A.R. (1985). *Persia and the Greeks.* London: Duckworth.

Cameron, G.G. (1948). *Persepolis Treasury Texts.* Chicago: University of Chicago Press.

Canepa, M. Seleucid sacred architecture, royal cult and transformation of Iranian culture in the Middle Iranian period. *Iranian Studies* 48: 71–97.

Cardascia, G. (1951). *Les archives de Murašu: une famille d'hommes d'affaires babyloniens à l'époque perse (455–403 av. J.-C.).* Paris: Imprimerie nationale.

Carey, C. and Edwards, M. (eds.) (2013). *Marathon – 2,500 Years: Proceedings of the Marathon Conference 2010.* London: University of London (Institute of Classical Studies, School of Advanced Study) (Bulletin of the Institute of Classical Studies Supplement 124).

Cerf, W.J. (2001). Thermopylai: myth and reality in 480 BBC. In: *Gab es das griechische Wunder?* (eds. D. Papenfuss and V.M. Strocka), 355–364. Mainz: Von Zabern.

Cross, F.M. (1978). A recently published Phoenician inscription of the Persian period from Byblos. *Israel Exploration Journal* 28 (4): 40–44.

Curtis, J. and Simpon, S.J. (eds.) (2010). *The World of Achaemenid Persia. History, Art and Society in Iran*. London: Tauris.

Curtis, J., Tallis, N., and André-Salvini, B. (2005). *Forgotten Empire: The World of Ancient Persia*. Berkeley: University of California Press.

Daryaee, T. and Mousavi, A. (2014). *Excavating an Empire*. Cosa Meza CA: Mazda.

De Graef, K. and Tavernier, J. (eds.) (2013). *Susa and Elam. Archaeological, Philological, Historical and Geographical Perspectives*. Leiden: Brill.

Depuydt, L. (1995). Murder in Memphis. The story of Cambyses' mortal wounding of the Apis Bull (ca.523 BCE). *Journal of Near Eastern Studies* 54: 119–126.

Drew, G.R. (2009). Honeymoon salad. Cambyses' Uxoricide according to the Egyptians (Hdt.3.32.34). *Historia* 58: 131–140.

Drews, R. (1974). Sargon, Cyrus and Mesopotamian folk history. *Journal of Near Eastern Studies* 33: 387–394.

Driver, G.R. (1957). *Aramaic Documents of the Fifth Century BC*. Oxford: Clarendon Press.

Dusinberre, E.R.M. (2003). *Aspects of Empire in Achaemenid Sardis*. Cambridge: Cambridge University Press.

Dusinberre, E.R.M. (2013). *Empire, Authority, and Autonomy in Achaemenid Anatolia*. Cambridge: Cambridge University Press.

Finkel, I. (2013). *The Cyrus Cylinder*. London: Tauris.

Finn, J. (2011). Gods, kings, men: trilingual inscriptions and symbolic visualizations in the Achaemenid empire. *Ars Orientalis* 41: 17–57.

Fitzpartick-McKinley, A. (2015). *Empire, Power and Indigenous Elites. A Case Study of the Nehemiah Memoir*. Leiden: Brill.

Fornara, C.W. (1983). *Archaic Times to the End of the Peloponnesian War*. Cambridge: Cambridge University Press.

Francfort, H.-P. (1988). Central Asia and Early Iran. In: *CAH IV²* (eds. J. Boardman, N.G.L. Hammond, D.M. Lewis and M. Ostwald), 165–193. Cambridge: Cambridge University Press.

Fraser, P. (1996). *Cities of Alexander the Great*. Oxford: Oxford University Press.

Garrison, M. (2011). By the favour of Ahuramazda: kingship and the divine in the early Achaemenid period. In: *More than Men, Less than Gods. Studies on Royal Cult and Imperial Worship* (eds. P.P. Iossif, A.S. Chankowski and C.C. Lorber), 15–104. Leuven: Peeters.

Garrison, M. and Root, M.C. (2001). *Seals on the Persepolis Fortification Tablets*. Chicago: University of Chicago Press.

Genito, B. (2001). Dāhān-i Ghulmān: una "vicina" periferia dell'Impero Achemenide. In: *Antica Persia. I tesori del Museo Nazionale di Teheran e la ricerca italiana in Iran* (eds. A. Gramiccia and G. d'Inzillo Carranza), XXXI–XXXV. Rome: De Luca.

Gibson, J.C.L. (1982). *Textbook of Syrian Semitic Inscriptions, vol. III: Phoenician Inscriptions Including Inscriptions in the Mixed Dialect of Arslan Tash*. Cambridge: Cambridge University Press.

Granerød, G. (2016). *Dimensions of Yahwism in the Persian Period. Studies in the Religion and Society of the Judaean Community at Elephantine*. Berlin: De Gruyter.

Gunter, A.C. (1993). *The Construction of the Near East*. Copenhagen: Academic Press.

Grayson, A.K. (1975). *Assyrian and Babylonian Chronicles*. Locust Valley, NY: J.J. Augustin.

Grayson, A.K. (1995). *Assyrian Rulers of the Early First Millennium BC II (858–745 BC)*. Toronto: University of Toronto (RIMA 3).

Hall, E. (1989). *Inventing the Barbarian*. Oxford: Oxford University Press.

Hall, E. (1993). Asia unmanned: images of victory in classical Athens. In: *War and Society in the Greek World* (eds. J. Rich and G. Shipley), 108–133. London: Routledge.

Hallock, R.T. (1969). *Persepolis Fortification Texts*. Chicago: University of Chicago Press.

Hallock, R.T. (1978). Selected fortification texts. *Cahiers de la Délégation Archéologique Française en Iran* 8: 109–136.

Hammond, N.G.L. (1986). *A History of Greece to 322 BC*. Oxford: Oxford University Press.

Harrison, T. (ed.) (2000). *Greeks and Barbarians*. Edinburgh: Edinburgh University Press.

Hartog, F. (1988). *The Mirror of Herodotus*. Berkeley: University of California Press.

Hegel, G.W.F. (1961/1822–1831). *Vorlesungen über die Philosophie der Geschichte*. Stuttgart: Reclam.

Held, W. (2011). Mischordnungen in Labraunda als Repräsentationsform persischer Satrapen. In: *Keleinai-Apameia Kobotos. Developpement urbain dans le contexte anatolien* (eds. L. Summerer, A. Ivantchik and A. von Kienlin), 383–390. Munich: Ugarit.

Held, W. and Kaptan, D. (2015). The residence of a Persian satrap in Meydancıkkale, Cilicia. In: *Mesopotamia in the Ancient World* (eds. R. Rollinger and E. van Dongen), 175–191. Münster: Ugarit (Melammu Symposia 7).

Held, W. and Kaptan, D. (2015). The residence of a Persian satrap in Meydancıkkale, Cilicia. In: *Mesopotamia in the Ancient World* (eds. R. Rollinger and E. van Dongen), 175–191. Münster: Ugarit. (Melammu Symposia 7).

Henkelman, W. (2008). The other gods who are: Studies in elamite-iranian acculturation based on the Persepolis fortification texts. PhD diss. University of Leiden.

Hesse, A. (2013). Electrical resistivity survey of the Shaur palace. In: *The Palace of Darius at Susa. The Great Royal Residence of Achaemenid Persia* (ed. J. Perrot), 373–403. London: Tauris.

Harrison, T. (ed.) (2002). *Gegenwelten zu den Kulturen Griechenlands und Roms in der Antike*. Munich: Saur.

Hoelteskamp, K.-J. (2001). Marathon – vom Monument zum Mythos. In: *Gab es das griechische Wunder?* (eds. D. Papenfuss and V.M. Strocka), 329–353. Mainz: Von Zabern.

Hornblower, S. (1998). Persia. In: *CAH IV²* (eds. J. Boardman, N.G.L. Hammond, D.M. Lewis and M. Ostwald), 45–96. Cambridge: Cambridge University Press.

Hornblower, S. (2001). Greeks and Persians. West against east. In: *War, Peace and World Orders in European History* (eds. A.V. Hartmann and B.V. Heuser), 48–61. London: Routledge.

Jacobs, B. (1994). *Die Satrapienverwaltung im Perserreich zur Zeit Darius III*. Wiesbaden: Ludwig Reichert.

Jacobs, B. (2000). Achaimenidenherrschaft in der Kaukasus-Region und in Cis-Kaukasien. *Archäologische Mitteilungen aus Iran und Turan* 32: 93–102.

Jacobs, B. (2011). Achaemenid Satrapies http://www.iranicaonline.org/articles/achaemenid-satrapies (accessed 9 June 2020).

Jacobs, B. (2017). Tradition oder Fiktion? Die "persischen" Elemente in den Ausstattungsprogrammen Antiochos' I. von Kommagene. In: *Persianism in Antiquity*, Oriens et Occidens 25 (eds. R. Strootman and M.J. Versluys), 235–248. Stuttgart: Franz Steiner.

Jacobs, B. and Rollinger, R. (eds.) (2010). *Der Achämenidenhof. The Achaemenid Court*. Basle: Harrassowitz.

Jacobs, B. and Rollinger, R. (eds.) (in press). *A Companion to the Achaemenid Empire*. Oxford: Wiley Blackwell.

Jigoulov, V.S. (2010). *The Social History of Achaemenid Phoenicia*. London: Routledge.

Kaptan, D. (2002). *The Dasyleion Bullae: Seal Images from the Western Achaemenid Empire*. Leiden: Nederlands Instituut voor het Nabije Oosten.

Kellens, J. (ed.) (1991). *La religion iranienne à l'époque achéménide*. Gent: Peeters.

Kellens, J. (2002). L'idéologie réligieuse des inscriptions achémenides. *Journal Asiatique* 290: 417–464.

Kleiss, W. (1980). Zur Entwicklung der achaemenidischen Palastarchitektur. *Iranica Antiqua* 15: 199–211.

Kleiss, W. (2000). Zur Planung von Persepolis. In: *Variatio Delectat. Iran und der Westen. Gedenkschrift für Peter Calmeyer* (eds. R. Dittman, B. Hrouda, U. Löw, et al.), 355–368. Münster: Ugarit (AOAT 272).

Knaus, F. (2006). Ancient Persia and the Caucasus. *Iranica Antiqua* 41: 79–118.

Knauss, F. (2011). Residenzen achaimenidischer Beamter und Vasallen. In: *Kelainai – Apameia Kibotos: Développement urbein dansle contexte anatolien* (eds. L. Summerer, A. Ivantchik and A. von Kienlin), 391–410. Bordeaux: Ausonius Éditions.

Kuhrt, A. (1983). The Cyrus Cylinder and Achaemenid imperial policy. *Journal for the Study of the Old Testament* 25: 83–97.

Kuhrt, A. (1987). Written sources available for the history of Babylonia under the later Achaemenids. *AchHist* 1: 147–157.

Kuhrt, A. (1995). *The Ancient Near East*, vol. 2. London: Routledge.

Kuhrt, A. (2003). Making history. Sargon of Agade and Cyrus the Great of Persia. *AchHist* 8: 347–361.

Kuhrt, A. (2007a). Cyrus the Great: images and realities. In: *Representations of Political Power: Case Histories from Times of Change and Dissolving Order in the Ancient Near East* (eds. M. Heinz and M.H. Feldman), 169–192. Winona Lake, IN: Eisenbrauns.

Kuhrt, A. (2007b). Problems in writing the history of Israel: the case of Cyrus the Great of Persia. In: *Understanding the History of Israel* (ed. H. Williamson), 107–127. Oxford: Oxford University Press for the British Academy.

Kuhrt, A. (2010). *The Persian Empire: A Corpus of Sources of the Achaemenid Period*. London: Routledge.

Kuhrt, A. and Sherwin-White, S. (1987). Xerxes' destruction of Babylonian temples. *AchHist* 2: 69–78.

Kwasman, T. and Lemaire, A. (2002). An Aramaic inscription from Kemaliye (Lydian Philadelphia). *Epigraphica Anatolica* 34: 185–187.

Lambert, W.G. (2013). *Babylonian Creation Myths*. Winona Lake, IN: Eisenbrauns.

Lanfranchi, G.B., Roaf, M., and Rollinger, R. (eds.) (2003). *Continuity of Empire (?): Assyria, Media, Persia*. Padova: S.a.r.g.o.n. Editrice e Libreria.

Lemaire, A. (2013). *Levantine Epigraphy and History in the Achaemenid Period (539–332 BCE)*. Oxford: Oxford University Press for the British Academy.

Lewis, D.M. (1977). *Sparta and Persia*. Leiden: Brill.

Lewis, D.M. (1987). The king's dinner (Polyaenus IV.3,32). *AchHist* 2: 79–87.

Lichtheim, M. (1980). *Ancient Egyptian Literature. Vol. III: The Late Period*. Berkeley: University of California Press.

Lincoln, B. (2012). *'Happiness for Mankind'. Achaemenid Religion and the Imperial Project*. Leuven: Peeters.

Liverani, M. (2003). The Rise and Fall of Media. In: *Continuity of Empire (?): Assyria, Media, Persia* (eds. G.B. Lanfranchi, M. Roaf and R. Rollinger), 1–12. Padova: S.a.r.g.o.n. Editrice e Libreria.

Luckenbill, D.D. (1926–1927). *Ancient Records of Assyria and Babylon*, 2 vols. Chicago: University of Chicago Press.

Lutz, H.F. (1928). An agreement between a Babylonian feudal Lord and his retainer in the reign of Darius II. *University of California Publications in Semitic Philology* 3 (9): 269–277.

Madreiter, I. (2012). *Stereotypisierung – Idealisierung – Indifferenz. Formen der Auseinandersetzung mit dem Achaimenidenreich in der griechischen Persika-Literatur*. Wiesbaden: Harrassowitz (Classica et Orientalia 4).

Malandra, W.W. (1983). *An Introduction to Ancient Iranian Religion*. Minneapolis: University of Minnesota Press.

Meiggs, R. and Lewis, D.M. (eds.) (1988). *A Selection of Greek Historical Inscriptions to the End of the Fifth Century BC*. Oxford: Oxford University Press.

Menant, J. (1887). *Le Stèle de Chalouf; essai derestitution du texte perse*. Paris: F. Vieweg.

Michel, E. (1954–1959). Die Assur-Texte Salmanassars III (858–824). *Welt des Orients* 2: 137–157. & 221–233.

Miller, M. (1995). Persians: the oriental other. *Source: Notes in the History of Art* 15: 38–44.

Miller, M. (1997). *Athens and Persia in the Fifth Century BC: A Study in Cultural Receptivity*. Cambridge: Cambridge University Press.

Miller, M. (2002). Greco-Persian cultural relations ii. *Encyclopaedia Iranica* 11: 301–319.

Miller, M. (2007). The poetics of emulation in the Achaemenid world: the figured bowls of the 'Lydian Treasure'. *Ancient West & East* 6: 43–72.

Miller, M. (2011). Town and country in the satrapies of western Anatolia. In: *Kelainai – Apameia Kibotos: Développement urbein dans le contexte anatolien* (eds. L. Summerer, A. Ivantchik and A. von Kienlin), 319–344. Bordeuax: Ausonius Éditions.

de Morgan, J. (1905). *Découverte d'une sépulture achéménide à Suse*, 29–58. Paris: Ernest Leroux (Mission de la Délégation Français en Perse 8).

Murray, O. (1988). The Ionian Revolt. In: *CAH IV²* (eds. J. Boardman, N.G.L. Hammond, D.M. Lewis and M. Ostwald), 461–490. Cambridge: Cambridge University Press.

Naveh, J. and Shaked, S. (eds.) (2012). *Aramaic Documents from Ancient Bactria*. London: The Khalili Family Trust.

Nieling, J. and Rehm, E. (eds.) (2010). *Achaemenid Impact in the Black Sea Region*. Aarhus: Aarhus University Press.

Nylander, C. (1993). Darius III – the coward king. Points and counterpoints. In: *Alexander the Great. Reality and Myth* (eds. J. Carlsen, B. Due, O.S. Due and B. Poulsen), 145–160. Rome: L'Erma di Bretschneider.

Perrot, J. (2013). The Franco-Iranian Programme. In: *The Palace of Darius at Susa. The Great Royal Residence of Achaemenid Persia* (ed. J. Perrot), 97–123. London: Tauris.

Pirngruber, R. (2017). *The Economy of Late Achaemenid and Seleucid Babylonia*. Cambridge: Cambridge University Press.

Porten, B. (2011). *The Elephantine Papyri in English. Three Millennia of Cross-Cultural Continuity and Change*, 2e. Leiden: Brill.

Porten, B. and Yardeni, A. (eds.) (1986). *Textbook of Aramaic Documents from Ancient Egypt: Letters*. Winona Lake, IN: Eisenbrauns.

Potts, D.T. (ed.) (2013). *The Oxford Handbook of Ancient Iran*. Oxford: Oxford University Press.

Potts, D., T. (2014). *Nomadism in Iran. From Antiquity to the Modern Era*. Oxford: Oxford University Press.

Potts, D.T. (2016). *The Archaeology of Elam. Formation and Transformation of an Ancient Iranian State*. Cambridge: Cambridge University Press.

Potts, D.T., Asgari Chaverdi, A., Petrie, C.A. et al. (2007). The Mamasani archaeological project, stage two: excavations at Qaleh Kali (Tappeh Servan/Jinjun [MS 46]). *Iran* 45: 287–300.

Radner, K. (2003). An Assyrian view of the Medes. In: *Continuity of Empire (?): Assyria, Media, Persia* (eds. G.B. Lanfranchi, M. Roaf and R. Rollinger), 37–64. Padova: S.a.r.g.o.n. Editrice e Libreria.

Ray, J.D. (1988). Egypt 525–404. In: *CAH IV²* (eds. J. Boardman, N.G.L. Hammond, D.M. Lewis and M. Ostwald), 254–286. Cambridge: Cambridge University Press.

Rhodes, P. (2007). The impact of the Persian Wars on Classical Greece. In: *Cultural Responses to the Persian Wars. Antiquity to the Third Millennium* (eds. E. Bridges, E. Hall and P.J. Rhodes), 31–45. Oxford: Oxford University Press.

Rhodes, P.J. and Osborne, R. (eds.) (2003). *Greek Historical Inscriptions 404–323 BC*. Oxford: Oxford University Press.

Roberto, D. (2015). *From the Armenian Highland to Iran*. Rome: Scienze e lettere.

Rollinger, R. and Wiesehöfer, J. (2009). Königlicher Haushalt, Residenz, und Hof. Der persische König und sein Palast. In: *Sprachen – Bilder – Klänge. Dimensionen der Theologie im Alten Testament und seinem Umfeld, Festschrift für S R. Bartelmus* (ed. C. Karrer-Grube), 213–225. Münster: Ugarit.

Rollinger, R., Truschnegg, B., and Bichler, R. (eds.) (2011). *Herodot und das persische Weltreich. Herodotus and the Persian Empire*. Wiesbaden: Harrassowitz.

Rollinger, R., Wiesehöfer, J., and Lanfranchi, G. (eds.) (2011). *Ktesias' Welt: Ctesias' World*. Wiesbaden: Harrassowitz.

Roosevelt, C.H. (2009). The archaeology of Lydia. In: *From Gyges to Alexander*. Cambridge: Cambridge University Press.

Root, M.C. (1979). *The King and Kingship in Achaemenid Art*. Leiden: Brill.

Roth, M. (1989). *Babylonian Marriage Agreements: 7th–3rd Centuries BC*. Neukirchen-Vlyn: Neukirchener Verlag.

Rudenko, I.S. (1970). *Frozen Tombs of Siberia. The Pazyrk Burials of Iron Age Horsemen*. Berkeley: University of California Press.

Sachs, A.J. and Hunger, H. (1988). *Astronomical Diaries and Related Texts from Babylonia I: Diaries from 652 BC to 262 BC*. Vienna: Verlag der Österreichischen Akadamie der Wissenschaften (ÖAW, Phil.-hist. Klasse, Denkschrift 195).

Sancisi-Weerdenburg, H. (1988). Was there ever a Median empire? *AchHist* 3: 197–212.

Sancisi-Weerdenburg, H. (1993). Alexander and Persepolis. In: *Alexander the Great. Reality and Myth* (eds. J. Carlsen, B. Due, O.S. Due and B. Poulsen), 177–188. Rome: L'Erma di Bretschneider.

Șare, T. (2013). The sculpture of the Heroon of Perikle at Limyra: the making of a Lycian king. *Anatolian Studies* 63: 55–74.

Schaudig, H. (2001). *Die Inschriften Nabonids von Babylon und Kyros' des Grossen samt den in ihrem Umfeld entstandenen Tendenzschriften. Textausgabe und Grammatik*. Münster: Ugarit (AOAT 256).

Schaudig, H. (2018). The magnanimous heart of Cyrus. The Cyrus Cylinder and its literary models. In: *Cyrus the Great. Life and Lore* (ed. R.M. Shahyegan), 16–25. Boston: Ilex Foundation.

Scheil, V. (1907). *Textes élamite-anzanites, troisième series*. Paris: Ernest Leroux (MDP IX).

Schmidt, E.F. (1953–1977). *Persepolis I-III*. Chicago: University of Chicago Press.

Schmitt, R. (1981). *Altpersische Siegelinschriften*. Vienna: Corpus Inscriptionum Iranicarum.

Schmitt, R. (1991). *The Bisitun Inscriptions of Darius the Great. Old Persian Text*. London: School of Oriental and African Studies.

Schmitt, R. (2009). *Die altpersischen Inschriften der Achämeniden*. Wiesbaden: Reichert.

Seibert, J. (1988). Darius III. In: *Zu Alexander d. Gr. Festschrift G. Wirth* (eds. W. Will and J. Heinrichs), 437–456. Amsterdam: Verlag Adolf M. Hakkert.

Seibert, J. (1998). 'Panhellenischer' Kreuzzug, Nationalkrieg, Rachefeldzug oder makedonischer Eroberungskrieg? Überlegungen zu den Ursachen des Krieges gegen Persien. In: *Alexander der Grosse. Eine Welteroberung und ihr Hintergrund* (ed. W. Will), 5–58. Bonn: Dr. Rudolf Habelt (Antiquitas Reihe I, Abhandlungen zur Alten Geschichte 46).

Shahbazi, S. (2003). Iranians and Alexander. *American Journal of Ancient History* 2: 5–38.

Shayegan, M.R. (2011). *Arsacids and Sasanians. Political Ideology in Post-Hellenistic and Late Antique Persia*. Cambridge: Cambridge University Press.

Shayegan, R., M. (2012). *Aspects of History and Epic in Ancient Iran*. Cambridge, MA: Harvard University Press.

Shayegan, R.M. (2017). Persianism: or Achaemenid reminiscences in the Iranian and Iranicate world(s) of antiquity. In: *Persianism in Antiquity* (eds. R. Strootman and M.J. Versluys), 401–455. Stutt-gart: Franz Steiner (Oriens et Occidens 25).

Shayegan, R.M. (ed.) (2018). *Cyrus the Great: Life and Lore* (Ilex Series 21). Cambridge, MA: Harvard University Press.

Shenkar, M. (2007). Temple architecture in the Iranian world before the Macedonian conquest. *Iran and the Caucasus* 11: 169–194.

Skjervø, P.O. (2014). Achaemenid religion. *Religious Compass* 8 (6): 175–187.

Smith, R.R.R. (2012). *The Gods of Nemrud. The Royal Sanctuary of Antiochus and the King of Commagene*. Istanbul: Ertug & Kocabiyik.

Strassmeier, J.N. (1890). *Inschriften von Cambyses, König von Babylon*. Leipzig: Pfeiffer.

Streck, M. (1916). *Assurbanipal und die letzten assyrischen Könige bis zum Untergang Niniveh's*. Leipzig: J.C. Hinrichs. (Vorderasiatische Bibliothek 7/1–3).

Stronach, D. (1969). *Pasargadae*. Oxford: Clarendon Press.

Summerer, L. (2007a). Picturing Persian victory: the painted battle scene on the Munich wood. *Ancient Civilizations from Scythia to Siberia* 13: 3–30.

Summerer, L. (2007b). From Tartalı to Munich: the recovery of a painted wooden tomb chamber in Phrygia. In: *The Achaemenid Impact on Local Populations and Cultures in Anatolia (Sixth–Fourth Centuries B.C.)* (eds. İ. Delemen, O. Casabonne, Ș. Karagöz and O. Tekin), 131–158. Beyoğlu, Istanbul: Turkish Institute of Archaeology.

Tarn, W.W. (2014). *Alexander the Great*. Cambridge: Cambridge University Press.

Taylor, D. (2013). *The Arshama Letters from the Bodleian Library, Vol. 2: Texts, Translations and Glossary*. Bodleian Libraries, University of Oxford. http://arshama.bodleian.ox.ac.uk/ (accessed 9 June 2020).

Tuplin, C. (1987). The administration of the Achaemenid empire. In: *Coinage and Administration in the Athenian and Persian Empires* (ed. I. Carradice), 109–166. London: British Archaeological Reports (BAR series 34).

Tuplin, C. (2013). *The Arshama Letters from the Bodleian Library, Vol. 3: Commentary*. Bodleian Libraries, University of Oxford. http://arshama.bodleian.ox.ac.uk/ (accessed 9 June 2020).

Waerzeggers, C. (2003/4). The Babylonian revolts against Xerxes and the "end of archives". *Archiv für Orientforschung* 50: 150–178.

Waerzeggers, C. (2010). Babylonians in Susa. Travels of Babylonian Businessmen to Susa Reconsidered. In: *Der Achämenidenhof. The Achaemenid Court* (eds. Jacobs and Rollinger), 777–813. Basle: Harrassowitz.

Waerzeggers, C. (2014). *Marduk-rēmanni. Local Networks and Imperial Politics in Achaemenid Babylonia*. Peeters: Leuven.

Walker, C. (1997). Achaemenid chronology and the Babylonian sources. In: *Mesopotamia and Iran in the Persian Period. Conquest and Imperialism 539–331 BC* (ed. J. Curtis), 17–25. London: British Museum Press.

Waters, M. (2000). *A Survey of Neo-Elamite History*. Helsinki: Neo-Assyrian Text Corpus Project (SAAS XII).

Waters, M. (2014). *Ancient Persia. A Concise History of the Achaemenid Empire 550–330 BCE*. New York: Cambridge University Press.

Weidner, E.F. (1931–1932). Die älteste Nachricht über das persische Königshaus. *Archiv für Orientforschung* 7: 1–7.

Weiskopf, M. (1989). *The So-Called Great Satraps' Revolt, 366–360 BC*. Stuttgart: Steiner (Historia Einzelschriften 63).

Wiesehöfer, J. (1980). Die 'Freunde' und 'Wohltäter' des Grosskönigs. *Studia Iranica* 9: 7–21.

Wiesehöfer, J. (1986). Iranische Ansprüche an Rom auf ehemals achaimendisichen Territorien. *Archäologische Mitteilungen aus Iran* 19: 177–185.

Wiesehöfer, J. (1993). "Denn es sind welthistorische Siege" – Nineteenth and Twentieth-Century Views of the Persian Wars. In: *The Construction of the Ancient Near East* (ed. A.C. Gunter), 61–83. Copenhagen: Academic Press.

Wiesehöfer, J. (1994). Zum Nachleben von Achaimeniden und Alexander in Iran. *AchHist* VIII: 389–397.

Wiesehöfer, J. (2001). *Ancient Persia: From 550 BC to 650 AD*, trans. A. Azodi, 231–242. London: Tauris.

Worthington, I. (2003). Alexander, Philip, and the Macedonian background. In: *A Companion to Ancient Macedonia* (eds. J. Roisman and I. Worthington) 2010, 69–98. Oxford: Wiley Blackwell.

Wuttman, M. and Marchand, S. (2005). Égypte. In: *L'archéologie de l'émpire achémenide* (eds. P. Briant and R. Boucharlat), 97–128. Paris: Persica.

Yarshater, E. (1971). Were the Sasanians heirs to the Achaemenids? In: *La Persia nel Medioevo*, 517–531. Rome: Accademia Nazionale dei Lincei.

Young, T.C. and Levine, L.D. (1974). *Excavations of the Godin Tepe Project. Second Progress Report*. Toronto: The Royal Museum. (Occasional Papers 26).

Zenzen, N., Hölscher, T., and Trampendach, K. (eds.) (2013). *Aneignung und Absterrung: wechselnde Perspektiven auf die Antithese von 'Ost' und 'West' in der griechischen Antike*. Heidelberg: Verlag Antike.

Index

Page numbers in *italics* refer to figures.

A History of Ancient Persia: The Achaemenid Empire, First Edition. Maria Brosius.
© 2021 John Wiley & Sons, Inc. Published 2021 by John Wiley & Sons, Inc.